Toward A More Balanced Approach: Rethinking and Readjusting Copyright Systems in the Digital Network Era

Jerry Jie Hua

Toward A More Balanced Approach: Rethinking and Readjusting Copyright Systems in the Digital Network Era

Springer

Jerry Jie Hua
Deacons (Hong Kong)
Hong Kong, China

ISBN 978-3-662-43516-8 ISBN 978-3-662-43517-5 (eBook)
DOI 10.1007/978-3-662-43517-5
Springer Heidelberg New York Dordrecht London

Library of Congress Control Number: 2014942649

Printed on acid-free paper

Springer is part of Springer Science+Business Media (www.springer.com)

Preface

The establishment of copyright protection systems aims to achieve two important purposes: to stimulate the incentive for creation by granting authors a series of exclusive rights on the one hand and promote the progress of culture and public welfare by establishing a series of limitations on these exclusive rights so that the flow of information and dissemination of knowledge will not be hindered on the other hand.

There is always a close relationship between technology development and copyright law. The emergence of personal computers and the Internet has brought about a distinct wave of technological innovation that has reshaped copyright laws by empowering anyone with a connection to flawless, inexpensive, and instantaneous reproduction and distribution of works of authorship. Such technological advancement changes the interests of copyright owners and public users. Users are exposed to more opportunities brought about by digital network technology to obtain access and exploit copyrightable works. If copyright laws do not expand their protected subject matters and categories of exclusive rights, authors cannot be adequately compensated under the digital network environment. Copyright laws can no longer function as an incentive for creation if there is a lack of revision and appropriate expansion. Hence, copyright laws need to extend protection to new subject matters, such as computer programs and databases; grant right holders new kinds of rights, such as right of rental and right to network dissemination of information; establish indirect infringing liability for Internet service providers; and expand protection to technological measures.

However, copyright expansion should not be unlimited and should cease when appropriate access to various works and future creations is at risk. Expansion of copyright protection is only justified when the access and use of works by the public threaten the incentive of authors to create and reap economic rewards. Overexpansion of copyright protection would again disrupt the balance if access to works is narrowly restricted. Overprotection of copyrights will not only obstruct access to original works but will also inhibit future creations based on the original works.

Based on comparative research on international and regional conventions as well as laws, regulations, policies, and cases among different jurisdictions, this book intends to suggest proposals to recover the balance of interests among copyright holders, technological intermediaries, and public users in terms of accessing, distributing, and exploiting copyright works. Four specific issues are discussed in the book: the anti-circumvention rules for protection of technological measures, indirect infringing liability for Internet service providers and safe harbor regulations, copyright limitations and exceptions especially under the digital network environment, and digital commons projects which promote distribution and adaptation of copyright works placed under voluntary licensing schemes. The analysis of these issues and corresponding proposals for reform are not only to reverse the worldwide copyright expansion trend so as to make copyright laws appropriately respond to digital network challenges and the emerging remix culture in general but also to induce China to rethink and amend her copyright system so as to restore a robust public domain where existing information and data can be used to produce future intellectual assets.

Hong Kong, China Jerry Jie Hua

Acknowledgments

This book is based on the doctoral thesis submitted to the University of Hong Kong for partial fulfillment of the PhD degree. The successful completion of PhD research is not an easy task. My journey in the pursuit of academic improvement was met with much confusion, exploration, distress, and joy. Many individuals were kind enough to lend me a hand, provide inspiration, and arouse courage in me on this journey. They are the recipients of my true appreciation and gratefulness.

First, I would like to express my gratitude to the University of Hong Kong, the institution that gave me the opportunity to start my academic research with a generous studentship and conference grant. My doctoral research is principally based on the collections housed in the university libraries and electronic databases.

My appreciation and gratitude belongs to Professor Li Yahong, my PhD supervisor, who dedicated her time and energy to reading my thesis, giving suggestions and correcting the errors in my expressions. She supported every opportunity to improve my legal study and academic research, regardless whether this was conducting visiting research abroad or taking part in an essay competition. She recommended my internship at the Hong Kong Intellectual Property Department and helped to secure my involvement with the Hong Kong Creative Commons as a student researcher. These experiences broadened my horizons, allowing me to become more familiar with Hong Kong copyright laws and the copyright community. I am also grateful to my thesis examiners, Professors Alice Lee and Zhao Yun of the University of Hong Kong as well as Professor Peter Yu of Drake University (USA), who raised thought-provoking questions and suggestions which helped me to more deeply ponder legal issues and better revise my work.

My gratitude is also extended to the Duke University School of Law (USA), Max Planck Institute for Intellectual Property and Competition Law (Germany), and Centre for Commercial Law Studies of Queen Mary University of London (UK). These institutions provided opportunities so that I was able to conduct visiting research by using their resources and facilities. The Max Planck Institute even provided a generous scholarship to aid my research and daily expenses in Munich, Germany. I would like to thank Professor Ulrich Loewenheim of the Frankfurt

University (Germany), Professor Silke von Lewinski of the Max Planck Institute for Intellectual Property and Competition Law, and Professor Jerome Reichman of the Duke University who inspired me and provided helpful comments toward my legal research. The academic discussions with them were always enlightening and pleasant.

I am also grateful to the organizers of the academic conferences and seminars that offered me the opportunity to present my research, as well as a couple of scholars and researchers who commented on my research and updated my knowledge-building in the research field by visiting research, journal editing, conferences, and seminars. Their insights from different angles and warm friendship added much joy to my journey toward the PhD degree.

Finally, true gratefulness goes to my family, especially my respected and beloved parents. Their unremitting support, encouragement, and love accompanied me during the entire journey in pursuit of my PhD degree. Without their love, I would not have successfully accomplished this difficult task. This book is dedicated to them.

Contents

1 **Copyright Law Changes and Developments in Digital Network Era** ... 1
1.1 Introduction ... 1
1.2 Interrelationship Between Technology Development and Copyright Laws ... 3
1.3 Amendment and Expansion of Copyright Protection Under Digital Network Environment ... 5
1.3.1 Amendment and Development of International Copyright Conventions ... 5
1.3.2 Changes and Amendments of Copyright Protection Systems in Developed Regions ... 9
1.3.3 New Stages of Copyright Reforms ... 13
1.3.4 Conclusion: Expansion of Copyright Protection Under Digital Network Environment ... 17
1.4 Should China Imitate or Innovate? ... 20
1.4.1 Development and Amendment of Copyright Protection System in China ... 21
1.4.2 Should China Imitate or Innovate? ... 31
1.5 Conclusion ... 35
References ... 36

2 **Balance of Interest in Copyright Systems and Imbalances Under Digital Network Environments** ... 39
2.1 Introduction ... 39
2.2 Balance of Interest in Copyright Systems ... 41
2.2.1 Philosophical Analysis of Intellectual Property Systems ... 41
2.2.2 Economical Analysis of Intellectual Property Systems ... 45
2.2.3 Origin and Development of Copyright Laws ... 48
2.2.4 Dual Goals of Copyright Systems ... 53

2.3 Current Imbalance of Interest in Copyright Systems ... 55
2.3.1 Borderline of Balance of Interests: Accessibility of Copyright Works ... 55
2.3.2 Justification of Expanding Copyrights ... 56
2.3.3 Current Imbalance of Interests in Copyright Systems ... 57
2.4 Conclusion ... 66
References ... 67

3 Toward a More Balanced Model: Revision of Anti-circumvention Rules ... 69
3.1 Introduction ... 69
3.2 Basic Understanding of Protection of Digital Rights Management and Technological Protection Measures ... 71
3.2.1 Conventional Protection of Technological Measures and Rights Management Information ... 72
3.2.2 Key Terms in the Protection of Technological Protection Measures ... 73
3.3 Balanced or Unbalanced: Anti-circumvention Rules of Digital Millennium Copyright Act ... 75
3.3.1 Contents of DMCA Anti-circumvention Rule ... 76
3.3.2 Balanced Designs: Exceptions Under the Anti-circumvention Rule ... 77
3.3.3 Unbalanced Designs: Existing Problems in the Anti-circumvention Rule ... 80
3.3.4 Conclusion: Balanced Designs Weighing Unbalanced Designs ... 87
3.4 Introduction of a More Balanced Model of Anti-circumvention Rule ... 88
3.4.1 Technological Design: Guaranteeing Minimum Use ... 90
3.4.2 Legislative Design: Inserting General Condition and Exception ... 91
3.4.3 Judicial Design: Reaching Decision Case by Case Based on Prerequisite and General Exception ... 94
3.4.4 Scheme Outside Intellectual Property Law: Importation of Anti-circumvention Rule into Competition Law ... 95
3.4.5 Suggestions for the New Round of Reform Regarding Anti-circumvention Rules in China ... 96
3.5 Conclusion ... 98
References ... 99

4 Establishing Certainty About Liability for Internet Service Providers and Safe Harbor Regulations ... 101
4.1 Introduction ... 101
4.2 Introduction on Internet Service Providers ... 103
4.2.1 Definition of Internet Service Providers ... 103
4.2.2 Importance of Establishing Certainty About Liability and Limitations for Internet Service Providers ... 106

4.3 Internet Service Provider Liability and Safe Harbor Rules Established by Common Law Cases 107
4.3.1 Sony Safe Harbor Rule 107
4.3.2 Contributory and Vicarious Liability Rules 108
4.3.3 Authorization or Joint Tortfeasor Liability of Commonwealth Jurisdictions 114
4.4 Internet Service Provider Liability and Safe Harbor Rules Established by Statutes 116
4.4.1 Notice and Takedown Regime 117
4.4.2 Counter Notification Regime 118
4.4.3 Subpoena Procedure or Norwich Pharmacal Order 120
4.5 New Development in Internet Service Provider Liability 122
4.5.1 New Conditions for Safe Harbors on Internet Service Provider Liability: The Graduated Response 122
4.5.2 Internet Service Provider Injunctions Ruled in European Courts 130
4.6 Conclusion: Recommendations for Establishing Certainty of Internet Service Provider Liability 136
References 139

5 Reconstruction of Copyright Limitations and Exceptions in Digital Network Age: Importation of Legal Flexibility and Certainty 141
5.1 Introduction 141
5.2 Theories of Copyright Limitations and Exceptions 144
5.2.1 Academic Arguments That Support Copyright Limitations and Exceptions 144
5.2.2 International Treaty Obligations 146
5.3 Reconstruction of Copyright Limitations and Exceptions 147
5.3.1 Importing Flexibility and Certainty into Copyright Limitations and Exceptions 149
5.3.2 Importing Four-Factor Balancing Test as Abstract Guidance 150
5.3.3 Importing Nonexclusive List of Exceptions as Minute Prescriptions 161
5.4 Supplementary Schemes 166
5.4.1 Compulsory Licensing Scheme 166
5.4.2 Copyright No Action Policy 171
5.4.3 Community Guidelines 172
5.5 Conclusion 172
References 173

6 Construction of Digital Commons and Exploration of Public Domain 175
6.1 Introduction 175
6.2 Alternative Schemes: Digital Commons 177

6.3 Construction and Promotion of Creative Commons 179
6.3.1 Creative Commons Licenses 179
6.3.2 Creative Commons in Greater China 182
6.3.3 Creative Commons China Mainland Licensing 183
6.3.4 Positive and Negative Impacts of Promoting Creative Commons in Mainland China 186
6.4 Impact of Digital Commons on Public Domain 190
6.4.1 Necessity of Public Domain 191
6.4.2 Shrinking Public Domain in Digital Age: Threats from Second Enclosure 193
6.4.3 Constructing Public Domain in Digital Age: Influence of Digital Commons 196
6.5 Conclusion 199
References 199

Conclusion 201
Main Findings 201
Contributions of the Study 204
Revision of Anti-circumvention Rule 205
Amending Internet Service Provider Liability and Safe Harbors 206
Importing Legal Flexibility and Certainty into Copyright Limitations and Exceptions 208
Promoting Digital Commons Projects 209
Concluding Remarks 210
Reference 210

List of Legislations 211

List of Cases 213

Bibliography 215

Introduction

Background

The establishment of copyright protection systems aims to achieve two important purposes: to stimulate the incentive for creation by granting authors a series of exclusive rights on the one hand and promote the progress of culture and public welfare by establishing a series of limitations on these exclusive rights so that the flow of information and dissemination of knowledge will not be hindered on the other hand.

There is always a close relationship between technology development and copyright law. The emergence of personal computers and the Internet has brought about a distinct wave of technological innovation that has reshaped copyright laws by empowering anyone with a connection to flawless, inexpensive, and instantaneous reproduction and distribution of works of authorship. Such technological advancement changes the interests of copyright owners and public users. Users are exposed to more opportunities brought about by digital network technology to obtain access and exploit copyrightable works. If copyright laws do not expand their protected subject matters and categories of exclusive rights, authors cannot be adequately compensated under the digital network environment. Copyright laws can no longer function as an incentive for creation if there is a lack of revision and appropriate expansion. Hence, the development of digital network technologies spurs the continuous expansion of copyright protection systems under which protected subject matters are increased, the categories of exclusive rights of copyright owners are widened, terms of protection are extended, indirect liability is imposed upon technological intermediaries such as Internet service providers (ISPs), protection is granted to digital locks such as technological measures, and copyright limitations and exceptions are restricted.

Developed countries and regions, such as the United States and the European Union, have pioneered to internally reform their copyright legislations in response to digital challenges and externally pressured international organizations to adopt higher standards as international conventional norms. These international conventional principles in turn came back to contracting parties in both developed and developing statuses as obligations which should be domestically fulfilled. In following the endeavors of their developed counterparts, developing countries, such as China, have quickened the process of updating their copyright system in the digital network age due to external pressures imposed by the obligation to implement international conventions on the one hand and the internal need to transform their legal system through legal transplant to match the developments in the information society and knowledge economy on the other hand.

However, copyright expansion should not be unlimited and should cease when appropriate access to works and future creations is at risk. Expansion of copyright protection is only justified when the access and use of works from the public threaten the incentive of authors to create and reap economic rewards. Overexpansion of copyright protection would again disrupt the balance if access to works is narrowly restricted. Overprotection of copyrights will not only obstruct access to original work but will also inhibit future creations based on the original works.

Whether a system shall be adjusted to more protect the interests of copyright owners or reflect that there is increased consideration given to consumer groups and future creators depends on the social values and perspectives of the policymakers. Policymakers should bear the idea that the purpose of establishing a copyright system is not to merely focus on stimulating creation by granting authors with exclusive proprietary rights but also concentrate on serving social welfare and advocating for progress by promoting access and dissemination of copyright works and encouraging future creations based on previous material. The design of a copyright system requires the attainment of social justice, not merely maximizing the protection of commoditization interests.

Social justice includes "not only access to, but also inclusion in, the social, cultural, and economic life of the country. Indeed, it extends beyond inclusion in social, cultural, and economic life to full participation in and ability to affect the direction of civil society in all its manifestations" [1, p. 83]. Social justice should be a part of the goals of intellectual property laws. In the spectrum of copyrights, social justice is realized when people not only have the ability to equally access and enjoy the works created by others but also have equal opportunity to participate in exploitation and creation based on previous works. The subsequent creations which have benefited from preexisting works and information form a benign chain which perpetuates the production of intellectual outputs, advances cultivation of cultural atmospheres, and finally, promotes social progress.

The emergence and rapid development of digital network technology have quickened the recreation chain, as the advancement of technology has simplified the reproduction and dissemination of works, provided mediocrity with the capability to modify and adapt works, enhanced the compactness of works in digital form, and strengthened ability to link and search for information through the Internet. These special features unprecedentedly enable the involvement of ordinary users in creations that are not only based on their own original ideas but also by making derivations and remixing of preexisting copyright material. Continuous recreations may further promote the formation of creative groups, such as fan fiction producers, and spur the spring-up of creative industries. The realization of such continuous recreations relies on a reasonable copyright legal system which grants appropriate copyright protection to the authors and guarantees adequate copyright limitations so that the users can continuously access and exploit copyright works.

The overprotection of proprietary rights in the digital network age will intensify the relationship among copyright holders, information disseminators, and end users, thus satisfying requests for strong copyright protection from powerful copyright industries by sacrificing the interests of technology developers and consumers. In the face of potential copyright infringement liability, technology intermediaries may hesitate to develop new technologies that facilitate information dissemination and adaptation, while consumers may no longer attempt to make full use of copyright works in the absence of clear authorization from the right holders. There is thus an imbalance of interests among the different stakeholders. Furthermore, overprotection will increase the digital divide which already exists between the developed and the developing countries, as well as between economically developed and rural areas. While residents in the more developed areas enjoy greater access to an abundance of information, locals in less developed regions do not have such benefits due to the lack of access to digital technology and the skills to effectively use the technology [1]. To address the conflicts in interest among the different stakeholders and the growing digital divide, copyright systems in the digital network age should be designed to better reflect social utility and social justice. Copyright laws not only cultivate incentives for creation but, more importantly, promote social advancement.

Literature Review

In response to digital network challenges and the difficulties in achieving a balance of interests, various jurisdictions around the world have taken unremitting measures to initiate legal reforms and promulgate new laws.

The United States enacted the Digital Millennium Copyright Act (DMCA) in 1998, with the objective to closely follow new technological developments and address copyright protection issues under the digital network environment. The key parts of the DMCA, namely, the anti-circumvention rules for the protection of technological measures and safe harbors for ISPs, had been incorporated as important sections in the Copyright Act of 1976. Much harsher measures against online piracy were proposed by the US Congress in recent amendment bills, the Protect IP Act (PIPA) and the Stop Online Piracy Act (SOPA). The European Union has issued a series of directives to protect digital copyright works and exclusive rights related to the digital network environment, including the Directive on the Legal Protection of Computer Programs, Directive on the Legal Protection of Databases, Directive on Certain Legal Aspects of Information Society Service in particular Electronic Commerce in the Internal Market, and Directive on the Harmonization of Certain Aspects of Copyright and Related Rights in the Information Society (thereafter, Information Society Directive). Guided by these directives, member countries in the

European Union have continuously updated their regulations and policies. Germany last revised its copyright law in 2008; France initiated a graduated response policy against rampant online piracy in 2009; and the United Kingdom issued the Digital Economy Act in 2010.

Jurisdictions outside North America or Europe have also taken steps to deal with digital copyright issues, especially in the areas of granting protection to exclusive rights related to information dissemination on the network, establishing liability for ISPs and prohibiting unauthorized circumvention of technological measures. Australia promulgated the Copyright (Digital Agenda) Amendment Act in 2000 so as to update its copyright law to fully adapt to the digital network environment. China enacted the Regulation on the Protection of the Right to Network Dissemination of Information in 2006, thus making digital copyright protection comply with national situations while assimilating certain approaches from the DMCA. The Hong Kong government launched public consultations to seek opinions from various sectors on how copyright protection should be strengthened in the digital age. They released the Preliminary Proposals for Strengthening Copyright Protection in the Digital Environment in 2008, the Proposals for Strengthening Copyright Protection in the Digital Environment in 2009, and Copyright (Amendment) Bill 2011. At the multinational level, the Anti-Counterfeiting Trade Agreement (ACTA) was reached and signed by various countries to strengthen protection on intellectual property rights in general and strike at infringement under the digital network environment in particular.

Although new laws, regulations, and treaties have been made to address digital network challenges, focus on these updated promulgations is mainly placed on the concerns and protection of the interests of copyright holders, since some of the provisions are released under pressure from media conglomerates through their lobbying activities. Although a few provisions have taken the concerns and interests of technological intermediaries and public users into consideration, they cannot adequately function well enough to balance the interests of public users against those of right holders.

Research Questions

In contrast to the predigital era when proprietary protection for creative expression was necessary to recover the cost of producing and disseminating information as well as compensate authors and intermediaries, in the participatory web age, strong proprietary protection on creative expression is no longer appropriate in the spirit of the Internet and participatory culture. Production expenses and distribution of information have significantly declined in the advancement of digital network technology. Internet surfers are more willing to engage in recreational activities online or other instrumental purposes rather than simply take in the existing information. Creation in the digital network era is more based on a model that has noncommercialized, nonmarketed, shared, and amateur-generated contents. To adapt to this new environment where recipients of creative products incorporate such into their own future creations, policymakers of copyright laws in the digital network age should further consider and address the following issues: (1) the extent that a copyright owner should restrict access, dissemination, and use of copyright works; (2) the extent that a technological intermediary is allowed to transmit copyright works; (3) the extent that a user is permitted to exploit copyright works and make new creations; and (4) the extent that massive participation in the mash-up and remix culture is tolerated or even encouraged by copyright laws. It is important to well resolve the abovementioned issues so as to alleviate the increasing tension between strong proprietary protection and permissible exploitation of copyright works.

Therefore, three concerns with regard to permissible activities by users should be appropriately addressed through the reform of copyright laws, namely, "user access permission," "user sharing permission," and "user creation permission." User access permission involves the variety of ways for users to obtain access to copyright works without being heavily restricted by technological measures established by copyright owners. In the absence of access to information, users cannot enjoy the lawful consumption of creative products, not to say any further exploitation and potential creation based on the original products. User sharing permission involves the extent of freedom of users to share information with certain social circles, such as family, friends, or peers. Not only are the creators of user-generated contents eager to share their works, but some mainstream content providers are also willing to do so or, at least to a certain degree, share their audiovisual or photographic works. Technology and network platforms should thus be available so as to cultivate a sharing-friendly environment. The use of stringent measures to address alleged copyright infringement of intermediaries and users in their online sharing of creative works will suffocate the desire and channels for information sharing. User creation permission involves the extent that users are allowed to exploit copyright works and copyright laws tolerate or even encourage the remix culture. Copyright limitations and exceptions are established to guarantee reasonable non-infringing use and exploitation of copyright works. The allowance of a broader scope of fair or non-infringing uses of copyright works will provide more opportunities for users to make derivative works. The acknowledgment of the transformative nature of subsequent works and parody is beneficial to further promote the user-generated culture and endorse the value of free speech, criticism, parody, and reporting through copyright laws with respect to cultural traditions [2]. In addition, alternative approaches based on contract law and voluntary licensing act as another approach to advance the dissemination and utilization of copyright works. These alternative approaches, such as the Creative Commons on the one hand, enrich the public domain and are freely exploited by users; yet on the other hand, they ensure that creators have some control over their works, such as reserving the right of attribution and noncommercial use.

Hence, copyright systems should be reformed toward a more balanced and relatively open model so that creative expression can be widely accessed, distributed, exploited, and recreated. It is necessary to reconsider and amend current legal designs with regard to anti-circumvention rules for the protection of technological measures, ISP liability and safe harbors, as well as copyright limitations and exceptions. Alternative approaches that are helpful for reserving the rights of intellectual commons deserve to be supported and promoted. Although there are concerns in many developing countries, such as China, on resolving rampant piracy and resisting pressure imposed by international criticism, a new model of creation based on nonmarket factors, user-generated contents, and a participatory culture has already been presented to the public and mass media, and policymakers should pay attention to this model. When the network age moves toward the development of a participatory culture and era, it is time for developing countries to think about reshaping their copyright regime to reflect cultural features and facilitate creation.

In terms of the future of copyright regimes, according to WIPO Director General Francis Gurry, "the central question facing the evolution of copyright policy is how to maintain a balance between availability of cultural works at affordable prices while assuring a dignified economic existence of creators and performers. There is no 'single magical answer' to the development of a successful policy response to the copyright challenges in the digital age, but a combination of 'law, infrastructure, cultural change, institutional collaboration and better business model.'"[1] Three main principles should guide the development of copyright policy responses. They are "neutrality to technology and to the business models developed in response to technology; comprehensiveness and coherence in the policy response; and the need of more simplicity in copyright."[2] Under Mr. Gurry's analysis, the purpose of copyrighting is to work with technologies to promote cultural exchanges and dynamism, not to preserve vested business interests. A comprehensive and global infrastructure needs to be established to legally permit the licensing of copyright works on the Internet. Attention should be given to the threat to "the financial viability of culture in the 21st century" if there lacks an effective and properly balanced copyright policy.[3]

Research Methodologies and Expected Value

My legal research primarily includes doctrinal, interdisciplinary, and comparative research methodologies.

The doctrinal research will be based on library sources, thus relying on existing information such as monographs, journal articles, case reports, legislations, treaties, and historical records. Collections from the university and institute libraries have provided this book with both common and civil law materials from a diversified range of jurisdictions, such as the United States, the United Kingdom, Hong Kong, Australia, Canada, India, Germany, France, Japan, Taiwan, and Mainland China,

[1] "WIPO Director General Addresses the Future of Copyright," available at http://www.wipo.int/pressroom/en/articles/2011/article_0005.html (visited May 15, 2012).

[2] Ibid.

[3] *See* n 1 above.

and digital and online databases, such as Westlaw, LexisNexis, HeinOnline, ChinaLawInfo, and the China National Knowledge Infrastructure (CNKI).

An interdisciplinary approach will be used to study the philosophical and economic theories with regard to the balance of interest doctrine in the spectrum of intangible property. In addition, since my research is intensively related to digital technology and the Internet, second-hand quantitative data will be used to demonstrate the development of the information network and its influence on the changes in copyright policymaking, advancement of copyright-related industries, and socioeconomic lives.

Another type of methodology covered in my research is the use of comparative study due to the growing importance of international intellectual property treaties and the increasing influence of Western countries on developing countries because the former has more advanced experiences. Due to the widespread importation of the DMCA legislative model with regard to the anti-circumvention rules for the protection of technological measures and ISP liability and safe harbors, my comparative research will focus on the United States, the first nation that exported its legislative approach, and several other jurisdictions, which have assimilated the American model, including Mainland China and Australia. When examining the particular regulations and policies, laws and practices in various other jurisdictions are also studied and analyzed. These jurisdictions include the United Kingdom, France, Germany, Canada, India, Japan, Hong Kong, and Taiwan. Although these countries or regions belong to different jurisdictions, which means that they have different copyright origins and systems, digital and cyberspace copyright issues have now become transnational. In a sense, the United States had pressured some of the countries to oblige to their international or regional convention commitments in terms of their digital and network copyright legislations. Laws and regulations on digital copyright issues in some countries are drawn on the experiences of the United States and the European Union through legal transplant. Therefore, a forefront discussion of copyright reflection and reconstruction in different jurisdictions could shed light on copyright reforms under the digital network environment.

Although many scholars, especially those from Western countries, have discussed digital copyright problems for a decade, copyright reforms that deal with digital network challenges are still new and necessary in developing countries, such as China. Due to the continuous expansion of copyright protection which imposes a threat to the access and dissemination of information as well as the advancement of knowledge and learning, it is time to rethink the current trends of development in copyright systems and amend copyright laws so that they are more balanced. These reflections have been continuously proposed and discussed by Western scholars, since Western countries are the pioneers in developing new technologies which often bring about new problems to information dissemination and copyright protection. However, discussions among Western scholars often focus on the laws, policies, and practices of domestic situations in developed societies with few comparative studies that have an international perspective and little attention on the law reforms and national situations in developing countries. This book intends to examine the digital network-related copyright issues under the balance of interest theory by including China as one of the important rising economies and comparatively analyzing the legal measures and policies among different jurisdictions. The proposals for the new rounds of copyright reforms after concluding on laws in various jurisdictions will be more multidimensional and take more into consideration the interests of developing countries.

As one of the rising economies, China increasingly endeavors to establish herself as an innovative state. In 2008, the Chinese government promulgated the *Outline of the National Intellectual Property Strategy*, with the goal to develop indigenous or self-driven intellectual property [3] and develop national copyright industries. The achievement of such a goal is based on a law reform that well reflects the interests of creators, industries, and consumers as well as the domestic needs both at the present and in the future. The development of communication technology and encouragement of public participation are important for advancing national and indigenous creations. Moreover, the emerging knowledge economy highly promotes the growth of information industries in general and digital libraries and related nonprofit institutes in particular, which meets the need for advancement of knowledge and learning in developing societies, such as China. Good development of information industries and digital educational institutions also requires open access to information and its effective dissemination. Thus, the establishment of a balanced copyright system by including exceptions into the anti-circumvention rules, setting up safe harbors for technology developers, expanding copyright limitations and exceptions, and adopting open-access initiatives may help to achieve the national strategic goal and the social function of copyright law and policies.

Book Structure

This book comprises an introduction, six principal chapters, and a conclusion. The introduction provides the research background and research questions in that a balance of interest among right holders, technological intermediaries, and public users should be recovered due to the continuous expansion of copyright protection. Guarantee of appropriate access, dissemination, and reuse of copyright works are necessary for encouraging future creations and promoting progress in literary, scientific, and art works. This part also explains the research methodologies, research value, and book structure.

Chapter 1 elaborates on the interrelationship of the changes in copyright laws with technology development and illustrates the continuous expansion of copyright protection in the digital network era. Since advancement in digital technologies simplifies and accelerates the reproduction and dissemination of information, authors thus demand more protection granted by copyright laws to safeguard their creations against pirating and their commercial interests from infringement. This chapter introduces the development and adaptation of international copyright conventions under the digital network environment by focusing on the World Intellectual Property Organization (WIPO) Internet Treaties and takes the DMCA of the United States and the Information Society Directive of the European Union as examples to discuss the changes and amendments in the copyright protection systems of the developed regions. The expansion of copyright protection has excessively focused on the interests of right holders and neglected the overall cultural construction and social progress based on free flow of information. By introducing updates in the copyright protection system in China based on legislative, administrative, judicial, and alternative perspectives, this chapter further points out the potential leadership role of the developing countries especially China in the new round of copyright reforms to recover a balance of interest between copyright holders and public users and to address public interests and social justice which are important purposes and functions of a copyright system.

Chapter 2 will discuss the public interest function of intellectual property and copyright systems and the current problem of the imbalance of interest in copyright systems under a digital network environment. This chapter will provide a discussion on the balance of interest that is embodied in intellectual property and copyright systems based on philosophical and economic theories, the origin and development of copyright laws, and the purposes for establishing copyright protection systems. This chapter will then carefully examine the imbalance of interest in current copyright systems from the angles of extended duration of protection, expansive scope of protection, constrained copyright limitations, increased protection for technological measures, aggravated liability of ISPs, and strengthened industry and media concentration. Further analysis and recommendation of proposals based on these issues will be given in the subsequent chapters.

Chapter 3 will analyze the protection of digital rights management (DRM) information and the anti-circumvention rules which prohibit unauthorized circumvention of technological measures. This chapter will first provide a basic understanding on the protection of DRM and technological measures by explaining the key terms that have been incorporated into the anti-circumvention provisions. This chapter will then examine the balanced and unbalanced aspects under the anti-circumvention rules provided by the DMCA of the United States. The balanced aspect is supported by general and specific exceptions as well as an ongoing administrative rulemaking proceeding with regard to the immunization of liability from circumvention acts. However, the problem of imbalance still exists, mainly due to prohibition against the circumvention of access-control measures and trafficking of circumvention-facilitated devices, which outweighs the balanced aspects. The chapter will finally recommend a more balanced model for anti-circumvention rules by including a technological component for minimalist use, a legislative component for general exceptions, a judicial component for case decisions, and an alternative scheme design for protecting technological measures under competition law.

Chapter 4 will analyze the infringement liability for ISPs and safe harbor regulations. This chapter will first provide a definition of ISPs and the significance of setting up the legal certainty of their liability and exemptions. This chapter will also analyze indirect liability and safe harbor rules for ISPs established by common law cases. The influential safe harbor rule developed by the *Sony* case, contributory and vicarious liability developed from American landmark cases, and authorization and joint tortfeasor liabilities developed from Commonwealth landmark cases will be discussed. This chapter will then proceed to analyze a couple of liability and immunization rules enacted by statutes, including the notice and takedown regime, counter notification regime, and the subpoena procedure or Norwich Pharmacal order. This chapter will then elaborate on the recent developments in the conditions for ISP safe harbors and the remedies against ISP indirect infringement, taking the graduated response policy from the French government and injunction orders against ISPs in European courts as example. In this part, the approach of the graduated response policy, the influence of such a policy on copyright owners, ISPs and public users, and China's response to such a policy will be further discussed. Typical cases in which ISP injunctions were granted will be analyzed to indicate the proportionality that courts should take into consideration when deciding whether to approve such remedies. This chapter will finally suggest recommendations to establish certainty for ISP liability and safe harbors in general and for China's digital copyright reform on ISP issues in particular. Recommendations include the establishing of certain standards for important factors in the indirect liability of ISPs, reforming notice and takedown regimes by incorporating a grace period and exceptions, adopting a Norwich Pharmacal procedure to guarantee the privacy of subscribers, and taking a multitude of approaches to better provide certainty for ISP liability.

Chapter 5 will analyze the copyright limitations and exceptions under the digital network environment and suggest the addition of legal flexibility and certainty. This chapter will first discuss academic theoretical analyses and international conventional obligations on copyright limitations and exceptions so as to explain the important function of limitations on exclusive rights that guarantee access to preexisting material and future creations based on borrowing. In light of the increasing convenience of exploitation of copyright works made possible by digital network technology, this chapter will then propose to reconstruct copyright limitations and exceptions by importing a four-factor balancing test based on the US copyright system with focus on the first and fourth factors, namely, the purpose and nature of the use and the influence of the original work on the market as a form of abstract guidance to guarantee legal flexibility and a list of a number of nonexclusive exceptions as minute prescriptions to guarantee legal certainty. The analysis is important because it gauges the transformative nature of user-generated contents and remix creations in the general guidance as well as typical situations in a specified list through comparative research on fair use/fair dealing legislations among different jurisdictions. This chapter will finally suggest several alternative schemes such as statutory licensing, no action notice, and community guidelines to supplement the fair use/fair dealing. Among them, statutory licensing is the most important scheme which can well balance the interests between different shareholders by guaranteeing fair compensation to copyright owners on the one hand and avoiding unfair prejudice to public users on the other hand.

Chapter 6 will analyze the emergence of digital commons based on voluntary licensing schemes and their influence on restoring the shrinking public domain. This chapter will first provide an introduction on anti-copyright tendencies and the birth of open-access projects which comprise digital commons. This chapter will then examine a well-known example of digital commons, namely, the Creative Commons, which provides authors with the opportunity to release their works under certain licenses. By publishing works under these licenses, authors give up a part of their copyright to allow free access and dissemination of their works. The Creative Commons has been launched and localized in many jurisdictions, including China, with the purpose of promoting information flow and encouraging amateur creations. Finally, the influence of digital commons represented by projects like the Creative Commons on the public domain which is shrinking due to the continuous expansion of copyright protection will be analyzed.

The conclusion will conclude on the main findings of the study and contributions by summarizing the problems and suggested proposals for digital copyright issues, including the anti-circumvention rules, ISP liability and safe harbors, copyright limitations and exceptions under the digital network environment, and advancement of digital commons and their influence in maintaining the public domain. In sum, the digital copyright system will be reviewed and amended by placing more emphasis on public interest and social justice with an appropriate response to the participatory culture and advancement of technology rather than overprotecting proprietary right holders.

References

1. Mtima, L., & Jamar, S. D. (2010/2011). Fulfilling the copyright social justice promise: Digitizing textual information. *New York Law School Law Review, 55*, 77–108.
2. Ricketson, S. (1999). *The law of intellectual property: Copyright, designs and confidential information.* Sydney: LBC Information Services.
3. State Council of People's Republic of China. *Outline of the national intellectual property strategy*. Available at http://english.sipo.gov.cn/laws/developing/200906/t20090616_465239.html. Visited 21 Jun 2008.

[illegible]

Chapter 1
Copyright Law Changes and Developments in Digital Network Era

1.1 Introduction

Copyright laws originate and develop with the advancement of technology. Technology updates dramatically change the ways in which works are accessible and disseminated. Thus, copyright systems are continuously revised to respond to new approaches of reproducing and distributing works brought about by technology and new requirements put forth by copyright owners to enforce their exclusive rights.

Developed countries and regions that experience rapid technological development, such as the United States and the European Union, bore the brunt of amending and reforming their original copyright systems in the face of new challenges. However, their domestic legal reforms cannot entirely solve the problems brought on by digital technologies anymore, since the Internet easily facilitates the transmitting of information and works beyond national borders and without permission from the copyright owners. A strong domestic copyright cannot guarantee the same level of protection against infringement by other countries. Thus, the pioneer jurisdictions called for the establishment of basic norms in international conventions and incorporation of new provisions to deal with digital challenges. The results of the international conventions and treaties were then taken back to these jurisdictions as obligations for compliance. The obligatory implementation of international conventions by various jurisdictions thus led to the enactment of a series of domestic and regional digital copyright laws, such as the DMCA in the United States and the Information Society Directive in the European Union.

As one of the leading developing countries, China is among the many jurisdictions that are amending and reforming their copyright protection mechanisms mainly through the domestic implementation of international obligations and legal transplant. In 1980, China joined the WIPO, an international agency that is dedicated to developing a balanced and accessible international intellectual property system [1]. Subsequently, China acceded to a couple of international conventions and agreements which are under the management and administration of the

J.J. Hua, *Toward A More Balanced Approach: Rethinking and Readjusting Copyright Systems in the Digital Network Era*, DOI 10.1007/978-3-662-43517-5_1,

WIPO, which range from substantive treaties that deal with copyrights, patents, and trademark issues to procedural treaties. The WIPO treaties in terms of copyright protection under which China is a contracting party are the Berne Convention for the Protection of Literary and Artistic Works (thereafter, the Berne Convention), Convention for the Protection of Producers and Phonograms against Unauthorized Duplication of Their Phonograms (Geneva Phonograms Convention), WIPO Copyright Treaty (WCT), and WIPO Performances and Phonograms Treaty (WPPT) [1]. With growth in trade that is linked to intellectual products, the World Trade Organization (WTO) is yet another forum that promotes the protection of intellectual property worldwide. China became a member of the WTO in 2001, therefore signatory to the Agreement on Trade-Related Aspects of Intellectual Property Rights (thereafter, the TRIPS Agreement).

The Chinese Copyright Law was issued in 1991 to fulfill the international obligations of protecting copyrights. In 2001, the Amendment to the Copyright Law was released under the pressure of resolving problems created by digital network technologies. By fulfilling conventional requirements and borrowing legislative approaches from developed societies, such as the United States and the European Union, China enacted a set of statutes, regulations, and judicial interpretations to better implement the Amendment.

This chapter will provide an introduction on the changes in copyright systems and their development trends in the digital network era. Then, there will be an elaboration on the interrelationship of copyright law changes with technological development, and the continuous expansion of copyright protection in the digital network era will be pointed out. Then, there will be a discussion of the international copyright protection system and the development trends under a digital network environment with focus on the WIPO Internet Treaties, which will demonstrate the changes in copyright laws and policies in response to digital technology advancement among typical jurisdictions, such as the United States and the European Union. An analysis of the DMCA in the United States and the Information Society Directive in the European Union will demonstrate the influence of these legislations on amendments in copyright systems in developing countries such as China under a digital network environment. Then, the latest developments in the Chinese copyright protection system will be outlined by examining the most updated copyright legislations and policies, administrative and judicial enforcement mechanisms, and alternative copyright protection schemes, such as collecting societies and alternative dispute resolutions. However, the systematic changes do not mean that China has reached an optimal level of copyright protection in the digital network era. On the contrary, this is just the first step in dealing with such issues. In the process of implementing the amended legislations and enforcement mechanisms, China will face more challenges than anticipated. Only by continually improving the legislation based on the changing environment as well as taking into consideration research on international conventions and the experiences of other countries will China be able to establish her own balanced copyright protection system in the digital network age.

1.2 Interrelationship Between Technology Development and Copyright Laws

There is always a close relationship between technology development and law reform. When advancement of technology brings about new changes to social lives and challenges existing legal relationships, the laws will often be amended and reformed to adapt to the new environment and address new problems. Such an interrelationship is especially reflected in the area of copyright laws. The birth and development of copyright laws have been continuously affected by technological advancements. The invention of the printing press spurred the emergence of copyright laws. The development of communication technology led to the birth of new inventions which accelerated the reproduction and distribution of various types of works, including sound recordings, photography, and motion pictures. These new communication and broadcasting technologies "triggered a second wave of expansions and adjustments to copyright" [2, p. 411]. The emergence of the personal computer and the Internet brought about "a third distinct wave of technological innovation reshaping copyright law" by empowering anyone with a connection to flawless, inexpensive, and instantaneous reproduction and distribution of works of authorship [2, p. 411].

In the fifteenth century, Gutenberg's invention of the printing press resulted in the efficient and costless reproduction of literary works. The printing technology generated the early publishing industries which demanded protection to safeguard their privileges and interests in reproducing literary works. The earliest form of protection was granted by the Venetian Republic as a patent right to print books in all Venetian territories for a limited period of time [2, p. 412]. The growth of publishing industries in the few decades that followed led to the recognition of the Venetian Cabinet as having the exclusive rights in printing particular books [2, p. 412]. After the printing press was imported to England and London became the center of trade, for the first time, England issued a royal decree that granted copyright protection to the publishing industry. The Stationers' Company was established and granted the exclusive right to control the printing business for an infinite amount of time [2, p. 413]. The call to terminate such exclusive rights, like that of the Stationers' Company, and the fierce competition in the printing market, stimulated the passing of the Statute of Anne in England in 1710 [3]. The Statute of Anne granted authors with the exclusive right to control the reproduction of their works for a limited time of 14 years, renewable for an additional 14 years. In the same period of time, continental Europe developed a different approach to protect the interests of authors by developing a parallel system which granted authors both economic and moral rights. Following the legislative model of the Statute of Anne, the first Copyright Act in the United States was passed by Congress in 1790. Under the Copyright Act of 1790, authors had exclusive rights over books, maps, and charts that they had created for 14 years which could be renewed for another 14 years [2].

Copyright laws have subsequently experienced numerous changes due to the emergence of new technologies. During the late nineteenth to the late twentieth century, new communication and broadcasting technologies, such as photography, sound recording, radio broadcasting, filming, television broadcasting, and satellite imaging, enriched the variety of works produced, increased ways of transmitting information, as well as spurred the establishment of a series of new copyright-related industries. Expressions of literary works were not merely confined to paper-based text but rather expanded to images, sound, and motion pictures. The rapid development of the music, film, and broadcasting industries imposed more concerns about the protection of newly emerging works. In response to these new changes, copyright laws expanded to cover an increased number of subject matters and exclusive rights and largely extended the terms of protection. For example, the United States Copyright Act of 1909 expanded the definition of protected literary works to "all writings" and amended the protection period from an initial 28 years renewable to an additional 28 years [2]. The Copyright Act of 1976 further expanded "all writings" to all written works "fixed in a tangible medium of expression," including literary, musical, drama, pantomime and choreographic, pictorial, graphic and sculptural works, motion pictures, sound recordings, and architectural works.[1] The protection period was further extended to the life of the author plus 50 years. During this period of time, a couple of significant international copyright conventions, such as the Berne Convention, were reached, under which certain minimum standards of copyright protection were established and imposed as international obligations to member countries.

Computers and the Internet were significant inventions in the late twentieth century that further accelerated information dissemination and reduced the expenses of reproduction and communication. The rapid development of digital network technology has generated a significant influence on various socioeconomic aspects, such as creation style, means of expression and communication, and the ways that businesses operate. The influence and challenges brought on by digital network technology can be summarized into several typical features. First, replication and transmission of works are simplified. The digital technology used to create and view digital work can be used to make multiple perfect copies of that work [4]. Facilitated by the Internet and mobile network, various works and perfect replications of these works can be quickly and cheaply distributed to almost every corner of the world where access to computers and the Internet is available. Secondly, digital network technology empowers people with the capability to easily modify or adapt works in the digital form [4]. With the aid of multimedia tools, ordinary users can manipulate digitalized works through editing, clipping, rerecording, and making adaptations and derivations. Such remixing of existing works has generated many new creations. Thirdly, digital network technology has greatly enhanced the compactness of works in the digital form [4]. Hundreds or thousands of copyright works in text, image, sound, or video formats can be stored onto one CD/DVD disk. This "feature also assists in the creation of new works or assemblages of printed and graphic

[1] The United States Copyright Act of 1976, s 102.

materials" [4, p. 11]. Finally, the information network has provided the means to connect and search. With connection to the Internet and use of search engines, individuals can quickly find the exact work that they need.

As digital network technology almost changes every stage in the value chain of copyright work production from reproduction to distribution, copyright owners and industries are more concerned about whether traditional copyright systems are able to protect their interests in the digital network age. Their demands and lobbying compelled governments to promulgate new copyright laws and regulations, particularly in addressing copyright protection issues under a digital network environment.

1.3 Amendment and Expansion of Copyright Protection Under Digital Network Environment

1.3.1 Amendment and Development of International Copyright Conventions

Among the many international copyright conventions and treaties, the most important three are the Berne Convention which has established some basic standards and minimum protection, the TRIPS Agreement which associates copyright protection with international trade, and the WIPO Internet Treaties which address copyright issues under a digital network environment.

As the first international copyright treaty, the Berne Convention has established some basic principles and minimum protection standards that have deeply influenced international copyright agreements established thereafter and the formation of domestic copyright legislations in many countries. These basic principles and minimum standards of protection clearly stipulate the works and rights to be protected and the duration of the protection. The protection of "literary and artistic works" in the Berne Convention covers "every production in the literary, scientific and artistic domain, whatever may be the mode or form of its expression."[2] The exclusive rights protected under the Berne Convention contain both economic and moral rights, including the right to translate; make adaptations and arrangements to the work; perform and recite the works in public; communicate the work to the public through drama, musical, or cinematographic performance; broadcast; reproduce in any manner or form; use the works as the basis for audiovisual works and reproduce, distribute, and perform in public or communicate the audiovisual works to the public,[3] as well as "the right to claim authorship of the work and the right to object to any mutilation or deformation or other modification of, or other derogatory

[2] Berne Convention for the Protection of Literary and Artistic Works, Art 2(1).

[3] Berne Convention for the Protection of Literary and Artistic Works, Arts 8, 9, 11, 11bis, 11ter, 12, and 14. *Also see* "Summary of the Berne Convention for the Protection of Literary and Artistic

action in relation to, the work which would be prejudicial to the author's honor or reputation."[4] The term of protection of these exclusive rights covers a period that is no less than 50 years after the author's death.[5]

As the first international treaty that incorporated intellectual property protection into an international trade framework, the TRIPS Agreement harmonizes intellectual property protection among different nations, expands protected subject matters to computer programs and databases, increases the minimum protection standards in previous conventions and treaties by providing right of rental to authors of computer programs and producers of sound recordings and films, and established mandatory dispute settlement procedures to permit the effective enforcement of rights protection.[6] The TRIPS Agreement has substantively borrowed from the principles of the WIPO international conventions in its own provisions and provides for a "consultative relation between the TRIPS Council and the WIPO."[7]

In the face of the challenges aroused by digital network technologies, more and more efforts were placed into driving the enactment of new international copyright conventions due to increased demand because the Berne Convention was not revised after 1971, as the last revision conference in Paris "had almost seen the complete breakdown of the international copyright system, as a huge gulf emerged between developed and developing countries" [5, p. 136]. The prevailing opinion of experts was that it would be risky to instigate a new revision process as there was the possibility that this could again lead to disengagement between different countries [5, p. 136]. Therefore, two new treaties were adopted by the WIPO in response to the demands and efforts, namely, the WCT and its companion, the WPPT.

In December 1996, the WCT and the WPPT were adopted at the WIPO international diplomatic conference in Geneva. These two treaties contained a general update of the legal principles that underpin the international protection of copyrights and the rights of performers and phonogram producers in cyberspace, more particularly in the world related to the Internet [3, p. 36]. Thus, together, they are dubbed the "WIPO Internet Treaties."

The WCT was established based on the Berne Convention so as to modernize international copyright systems and usher those systems into the digital network age. Article 1 of the WCT explicitly states that the treaty is "a special agreement within the meaning of Article 20 of the Berne Convention" and the treaty "shall not have any connection with treaties other than the Berne Convention, nor shall

Works (1886)," available at http://www.wipo.int/treaties/en/ip/berne/summary_berne.html (visited Oct 18, 2011).

[4] Berne Convention for the Protection of Literary and Artistic Works, Art 6bis(1). *Also see* "Summary of the Berne Convention for the Protection of Literary and Artistic Works (1886)," available at http://www.wipo.int/treaties/en/ip/berne/summary_berne.html (visited Oct 18, 2011).

[5] Berne Convention for the Protection of Literary and Artistic Works, Art 7(1).

[6] TRIPS Agreement, Arts 9–14 and 64.

[7] TRIPS Agreement, Art 68.

it prejudice any rights and obligations under any other treaties."[8] The treaty also provides that "any Contracting Party (even if it is not bound by the Berne Convention) must comply with the substantive provisions of the 1971 (Paris) Act of the Berne Convention."[9]

Built on the minimum standards of protection under the Berne Convention, the WCT modernizes and expands copyright protection to the digital network environment. First, the treaty adds two more subject matters that are to be protected by copyright, namely, computer programs and compilation of data or other materials (so-called databases) provided that "the selection or arrangement of their contents constitutes intellectual creations."[10] However, the protection of databases does not extend to the data or materials themselves contained thereof.

Secondly, the treaty expands three kinds of rights, namely, the right of distribution, rental, and communication to the public. Article 6 of the WCT indicates that the right of distribution is the right to authorize "the making available to the public of the original and copies of their works through sale or other transfer of ownership." It gives the contracting party the freedom to determine conditions or exceptions of the distribution right, such as the exhaustion of the right after the first sale and other transfer of ownership of the work.[11] While the right of distribution under the Berne Convention only applies to cinematographic works, this right in the WCT is extended to works in all categories. The right of rental is stated in Article 7 of the WCT as the right to authorize commercial rental to the public of the originals or copies of three kinds of works, including computer programs, cinematographic works, and works embodied in phonograms.[12] The protection of such a right does not apply where the computer program is not the essential object of the rental and in the case of cinematographic works, commercial rental does not lead to widespread copying of the works thus materially impairing the right of reproduction.[13] Article 8 of the WCT introduces a somewhat new right, that is, the right of communication to the public which particularly deals with the copyright infringement issue under the Internet environment. The article grants authors with the exclusive right to "authorize any communication to the public of their works, by wire or wireless means, including the making available to the public of their works in such a way that members of the public may access these works from a

[8] WIPO Copyright Treaty, Art 1(1). Article 20 of the Berne Convention provides that "countries of the Berne Union reserve the right to enter into special agreements among themselves, in so far as such agreements grant to authors more extensive rights than those granted by the Convention, or contain other provisions not contrary to this Convention."

[9] "Summary of the WIPO Copyright Treaty (WCT) (1996)," available at http://www.wipo.int/treaties/en/ip/wct/summary_wct.html (visited Oct 19, 2011).

[10] Ibid. *Also See* WIPO Copyright Treaty, Arts 4 and 5.

[11] WIPO Copyright Treaty, Art 6(2).

[12] WIPO Copyright Treaty, Art 7.

[13] Ibid.

place and at a time individually chosen by them."[14] It covers in particular, on-demand, interactive communication through the Internet.[15]

Thirdly, the treaty grants protection to technological measures and rights management information. It obliges the contracting parties to provide adequate and effective legal remedies against the circumvention of effective technological measures, such as encryption, which is used by authors in connection with the exercise of their rights and against the removal and alteration of electronic rights management information or the distribution, importing, broadcasting, or communicating to the public of works that have their rights management information removed.[16] The electronic rights management information includes certain data that identifies the works or their authors or is necessary for the copyright owners to exercise the management of their rights, such as licensing, collecting, and distribution of royalties.[17]

Fourthly, similar to the Berne Convention and TRIPS Agreement, the WCT stipulates limitations and exceptions to the exclusive rights of copyright owners as a three-step test, which provides that limitations and exceptions shall be "in certain special cases that do not conflict with a normal exploitation of the work and do not unreasonably prejudice the legitimate interests of the author."[18]

Finally, the WCT obliges the contracting parties to provide effective measures that ensure the application of the treaty with enforcement procedures available in the domestic laws.[19] Where necessary, expeditious remedies shall be granted to prevent infringement and deter further infringing actions.

As a counterpart of the WCT, the WPPT mainly deals with the protection of the neighboring rights of two types of beneficiaries, performers and phonogram producers, under the digital network environment. The WPPT grants a broad right of reproduction that "authorize(s) direct or indirect reproduction of the phonogram in any manner or form"[20] to producers of phonograms and performers whose performances are fixed in phonograms. It also provides the two beneficiaries with some new rights, such as the right of distribution, rental, and making available of fixed performances and phonograms similar to the counterpart provisions in the WCT.[21] In the case that the performances are unfixed, the WPPT grants three kinds of economic rights, namely, the right of broadcasting, communication to the public, and fixation of the unfixed performances.[22] In contrast to the former international conventions that protect neighboring rights, the WPPT protects the moral rights of

---

[14] WIPO Copyright Treaty, Art 8.

[15] "Summary of the WCT," (*see* n 9 above).

[16] WIPO Copyright Treaty, Arts 11 and 12.

[17] Ibid. "Summary of the WCT," (*see* n 9 above).

[18] WIPO Copyright Treaty, Art 10.

[19] WIPO Copyright Treaty, Art 14.

[20] WIPO Performances and Phonograms Treaty, Arts 7 and 11. *Also see* "Summary of the WIPO Performances and Phonograms Treaty (WPPT) (1996)," available at http://www.wipo.int/treaties/en/ip/wppt/summary_wppt.html (visited Oct 19, 2011).

[21] WIPO Performances and Phonograms Treaty, Arts 8, 9, 10, 12, 13, and 14.

[22] WIPO Performances and Phonograms Treaty, Art 6.

performers for the first time. Performers have the right to claim to be identified as performers and object to any distortion, mutilation, or other modifications of their performances that would be prejudicial to the reputation of the performers.[23] Similar to the WCT, the WPPT also provides legal remedies against the circumvention of technological measures and removal or alteration of rights management information.[24] Enforcement of the treaty is also obliged on the contracting parties to stem the infringement of rights.[25]

The WCT and WPPT came into force on March 6, 2002 and May 20, 2002, respectively.[26] Each treaty had to be ratified or acceded by 30 countries before it could be effective.[27] The current contracting parties of both treaties come from various regions of the world, including both developed and developing countries. In other words, the establishment of the WIPO Internet Treaties was a cornerstone in the updating and improving of existing copyright protection systems to match the development of digital network technologies.

1.3.2 Changes and Amendments of Copyright Protection Systems in Developed Regions

In the process of implementing international conventional obligations, some developed countries and regions reacted quickly to address copyright challenges that were transpired by the rise in digital network technologies by introducing new policies and drawing up new laws. The United States and the European Union are the two regions which led the process.

As one of the information technology powers, the United States expediently responded to digital copyright challenges after recognizing the emerging significance and influence of new media and Internet technologies. President Clinton formed the Information Infrastructure Task Force (IITF) in February 1993 to fulfill the goal of the administration to dramatically enhance public access to information through the National Information Infrastructure (NII). The Working Group on Intellectual Property Rights (thereafter, the Working Group) was established within the Information Policy Committee of the IITF. From 1994 to 1996, the Working Group examined whether the current intellectual property regime was appropriate for maintaining a proper balance between the public interest in free flow of information and the economic interest of the creators. The efforts of the Working Group resulted in a report called the White Paper in 1995. Based on the White Paper, an influential legislation, the DMCA, was later promulgated in 1998 by Congress,

---

[23] WIPO Performances and Phonograms Treaty, Art 5.

[24] WIPO Performances and Phonograms Treaty, Arts 18 and 19.

[25] WIPO Performances and Phonograms Treaty, Art 23.

[26] "Summary of the WPPT" (*see* n 20 above).

[27] Ibid.

which implemented the WIPO Internet Treaties and addressed digital copyright issues from various angles.

The development of digital technology also increased the supply of intellectual goods and services as well as multinational trade in the European Union. The increase in trade caused serious piracy issues over intellectual goods and the protection of intellectual property rights. In order to stifle piracy and illegitimate trade, the European Committee began to introduce intellectual property or copyright policies to guarantee the free and legitimate flow of goods and services. The Green Paper on Copyright and the Challenges of Technology was issued in 1988 under such a circumstance, which outlined issues such as piracy, home-recording of audiovisual works, and copyright protection of computer programs and databases [6]. The subsequent revision to the first Green Paper was the Follow-up to the Green Paper: Working Programme of the Commission in the Field of Copyright and Neighbouring Rights, released in 1991 [6]. The second Green Paper was issued to update the first version in 1995 with a follow-up document released in 1996. These documents laid the foundation for the later development of a series of copyright directives which addressed issues in the digital network environment. Relevant copyright directives included, but were not limited to, the Directive on the Legal Protection of Computer Programs[28]; Directive on Rental Right and Lending Right and on Certain Rights Related to Copyright in the Field of Intellectual Property[29]; Directive on the Legal Protection of Databases[30]; Directive on Certain Legal Aspects of Information Society Services, in Particular Electronic Commerce, in the Internal Market[31]; and Information Society Directive.[32] Among them, the last directive, namely, the Information Society Directive, is the most important directive to implement the WIPO Internet Treaties in the European region.

1.3.2.1 Digital Millennium Copyright Act

The DMCA of the United States was signed into law in 1998 and comprised five parts, including the "WIPO Copyright and Performances and Phonograms Treaties Implementation Act of 1998," "Online Copyright Infringement Liability Limitation Act," "Computer Maintenance Competition Assurance Act," six miscellaneous provisions, and the "Vessel Hull Design Protection Act."[33] The most important parts are the former two which were later incorporated into the United States Copyright Act of 1976 as Chapter 12 and Section 512, respectively, to

[28] 91/250/EEC, 1991.

[29] 92/100/EEC, 1992.

[30] 96/9/EC, 1996.

[31] 2000/31/EC, 2000.

[32] 2001/29/EC, 2001.

[33] "The Digital Millennium Copyright Act of 1998: U.S. Copyright Office Summary," available at http://www.copyright.gov/legislation/dmca.pdf (visited Oct 20, 2011).

address the issues of protection on technological measures and exceptions for indirect infringing liability of ISPs.

In order to implement the WIPO Internet Treaties and link domestic laws to the treaties, Title I of the DMCA led to two new prohibitions in its Copyright Act, Chapter 12; one prohibition was on the circumvention of technological protection measures (TPMs) adopted by copyright owners to prevent the unauthorized use of their works, and the other was on the removal or alteration of DRM information used to identify copyrighted works and their authors. Generally, the amended law protects two kinds of TPMs, those that control access to copyrighted works and those that control the copying of the works. The circumvention of the former and trafficking of devices which are used to circumvent both types of TPMs are prohibited. A few exceptions are embodied under anti-circumvention rules. The first exception is a general provision for law enforcement, intelligence, and other governmental activities.[34] The second exception established a triennial "rule-making proceeding to evaluate the impact of the prohibition against the act of circumventing such access-control measures."[35] The third exception lists seven detailed situations, including use by nonprofit libraries and education institutions, reverse engineering, encryption research, protection of minors, personal privacy, and security testing.

DRM information is protected by prohibiting the providing, distributing, or importing of false DRM information with the intent to induce, enable, facilitate, or conceal infringement, intentional removal, or alteration of DRM information without authority, as well as distribution or importing for distribution of works or copies of works, knowing that the DRM information has been removed or altered without authorization.[36] A general exception also applies to the protection of DRM information for law enforcement, intelligence, and other governmental activities.[37] In addition, exceptions also apply to broadcast stations and cable systems under certain circumstances where there is no intent to induce, enable, facilitate, or conceal infringement.[38]

Title II of the DMCA provided a new section, Section 512, which was added to the Copyright Act, and contained limitations on the indirect liability of ISPs for the copyright infringement of Internet subscribers. These limitations are based on four categories of ISP conducts: transitory communication where the ISP merely acts as a data conduit, transmitting of digital information from one point on a network to another at someone else's request; system caching where the ISP retains copies, for a limited time, of material that has been made available online by a person other than the ISP and then transmitted to a subscriber under his/her direction; storage of information on systems or networks under the direction of the users; and information location tools where the ISP refers or links users to a

[34] Ibid.

[35] *See* n 33 above, p. 5.

[36] *See* n 33 above. *Also see* The United States Copyright Act of 1976, ss 1202(a)–(b).

[37] *See* n 33 above. *Also see* The United States Copyright Act of 1976, s 1202(d).

[38] *See* n 33 above. *Also see* The United States Copyright Act of 1976, s 1202(e).

site that contains infringing material by providing information location tools, such as search engines, hyperlinks, or online directories.[39]

1.3.2.2 Information Society Directive

The Information Society Directive is the most important directive in the European Union which implements the WIPO Internet Treaties. As the directive encompasses more information, the member states must implement the Information Society Directive before they can implement the Internet Treaties. The Information Society Directive came into effect in 2001 with the main purpose of updating the terms of copyright protection and neighboring rights in the digital network environment and harmonizing certain economic rights.

Among the four chapters in the Information Society Directive, the second and third chapters are significant as they contain certain economic rights and exceptions as well as protection of technological measures and rights management information, respectively.

The Information Society Directive basically regulates three categories of economic rights, namely, reproduction, communication to the public or made available to the public, and distribution. With respect to the right to reproduce, the Information Society Directive articulates that temporary reproduction by any means and in any form is covered under the right to reproduce.[40] In terms of communication to the public, the Information Society Directive adapts this right to a digital network environment by echoing the WIPO Internet Treaties: "Member States shall provide authors with the exclusive right to authorize or prohibit any communication to the public of their works, by wire or wireless means, including the making available to the public of their works in such a way that members of the public may access them from a place and at a time individually chosen by them."[41]

Article 5 of the Information Society Directive lists some exceptions and limitations, including 1 compulsory exception and another 20 optional exceptions. The compulsory exception allows temporary reproduction which is transient or incidental and an integral and essential part of a technological process, and its sole purpose is to enable a transmission in a network between third parties or a lawful use of a work without any independent economic significance.[42] In essence, this compulsory exception provides protection to ISPs by immunizing them from infringing liability in their conducts such as transitory and automatic reproduction of works for the purpose of transmission over the internet. As for the non-mandatory exceptions, 5 of them cater to the right to reproduce and the other 15 are for both the right to reproduce and communication to the public.[43]

---

[39] The United States Copyright Act of 1976, ss 512(a)–(d).

[40] Information Society Directive of the European Union, Art 2.

[41] Information Society Directive of the European Union, Art 3(1).

[42] Information Society Directive of the European Union, Art 5(1).

[43] Information Society Directive of the European Union, Arts 5(2)(3).

Similar exceptions and limitations may also apply to the right of distribution to the extent justified by the purpose of the authorized act of reproduction.[44] The adoption of detailed non-mandatory exceptions reflects the different interests and needs of different member states. Influenced by the three-step test in the Berne Convention and the TRIPS Agreement, the Information Society Directive includes the same wording as those in the international conventions and narrows the scope for both the mandatory and voluntary exceptions, to include "certain special cases which do not conflict with a normal exploitation of the work or other subject-matter and do not unreasonably prejudice the legitimate interests of the rightholder."[45]

Chapter III of the Information Society Directive grants protection to technological measures and rights management information, which implements relevant provisions in the WIPO Internet Treaties and establishes a legislative model similar to that of the DMCA in the United States.

1.3.3 New Stages of Copyright Reforms

The period during late 2011–2013 witnessed a new stage in copyright reforms that took place among different jurisdictions worldwide with the goal to seriously address infringement under the digital network environment. Some of the new legal proposals initiated unexpected leapfrog steps to strike online piracy, which have been widely criticized and opposed by technology industries, technical experts, and scholars as they are considered to be biased and ill-considered.

In the United States, the PIPA and SOPA bills were introduced in May 2011 and October 2011, respectively, with the purpose of empowering the government and copyright holders to bridle access to infringing websites. The PIPA attacks "rogue websites operated and registered overseas" [7]. Under the PIPA, the United States Department of Justice (DOJ) can seek court orders against infringing websites and require financial transaction providers, Internet advertising services, ISPs, and information location tools to stop financial transactions with these websites and remove links to them.[46] In addition, the court order requested by the Attorney General of the DOJ can prompt non-authoritative domain name servers to take the least burdensome, most technically feasible and reasonable measures to prevent the domain name from resolving to the Internet protocol address of a website which has been found to be infringing.[47] Copyright holders who are negatively affected by the infringing activities of websites can also apply for court orders to require financial transaction providers and Internet advertising services to stop transactions and

[44] Information Society Directive of the European Union, Art 5(4).

[45] Information Society Directive of the European Union, Art 5(5).

[46] Protect IP Act, s 3(d)(2).

[47] Protect IP Act, s 3(d)(2)(A)(i).

advertising on infringing websites, but cannot prompt domain name servers to take remedy measures that are available to the DOJ.[48]

SOPA provides similar proceedings as PIPA by empowering the DOJ to seek court order against overseas websites that are dedicated to enabling or facilitating copyright infringement and to prevent online advertising networks, payment facilitators, search engines, and ISPs from conducting business with infringing websites, as well as providing linkages and access to them.[49] As for the remedies for copyright holders, the SOPA provides a two-step procedure under which copyright holders must first notify the payment facilitators and advertising networks of the infringing websites and then allow them to send notification to the identified websites and possibly suspend their services.[50] If payment facilitators and advertising networks fail to suspend services, or if the identified websites provide counter arguments of their charges, the copyright holders can then sue for limited injunctive relief against the website operators.[51]

Apart from domestic reforms of legislations, a multilateral treaty, the ACTA, was also reached to strengthen intellectual property protection and enforcement outside traditional multinational forums, such as the WIPO and WTO. The ACTA was first signed in October 2011 by Australia, Canada, Japan, Morocco, New Zealand, Singapore, South Korea, and the United States and later signed in January 2012 by the European Union and 22 other countries which are member states of the European Union.[52] One of the important issues that are handled by the ACTA is the enforcement of intellectual property protection in the digital environment. Under the ACTA, civil and criminal enforcement should be available under domestic laws to permit effective action against infringement of intellectual property in the digital environment.[53] Competent authorities of member countries can order ISPs to expeditiously disclose information of alleged infringing subscribers to the right holders where sufficient claims of infringement have been filed by the right holders for the purpose of protecting their rights.[54] The ACTA prohibits the unauthorized circumvention of copy-control technological measures and trafficking of circumvention devices, as well as unauthorized removal of DRM information and knowing distribution of works which have their DRM information altered.[55]

---

[48] Protect IP Act, s 4(d)(2).

[49] "Stop Online Piracy Act," available at http://en.wikipedia.org/wiki/Stop_Online_Piracy_Act (visited July 13, 2012).

[50] "Bill Summary & Status, 112th Congress (2011–2012), H.R. 3261, CRS Summary," available at http://www.webcitation.org/643NehNoc (visited July 13, 2012).

[51] Ibid.

[52] "Anti-Counterfeiting Trade Agreement," available at http://en.wikipedia.org/wiki/Anti-Counterfeiting_Trade_Agreement (visited July 12, 2012).

[53] Anti-Counterfeiting Trade Agreement, Art 27 paragraph 1.

[54] Anti-Counterfeiting Trade Agreement, Art 27 paragraph 4.

[55] Anti-Counterfeiting Trade Agreement, Art 27 paragraphs 5–7.

Despite efforts to combat the infringement of intellectual property rights on the internet, the PIPA, SOPA, and ACTA have been criticized by opponents as lacking transparency; having adverse influences on fundamental civil rights, such as freedom of speech and protection of privacy; and suffocating the advancement of technology and the internet. The negotiation process of the ACTA was kept a secret before it was leaked out on the internet, in which it was found that the ACTA had excluded the developing countries and civil societies [8]. Although the ACTA provides that the protection of intellectual property rights in the digital environment should be enforced in a manner that preserves "fundamental principles such as freedom of expression, fair process and privacy,"[56] the briefness of the article without any further explanations or details on exceptions cannot well guarantee these fundamental civil rights which are endangered by the risk of Internet censorship and random surveillance from network operators. The opponents believe that all of the three legal proposals create unreasonably harsh legal standards that neglect safe harbors which have already been incorporated into existing laws to protect ISPs from infringement liability under certain conditions. The three proposals leave no options for ISPs which thus must comply with the provisional requirements to invade the privacy or freedom of expression of their subscribers. Due to the ubiquitous protests against the three proposals, none of them have been implemented. Further official discussions with regard to the three proposals will also be shelved if further consensus cannot be reached.

In contrast to the severe reprimanding of online piracy put forth by the PIPA, SOPA, and ACTA, some developed jurisdictions are attempting to amend their copyright legislations in a more balanced manner by taking copyright limitations and exceptions into consideration. Hong Kong is one of these jurisdictions. In the Copyright (Amendment) Bill 2011, a technology-neutral exclusive right is introduced "for copyright owners to communicate their works through any mode of electronic transmission" on the one hand, and exceptions are provided "for better preservation of works and dissemination of knowledge" on the other hand.[57] The exceptions include safe harbors for ISPs, exceptions granted to ISPs for temporary reproduction of copyright works, and exceptions given for media shifting of sound recordings for private and domestic use.[58] Under the proposed safe harbor rule, ISPs will not be required to actively supervise their service platforms to qualify for safe harbor protection.[59] ISPs are requested to initiate action against the specified infringement upon receiving proper notifications from the copyright owners.[60] A non-statutory code of practice sets out the practical guidelines and procedures for

[56] Anti-Counterfeiting Trade Agreement, Art 27 paragraphs 2–4.

[57] Legislative Council Brief of Copyright (Amendment) Bill 2011, p. 2.

[58] Ibid.

[59] Legislative Council Brief of Copyright (Amendment) Bill 2011, p. 5

[60] Ibid.

ISPs to follow, which imports the "notice and notice"[61] and the "notice and takedown"[62] systems that already exist in other jurisdictions, such as Singapore and the United States.[63] Although the amendment proposal initiated by the Hong Kong government seeks a more balanced way to resolve digital network challenges, opponents still challenge its broad and vague definition of technology-neutral exclusive rights under which "copyright infringement can mean whatever the authorities want it to mean" and its criminal sanction against any unauthorized communication of copyright works to the public.[64] Finally, because of the strong opposition and protest from the public, the amendment has not been made effective yet. The Hong Kong government issued the Copyright (Amendment) Bill 2014 on 18 June 2014 to continually update Hong Kong's copyright reform. However, whether this updated amendment can be made effective finally is still uncertain.

At an international level, WIPO successfully concluded on June 28, 2013 a new international IP treaty, Marrakesh Treaty to Facilitate Access to Published Works for Persons who are Blind, Visually Impaired, or otherwise Print Disabled.[65] The Marrakesh Treaty does not change the current mechanism of copyright limitations and exceptions, but rather works as an international legal basis for the first time from the right holder perspective to facilitate access to works in perceivable form for visually impaired persons or persons with print disabilities. In addition, the Marrakesh Treaty encourages member countries to establish network for the cross-border exchange of accessible format of copies of works.[66] The conclusion of the Marrakesh Treaty in fact provides copyright exceptions for a special class of persons and counterbalances the continuous expansion of copyright protection to a certain degree.

---

[61] Under the "notice and notice" system, ISPs are required to forward notices of alleged infringement that they have received from copyright owners to their users or subscribers.

[62] Under the "notice and takedown" system, ISPs are required, upon receipt of a notice from the copyright owner concerned, to (a) take down or disable access to materials identified as infringing and (b), where applicable, notify the alleged infringer who is making the material available. The alleged infringer could file a counter-notice to the ISP if s/he disagrees with the accusation of infringement. Upon receipt of the counter-notice, the ISP is required to reinstate the materials or restore access.

[63] *See* n 59 above.

[64] "Hong Kong Copyright (Amendment) Bill 2011 Criminalises Parody and Uploading/Posting of Unauthorised Copyrighted Materials including News Articles/AFP's Misleading Report on Hong Kong Copyright Amendment," available at http://badcanto.wordpress.com/2012/04/27/hong-kong-copyright-amendment-bill-2011-criminalises-parody-and-posting-of-unauthorised-coyrighted-materials-including-news-articles/ (visited July 14, 2012).

[65] "Diplomatic Conference to Conclude a Treaty to Facilitate Access to Published Works by Visually Impaired Persons and Persons with Print Disabilities," available at http://www.wipo.int/dc2013/en/ (visited Nov 16, 2013).

[66] "Analysis of WIPO Marrakesh Treaty to Facilitate Access to Published Works for Persons who are Blind, Visually Impaired, or otherwise Print Disabled," available at http://www.ifrro.org/content/analysis-wipo-marrakesh-treaty-facilitate-access-published-works-persons-who-are-blind-visua (visited Nov 6, 2013).

1.3.4 Conclusion: Expansion of Copyright Protection Under Digital Network Environment

The establishment of copyright protection systems aims to achieve two important purposes: one is to stimulate the incentives for creation by granting authors with a series of exclusive rights on the one hand and, on the other hand, promoting the progress of culture and public welfare by setting up a series of limitations to these exclusive rights so that flow of information and dissemination of knowledge will not be hindered.

Although copyright laws prior to the digital network age witnessed the unceasing expansion of copyright protection, the limitations embodied in the copyright system still function well to balance copyright protection and access to information. These limitations include the idea/expression dichotomy, limited duration of protection, fair use or fair dealing, and compulsory licensing. Copyright laws do not protect ideas themselves. Only the expressions of ideas are copyrightable. The idea/expression dichotomy guarantees free borrowing of ideas in existing works by subsequent creators. The protection of the exclusive rights of the authors is subject to a time limitation, often his/her life plus 50 years.[67] Some jurisdictions have extended their duration to the author's life plus 70 years, such as the United States and the European Union. Upon expiration of the term of protection, copyright works will enter into the public domain and be free for all to use. The fair use or fair dealing doctrine permits the use of copyright works without authorization from the owners and paying remunerations to the right holders. This type of right restriction aims to provide leeway for the purposes of teaching, research, news reporting, criticism and comments [2]. With similar functions as the fair use or fair dealing doctrine, the compulsory licensing scheme offers exceptions for certain situations, such as secondary transmission by cable systems, digital audio transmission of sound recordings, or fulfilling of national compulsory education programs [2]. Under the compulsory licensing scheme, users have to pay remuneration to copyright owners but can then exploit the work without prior authorization. In addition, the exclusive rights of authors found in traditional copyright systems have a limited scope. Certain private uses are not prohibited by copyright laws, such as private performance and display of works.

The expansion of copyright protection both at the international and domestic levels in the digital network era significantly changes the situation and disrupts the balance of interest between copyright owners and public users. Due to continual strong lobbying from powerful copyright entrepreneur holders, copyright legislations are amended and reformed to strengthen the protection of the interests of copyright owners by increasing protected subject matters and exclusive rights, introducing protection on newly emerging copyright protection measures such as

[67] Berne Convention for the Protection of Literary and Artistic Works, Art 7(1).

technological measures and DRM information, developing the principle of indirect liability for technological intermediaries such as ISPs, and restricting current copyright limitations. Although digital network technology enhances the production and dissemination of information, the expansion of copyright protection subjects quite a number of unauthorized duplication and dissemination of copyright works to infringement liability and thus, to a certain degree, suffocates the free flow of information and knowledge. Users can no longer enjoy privileges that were guaranteed under traditional copyright systems.

In consideration of digital network challenges, international copyright conventions and national copyright laws in many jurisdictions have expanded the subject matters to computer programs and databases. Although developing countries prefer to grant other types of protection, such as applied art protection or sui generis right for computer programs, computer programs were finally approved as copyright works under major intellectual property or copyright conventions, such as the TRIPS Agreement and the WCT, due to the insistence of some of the developed countries. Copyright protection is granted to computer programs regardless of the mode or form of expression.[68] In addition, copyright protection is extended to databases, that is, compilations of data or other material in any form, as long as the selection or the arrangement constitutes creation.[69] Thus, non-copyrightable data or materials are subject to copyright protection if they constitute parts of a database.

Similar to the expansion of subject matters, the scope of the exclusive rights of copyright owners was also widened. Two fundamental rights, reproduction and distribution, were revised by international copyright conventions to include more situations. Two new rights, the right of rental and the right of making available, were added to the list of exclusive rights. The right of reproduction was amended by copyright conventions to include temporary reproductions caused by technical or automatic acts.[70] The WCT expanded the parameters of the right of distribution to include all copyright works instead of only cinematographic works.[71] The right of rental is applicable to certain categories of works, namely, cinematographic works, computer programs, and phonograms.[72] The right of making available grants copyright owners the exclusive privilege to control dissemination such that members of the public may access the works from a place and at a time individually chosen by them.[73] This kind of right not only covers simultaneous communication to the public but also contains subsequent access to the work offered through the internet.

The WIPO Internet Treaties, for the first time, granted protection to technological measures, which are used by copyright owners to control access and copying of protected works. Under the treaties and domestic laws of some of the jurisdictions which have implemented the international obligations, the circumvention of

---

[68] TRIPS Agreement, Art 10(1); WIPO Copyright Treaty, Art 4.

[69] TRIPS Agreement, Art 10(2); WIPO Copyright Treaty, Art 5.

[70] *See* n 40 above.

[71] WIPO Copyright Treaty, Art 6.

[72] WIPO Copyright Treaty, Art 7.

[73] WIPO Copyright Treaty, Art 8; WIPO Performances and Phonograms Treaty, Arts 10 and 14.

access-control technological measures is prohibited.[74] In addition, the prohibition also includes the acts of producing and distributing technologies and devices that facilitate circumvention of both access-control and copy-control technological measures.[75] These controls against the circumvention of technological measures seriously restrict users from accessing copyright works, which were previously not limited. Although there are several kinds of exceptions under anti-circumvention rules, users are not guaranteed their previous privileges, such as fair use or fair dealing because they can neither access the work at their free will nor conduct circumvention with the aid of related devices to carry out non-infringing uses. Furthermore, the adoption of technological measures may impede access to non-copyrightable material which has been combined with copyright works.

To enforce the right of making available and control online piracy, many jurisdictions have resorted to reviewing the indirect copyright infringement liability of technological intermediaries, such as ISPs. In the development of case law, ISPs will be held liable for contributory, vicarious, or authorization infringement in the event that there is copyright infringement on the part of their Internet subscribers, that is, if they should know or are aware of the primary infringement, have made material contributions, obtained direct financial benefits, have the right and ability to supervise or control subscriber activity, or had authorized subscriber activity that commits copyright infringement.[76] Some of these factors have been imported into statutes in civil law jurisdictions such as China. In order to be safeguarded against indirect infringement liability, ISPs must follow certain statutory requirements, such as the notice and takedown procedure which demands ISPs to immediately take down the alleged infringing material on their systems upon receiving proper notification from the copyright owners.[77] Although a counterbalance mechanism is also established to protect the interest of subscribers, it cannot completely eliminate the negative effects brought on by an immediate takedown requirement which denies them of the opportunity for refutation and places ISPs in a dilemma to either comply with the statutory procedure so that they are safeguarded from liability but lose customers or protect the interest of their customers but lose immunity under the safe harbor system. In addition, the releasing of subscriber information to copyright owners upon request elicits the problems of privacy protection.

As aforementioned, copyright systems have embodied limitations which are used to balance access to information and promote the progress of culture and useful arts. The United States has established the fair use doctrine based on a balancing

[74] Examples of legislations include the United States Copyright Act of 1976, s 1201 and the Regulation on the Protection of the Right to Network Dissemination of Information of China, Arts 4–5 and 18–19.

[75] Ibid.

[76] Examples of legislations include the United States Copyright Act of 1976, s 512, the Regulation on the Protection of the Right to Network Dissemination of Information of China, Arts 22–23, and Australia Copyright (Digital Agenda) Amendment Act 2000, s 36.

[77] Examples of legislations include the United States Copyright Act of 1976, s 512 and the Regulation on the Protection of the Right to Network Dissemination of Information of China, Arts 20–23.

test which provides four guiding factors for judges to make decisions, namely, the purpose and character of the use, nature of the copyrighted work, amount and substantiality of the portion used, and effect on the potential market.[78] Whether a particular unauthorized use of copyrighted work will be considered fair depends on how these factors shall be balanced and weighed. Commonwealth jurisdictions, such as the United Kingdom and Canada, have adopted fair dealing that encompasses specific situations under which uses are deemed fair.[79] Similar to fair dealing, the Chinese copyright law also includes specific exceptions, but in a much simpler way.[80] Regardless of the legislative models, limitations are subjected to a "three-step test" in international conventions under which limitations shall be confined to certain special cases that do not conflict with the normal exploitation of the work and do not unreasonably prejudice the legitimate interests of the author.[81] This three-step test in turn restricts the limitations on the exclusive rights of copyright owners. The adoption of technological measures and anti-circumvention rules as well as the commencement of a large number of user-generated contents and fan fictions further create problems with regard to current copyright limitations. On the one hand, the specific exceptions cannot cover all possible situations in an era where digital network technologies are developing quickly. On the other hand, the seemingly flexible fair use doctrine is questioned about its uncertainty, as no guidance is provided as to how these different factors shall be balanced and weighed. Without further interpretation, many of the uses that are fostered by digital technology and the remix culture fall into a grey zone area where it becomes difficult to determine fairness and make justifications.

1.4 Should China Imitate or Innovate?

Unlike the developed countries which have led the digital copyright reform due to the push for a balance of interests among the different stakeholders, the developing countries followed them and amended their copyright systems mainly through legal transplant. On the one hand, developing countries face external pressure to fulfill the obligations of international conventions and treaties which they have taken part and, on the other hand, face internal demand to borrow the advanced and effective legislations from the developed areas to accelerate the reform process as well as save on costs. China is one of these developing countries which have endeavored to conduct both externally dictated transplant and internally cost-saving transplant [9].

---

[78] The United States Copyright Act of 1976, s 107.

[79] Copyright, Designs and Patents Act 1988 of the United Kingdom, ss 29–30 and Canadian Copyright Act, ss 29–32.2.

[80] Copyright Law of People's Republic of China (2010 Amendment), Art 22.

[81] Berne Convention for the Protection of Literary and Artistic Works, Art 9(2); WIPO Copyright Treaty, Art 10; the TRIPS Agreement, Art 13.

1.4.1 Development and Amendment of Copyright Protection System in China

As one of the leading developing countries, China continuously endeavors to be involved in the international community and amends her legal system to comply with international norms and customs. Intellectual property protection is one of the most prioritized issues which China intends to rival with that of her developed counterparts. In order to increase the protection of intellectual property in general and establish the most updated practices in copyright protection under the digital network environment in particular, China has reformed its intellectual property and copyright protection system from various aspects by implementing international conventions and treaties on the one hand and borrowing from the experiences of developed countries on the other hand. Based on amendments in the legislative, administrative, and judicial regimes, China has established a modern copyright system with its own characteristics.

1.4.1.1 Influence of International Conventions on Copyright Protection System in China

In terms of the status of international treaties in China's domestic legal system, the Constitution of the People's Republic of China does not address the issue. However, the prevailing effect of international treaties was stipulated in some of the major laws at a lower level. The General Principles of Civil Law expresses that "if any international treaty concluded or acceded to by the People's Republic of China contains provisions differing from those in the civil laws of the People's Republic of China, the provisions of the international treaty shall apply, unless the provisions are ones on which People's Republic of China has announced reservations."[82] Therefore, when conflicts arise between an international treaty provision without reservations and the relevant Chinese domestic legal provision, the former shall prevail and will apply to the case. Despite the minor occasions when domestic legislations conflict with international treaties, laws in China are made and amended from time to time so as to comply with international intellectual property standards and developments.

When the Copyright Law Draft in China was under discussion in the 1980s, one of the major debates revolved around whether China should become a member of the WIPO copyright conventions. Some of the government officers opined that China would be better off if she did not participate in the copyright conventions because impracticality of the high standards of copyright protection would result in difficulties during the importing of foreign science and technology works and would further negatively impact the development of science, technology, and education [10]. Although this view was overridden by the importance of

[82] The General Principles of the Civil Law of the People's Republic of China, Art 142.

restoring a normal copyright trade relationship with foreign countries, it reflected the reality of deficient intellectual property protection and modern cultural resources in China as a developing country. In the negotiation process of joining the Berne Convention, the former WIPO Director General Arpad Bogsch provided a suggestion that China could join the Berne Convention on the basis of its Copyright Law which was released in 1990, since the primary principles under the Copyright Law already complied with the Berne Convention. Existing conflicts in some of the details could be eliminated by reasonable interpretation of the law and by implementing regulations. Therefore, Chinese officers suggested the stipulation of a special regulation which could incorporate conflicting provisions in the Berne Convention into domestic law that would be solely applicable to foreigners. China filed an application to join the Berne Convention and the Universal Copyright Convention to the WIPO in 1992. Shortly before the treaties came into effect in China in the same year, the State Council of China enacted the Provisions on the Implementation of International Copyright Conventions so as to guarantee sufficient protection for foreign works in China. Thus, the protection of foreign works is stronger than that for domestic works. The double standard of protection suited the early transition period of China's participation in the international copyright conventions but was no longer appropriate when domestic cultural industries developed and required equal protection. The amendment of the Copyright Law in 2000 has resolved this problem.

In the negotiation process for entering the WTO, China made it clear that she would implement the WTO Agreements by revising existing domestic laws and enacting new ones that fully comply with the WTO Agreements [11, p. 155]. Shortly after the conclusion of the agreement between China and the United States on China's accession to the WTO in November 1999, China conducted an intensive work program to examine and revise intellectual property related laws and regulations so as to fulfill China's accession commitments. Amendments were made to major intellectual property laws, including the Copyright Law, Patent Law, and Trademark Law, as well as to relevant Implementing Regulations. The amended intellectual property laws, regulations, and rules together constitute an updated intellectual property protection regime that is compatible with the TRIPS Agreement. In cases where there are conflicts between the domestic laws and the TRIPS Agreement, the TRIPS Agreement provisions shall apply.

With the intent to join the WIPO Internet Treaties, the State Council began to draft the Regulation on the Protection of the Right to Network Dissemination of Information as early as 2004, which was an important preparatory legislative work in compliance with the treaties.[83] The regulation was issued in 2006, which incorporated the basic concepts and norms in the WIPO Internet Treaties so as to address serious online copyright infringements. After the intent to join the WIPO Internet Treaties was made evident, China filed the application and became a member in 2007.

[83] "China Will Join the WIPO Internet Treaties in the Second Half Year," (in Chinese), available at http://www.wangchao.net.cn/bbsdetail_1421857.html (visited Jan 17, 2010).

Aside from the problem of incorporating international intellectual property agreements into domestic legislation, another major issue was the enforcement of an international IP-compatible framework in the jurisdiction. Although China is a centralized country, the regions tremendously differ in terms of economic prosperity, degree of receptiveness, cultural traditions, governance structure, and so on [11, p. 158]. Each region can issue its own regulations and rules and enjoy discretionary power with regard to the application of law. Thus, law enforcement differs among the various regions, which results in the difficulty of uniformly enforcing and protecting international intellectual property standards. Although the State Council takes the leading role in implementing laws and international conventions, the problems caused by the regional variance cannot be addressed in a short amount of time. Continuous efforts are needed to address law enforcement along with social development in the long run.

1.4.1.2 Legislative System of Copyright Protection in China

Existing Chinese laws can be divided into those which have been approved and adopted by the National People's Congress and the Standing Committee of the National People's Congress (state laws); administrative laws and regulations of the State Council (state regulations); local regulations promulgated by the various people's congresses of the provinces, major cities, and special economic zones and their respective standing committees (local regulations); and departmental rules implemented by ministries and commissions, the People's Bank of China, and the Auditing Administration under the State Council as well as agencies directly under the control of the State Council (departmental rules) [12, pp. 34–35]. The laws, regulations, rules, decisions, and orders made at the national legislature and administrative levels establish judicial standards for all Chinese courts. Chinese courts can also refer to local regulations and departmental rules whenever necessary in making judicial decisions, but they cannot reach a decision merely based on these regulations and rules.

The consciousness of copyright protection in China originated from the reform and open door policy in the 1980s. The initial basis for judicial enforcement on copyrights was the General Principles of Civil Law adopted by the National People's Congress in 1986 under which authors enjoy the right to be named in connection with their work, to issue and publish their work and be remunerated for the work's exploitation. To protect these rights, authors can file litigation against an infringing party, demanding that they stop the infringement, eliminate the negative effects, and compensate for damages. Besides the General Principles of Civil Law, the primary law in the copyright field is the Copyright Law issued by the National People's Congress on September 7, 1990, which came into effect on June 1, 1991. The birth of the Copyright Law was influenced by domestic demands for the encouragement of creations and overseas pressure to comply with international standards of protection. The Copyright Law of 1991 primarily integrated the copyright perspectives and theories from continental Europe, distinguishing between the moral rights of publication, attribution, revision and prevention of mutilation, and economic exploitation rights as well as clear differentiations between the author's copyright and the neighboring rights of performers, phonogram producers, broadcasters, and publishers [13, p. 211]. In order to guarantee the administrative enforcement of the copyright protection, the State Council released the Regulation on the Implementation of the Copyright Law on May 24, 1991, which came into force on June 1, 1991. Despite its progressiveness, the Copyright Law of 1991 soon showed its deficiencies due to swiftly changing technology. Shortly before China's accession to the WTO, the Ninth National People's Congress promulgated the Decision on the Amendment of the Copyright Law on October 27, 2001, which came into force on the same day [13]. Accordingly, the Regulation on the Implementation of the Copyright Law was amended on August 2, 2002, and became effective on September 15, 2002. The second revision of the Copyright Law took place on February 26, 2010, and became effective on April 1 of the same year.

Other important administrative laws and regulations promulgated by the State Council or various ministries and departments under the State Council include Regulation on the Protection of Computer Software; Regulation on the Collective Administration of Copyright, Regulation on the Protection of the Right to Network Dissemination of Information, Measures for the Registration of Computer Software Copyright issued by the National Copyright Administration of China, Measures for the Administrative Protection of Internet Copyright issued by the National Copyright Administration of China and former Ministry of Information Industry, Administrative Measures for Software Products issued by Ministry of Industry and Information Technology, and Measures for the Implementation of Copyright Administrative Punishment issued by the National Copyright Administration of China. These administrative laws and regulations form a systematical copyright protection framework along with the primary Copyright Law.

It is commonly recognized that the purpose for the enactment of the Chinese Copyright Law of 2001 was to satisfy the requirements of the TRIPS Agreement under the WTO framework and extend copyright protection under the digital network environment [14, p. 5]. Under the updated copyright law and regulations, new subject matters are included as part of copyright works, including computer software and electronic databases; new kinds of exclusive rights are granted to copyright owners, including the right of rental for particular works and the right to network dissemination of information; the indirect liability of ISPs is for the first time stipulated in law; and protection is granted to technological measures and DRM information which guaranteed the control of copyright owners over access and use of works.

The Copyright Law of 2001 includes computer software as a subject matter of protection, as long as the software shows "originality and already be fixed in physical objects,"[84] thus removing the requirement for registration as a prerequisite for protection. Copyright protection is also extended to electronic databases

[84] Computer Software Regulations of the People's Republic of China, Art 5.

as long as the compilation is original, regardless whether the selected materials are copyrightable or not.[85]

The Copyright Law of 2001 gives works in the digital form the same protection as other traditional works listed under Article 3[86] and recognizes the nature of the digitalization of works as reproduction. The digitalization of sound or video recordings is also regarded as reproduction. Article 10 of the Copyright Law defines the right of reproduction as "the right to reproduce one or more copies of a work by printing, photocopying, lithographing, making a sound recording or video recording, duplicating a recording, or duplicating a photographic work or by any other means." Digitalization is included in the non-exclusive "any other means." An explicit and independent right of rental has been added to the Copyright Law of 2001, which was no longer embodied in the right of distribution and applies to three categories of works, namely, cinematographic and other audiovisual works, and computer software.

A new kind of exclusive economic right, namely, the right to network dissemination of information, has been created to resolve the piracy problem brought about by increasing computer and network users. Taking into consideration the flexibility of the right to cover the ever-developing technology, the National People's Congress did not restrict the right to merely providing works to the public on the Internet, but rather formulated the expression in a similar way to that in the WCT; thus, it is the right to "provide to the public of a work, by wire or wireless means, so as to make the work available to the public in such a way that members of the public may access the work from a place and at a time individually chosen by them."[87] However, the law does not give any detailed provision to address digital network challenges and the protection of the right to network dissemination of information. In compliance with Article 58 of the Copyright Law of 2001 which stipulates that "regulations for the protection of computer software and the right to network dissemination of information shall be established separately by the State Council," the State Council enacted a detailed rule on the protection given by the right to network dissemination of information in 2006, that is, the Regulation on the Protection of the Right to Network Dissemination of Information (thereafter, the 2006 Regulation).[88]

---

[85] Copyright Law of the People's Republic of China (2010 Amendment) Art 14 stipulates that "works, created by compiling a number of works, parts of works or uncopyrightable data or other materials, are compilation works, provided that the selection or arrangement of their contents constitute intellectual creations."

[86] The works listed under Article 3 of Copyright Law include written works; oral works; musical, drama, quyi (Chinese performance art), choreographic, and acrobatic works; artistic and architectural works; photographic works; cinematographic works and works created by virtue of an analogous method of film production; drawings of engineering and product designs, illustrations, maps and the like, graphic works, and models; computer software; and other works as provided for in the laws and administrative regulations.

[87] Copyright Law of the People's Republic of China (2010 Amendment), Art 10(12).

[88] The Regulations on the Protection of the Right to Network Dissemination of Information was amended on 30 January 2013 and the amendment became effective from March 1, 2013. However, the amendment only revised Articles 18 and 19 which increase penalties for infringing activities. Therefore, the abbreviation for the Regulations in this book is still "the 2006 Regulation."

The 2006 Regulation mainly focuses on three issues, namely, the anti-circumvention rules, ISP liability, and copyright limitations under the digital network environment. However, it only provides general guidance for these issues, since there are only 27 articles and many of them are not specific enough.

For the first time, TPM and DRM information have been granted protection in copyright regulations. The unauthorized circumvention of TPMs and the removal or alteration of DRM information could be considered as infringements. Under Article 4, no organization or individual can intentionally circumvent technological measures or trafficking devices that can circumvent technological measures. Article 26 provides a definition for technological measures, which are "efficient techniques, devices and components that are applied to preventing or restricting the browse or appreciation of the work ... in the absence of the relevant owner's permission or in providing the works ...to the general public through the information network in the absence of the relevant owner's permission." However, the wording is very vague and does not clarify whether the technological measures are used against access or copying. The words "browse or appreciation" and "providing the works to the general public" indicate that technological measures in this Chinese regulation refer to both access and copy controls. Exceptions only apply to the circumvention act itself, not for trafficking of circumvention devices. Article 12 only lists four exceptions, including classroom teaching and scientific research, supply of works to blind people, governmental official duties, and security testing.

Also for the first time, the laws and regulations stipulate the obligation and liability of ISPs who play a central role in network data and information transmission and online copyright protection. ISPs are not clearly defined in the 2006 Regulation, but similar to Section 512 in the DMCA, there are four categories that govern the provision of services by ISPs which include: (1) the providing of automatic access or transmission of works in accordance with instructions from subscribers, which is similar to the transitory communication services in the DMCA; (2) the automatic storing of works supplied by other ISPs and automatic transmittance of the works to subscribers, which is similar to the system caching services outlined in the DMCA; (3) the providing of information memory space for subscribers when they supply their works, which is similar to the service of storing information on systems or networks at the direction of users in the DMCA; and (4) the providing of searching or linking services to recipients, which is similar to the provision of information location tools in the DMCA.[89]

As for copyright limitations, the Copyright Law of 2001 explicitly lists all foreseeable situations. These exceptions are basically for private study, reporting of current events, teaching and research, carrying out of governmental official duties, and use by nonprofit organizations. The 2006 Regulation adopts the list that exists in the Copyright Law and selects situations that exist under the digital network environment, including the providing of any publicized work through information networks for the purposes of introduction or commenting of works; news reporting;

[89] Regulation on the Protection of the Right to Network Dissemination of Information, Arts 20–23.

teaching or scientific research; fulfillment of the duties of state organs; translating Chinese into languages of ethnic minority groups; making the work accessible to the blind; providing articles on current affairs, such as political and economic issues; delivering a public speech; and providing digital copies of works in library, archives, memorials, museums, and art galleries.[90]

To address the need for a holistic response to the challenges posed by the digital network environment, China launched the third revision of the Copyright Law. The National Copyright Administration of China released the first, second, and third Modified Drafts in March, July, and October 2012, respectively. The third draft was submitted to the Legislative Affairs Office of the State Council for further review and then submitted to the Standing Committee of the People's Congress for the final review and promulgation.[91] Based on the third draft, the Reviewing Modified Draft was released in June 2014 for seeking public opinions by 5th July 2014.

The Modified Drafts comprise eight chapters: "General Provisions, Copyright, Neighboring Rights, Limitations of the Rights, Exercise of the Rights, Technological Protection Measures and Rights Management Information, Protection of the Rights, and Supplementary Provisions."[92] One of the important features of the Modified Drafts is that they completely respond to copyright issues under the digital network environment. This is reflected in several aspects: (1) under the economic rights granted by the draft, the right of reproduction clearly includes digitalization as a way of reproducing work; the right to network dissemination of information additionally contains situations of live and relay broadcasting; the right of alteration is added to deal with alterations made to computer programs[93]; (2) under the neighboring rights, a performer can authorize his/her performance to the public under the information network environment, by wire or wireless means in such a way that members of the public may access these performances from a place or at a time individually chosen by them, and communicate to the public the work provided in the aforementioned manner by technical equipment; such right to the network dissemination of information also applies to the producer who provides phonogram

---

[90] Regulation on the Protection of the Right to Network Dissemination of Information, Arts 6–7.

[91] "China's Proposed Copyright Reforms Prompt Widespread Comment," available at http://the-1709blog.blogspot.com/2012/04/chinas-proposed-copyright-reforms.html (visited May 12, 2012).

[92] Copyright Law of People's Republic of China (First Modified Draft) (in Chinese), available at http://www.gapp.gov.cn/cms/cms/upload/info/201203/740607/133317987342298209.doc (visited May 17, 2014).

[93] Copyright Law of People's Republic of China (Second Modified Draft), Art 11 Paragraph 3(1): the right of reproduction, that is, the right to fix a work on the physical carrier by printing, photocopying, recording, duplicating a photographic work, digitalization or by any other means; Art 11 Paragraph 3(7): the right to network dissemination of information, that is, the right to communicate to the public a work under the information network environment, by wire or wireless means, in such as a way that members of the public may access these works from a place or at a time individually chosen by them, and communicate to the public the work provided in the aforementioned manner by technical equipment; Art 11 Paragraph 3(8): the right of alteration, that is, the right to change the work to a new work in different genre, types, or forms other than audiovisual works or supplement or abridge the computer programs or to change the sequence of instructions or statements.

productions[94]; (3) under the limitation of the rights, several specific limitations and exceptions apply to computer programs[95]; (4) the protection of technological measures and rights management information is regulated under a specific chapter; administrative and criminal liability will be imposed on infringing acts that circumvent or destroy technological measures and trafficking of circumvention devices[96]; and (5) the notice and takedown procedure is included with regard to ISP liability and safe harbors.[97]

It is a leapfrog step that China has taken in the revision of the Copyright Law which fully responds to the need for rights protection under a digital network environment. An amendment was also made to the Modified Drafts with regard to the issues of the anti-circumvention rules for the protection of technological measures, ISP liability and safe harbors, and copyright limitations and exceptions. However, the amendment is too minimal to have a substantial impact on the relevant provisions under the current copyright regime. The Modified Drafts directly incorporated the provisions related to the anti-circumvention rules and protection of DRM information in the 2006 Regulation with subtle changes, included only one provision for ISP liability and safe harbors, imported a general provision of copyright limitations from the Regulation on the Implementation of the Copyright Law and made a slight amendment to the specified list of exceptions. The problems of balancing interests and realizing the ultimate goal of advancing knowledge and learning still exist in the Modified Drafts. Therefore, further revisions should be made to the Copyright Law of China.

[94] Copyright Law of People's Republic of China (Second Modified Draft), Art 33 Paragraph 1(6); Art 38 Paragraph 1(4): a producer of sound recordings or video recordings shall have the right to permit others to disseminate to the public the phonogram productions under the information network environment, by wire or wireless means in such as way that members of the public may access the phonogram production from a place or at a time individually chosen by them, and communicate to the public the work provided in the aforementioned manner by technical equipment.

[95] Copyright Law of People's Republic of China (Second Modified Draft), Art 43: licensees of computer programs are entitled to enjoy the following rights: (1) to install and store the computer program in devices with information processing capabilities, such as computer, according to the need of the use; (2) to make backup copies against damage, provided that such licensee does not offer others in any way the backup copies for their use and that he destroys the copies once he loses the legal license; (3) to make necessary alterations to the computer program in order to implement it in an actual environment of computer application or to improve its functions or performance, provided that such licensee does not offer any third party the altered computer program without permission from the copyright owner of the computer program; Art 44: computer program may be used by its installing, displaying, transmitting, or storing for the purposes of studying or researching the design ideas or principles embodied therein, without permission from and without payment of remuneration to the copyright owner of the computer program; Art 45: licensee of the computer program may reproduce and translate part of the contents relevant to compatibility information in the program without permission from the copyright owner of the computer program, provided that such licensee does not use the information obtained through abovementioned method for purposes other than compatibility of computer program or provide the information to other or use the information to develop, produce, or sell computer programs with substantial similarity or use the information to infringe copyright.

[96] Copyright Law of People's Republic of China (Second Modified Draft), Arts 64–67 and Art 74.

[97] Copyright Law of People's Republic of China (Second Modified Draft), Art 69.

1.4.1.3 Administrative System of Copyright Protection in China

The administrative system is the most efficient and effective organ to enforce copyright protection. Various ministries and departments under the State Council are responsible for different kinds of intellectual property enforcement and administration. Ministries and departments relevant to copyright administration and protection include the National Copyright Administration of China which is responsible for copyright administration, the Ministry of Commerce which is responsible for intellectual property issues in international trade, the Ministry of Science and Technology which is responsible for intellectual property issues related to technology, and the General Administration of Customs which is responsible for intellectual property related to import–export goods. In addition to the state administrative organs at the national level, provincial and municipal administrative branches also take responsibility for intellectual property enforcement in their local regions.

The administrative organs have made many achievements in recent years. Special intellectual property enforcement activities, such as the "Eagle" and "Blue Sky" campaigns initiated in 2005 and 2007, respectively, and coordinated by different state administrative departments, have launched investigations, taken provisional measures, and imposed sanctions at various periods of time in numerous administrative regions with the purpose to efficiently address infringement and penalize piracy producers.

Despite that there have been improvements and achievements made by Chinese administrative organs, many critics still emphasize on their administration shortcomings and are concerned about the comparatively weak enforcement of intellectual property. One major problem is that the lack of effective supervision could result in corruption in the administration system. Another key problem stems from the mismanagement of law enforcement due to the large number of administrative ministries and departments and their complexity. Therefore, it is essential to prevent corruption and mismanagement in order to strengthen administrative enforcement to protect intellectual property.

1.4.1.4 Judicial System of Copyright Protection in China

In addition to intellectual property enforcement by the administrative system, filing litigations to the people's courts is another important way to enforce the protection of intellectual property rights and reasonably compensate for the loss of the owners of intellectual property rights. There are four levels of people's courts in China: the Supreme Court and the high, intermediary, and district courts.

The Supreme Court is the highest judicial organ. Its responsibilities include the hearing of significant cases at the national level, making the final judgment on appellant cases, supervising the judicial works of lower courts, and releasing judicial interpretations in the application of laws. The Intellectual Property Chamber in the Supreme Court shoulders the responsibility of deciding on various intellectual property civil cases and some of the administrative cases that stem from disputes with regard to authorization and confirmation of patents and trademark rights. In 2011, the total number of cases received by the Supreme Court reached 420, a 34.19 % increase over the previous year.[98]

The judicial interpretations issued by the Supreme Court are important and binding within the judicial system. Although they are not legislations, judicial interpretations can quickly match social developments and close loopholes in the legislations. The major judicial interpretations with regard to copyright protection under the digital network environment are the Interpretations on Several Issues Concerning the Application of Law in the Trial of Cases Involving Copyright Disputes over Computer Network (thereafter Interpretations) which was amended for the first time in 2003 and for the second time in 2006 and the Provisions of the Supreme People's Court on Certain Issues Related to the Application of Law in the Trial of Civil Cases Involving Disputes over Infringement of the Right to Network Dissemination of Information (thereafter Provisions) which was released in 2012 and took into force on January 1, 2013. The Interpretations and the Provisions deal with frontier copyright issues, such as copyright protection for works in the digital form, ISP liability, and protection of technological measures. Apart from the judicial interpretations, the Supreme Court publishes typical cases that have been decided by the people's courts at different levels in its monthly gazette, which influence the judgment of similar cases later on.

High courts are generally found at the provincial level, which hear influential intellectual property cases in the jurisdictions of the provinces as well as make guidelines on the application of law. Intermediary courts shoulder the obligation of hearing the first trial of most intellectual property cases. District courts are at the lowest level and the first instance courts for simple copyright dispute cases.

1.4.1.5 Other Copyright Enforcement Mechanisms in China

Other copyright enforcement mechanisms in China include collecting management societies and alternative dispute resolutions. Despite that they lack compulsory enforcement power, these mechanisms can help copyright holders better manage their rights and resolve disputes.

Currently, there are five collecting management societies established in China, namely, the Music Copyright Society of China (MCSC), China Audio-Video Copyright Association (CAVCA), China Written Works Copyright Society (CWWCS), Images Copyright Society of China (ICSC), and China Film Copyright Association (Collective) (CFCAC). The establishment of these copyright collecting societies largely enhances the capability of copyright owners in preventing

[98] "Annual Report of the Intellectual Property Cases in the Supreme People's Court (2011)," (in Chinese), available at http://www.hljcourt.gov.cn/lawdb/show.php?fid=147063 (visited Nov 6, 2013).

infringement and managing copyright transactions under the information network environment.

One of the typical alternative dispute resolutions is arbitration. In contrast to litigations in the judicial system, arbitrations do not have jurisdiction requirements to file applications and can efficiently settle disputes and save on costs. In 2008, the Intellectual Property Court of Arbitration was established in Shanghai and the Intellectual Property Center was launched under the Guangzhou Court of Arbitration.

1.4.2 Should China Imitate or Innovate?

Legal transplant is a double-edged sword. The less developed recipient countries can save both time and resources by absorbing the legislative results of socioeconomically developed countries based on an appropriate and well-selected legal transplant. By introducing the principles and norms of developed trading partners into domestic legal systems, developing countries can better face the pressure that is continuously imposed upon them by the economic powers to heighten intellectual property protection standards and fulfill international conventional obligations. However, hasty legal transplants lack careful analysis and evaluation of laws in the source countries which will import any disadvantages of these foreign systems at the same time when borrowing the beneficial factors. Even worse, direct legal transplant without appropriate localization may render an advanced legal system incompatible to the national socioeconomic situations of the recipient countries.

With the growth of the knowledge economy and involvement in economic globalization, developing countries such as China cannot expedite national socioeconomic development without adopting intellectual property protection systems from others. Due to the lack of suitable intellectual property laws and policies, these newly emerging economic entities cannot efficiently convert intangible intellectual outputs into commercial products and encourage the rise of knowledge-economic industries. Nevertheless, the experiences of developing economies have shown that an imbalance with overprotection of intellectual property rights would impede the introduction of technology and suffocate future innovation. In the area of copyright law, inappropriate overprotection will hinder the dissemination of knowledge and culture and badly affect future creations. This will seriously damage the cultural construction of the less developed countries which have poor resources. Therefore, when developing countries intend to reform their legal systems through legal transplant, they should try to balance the system by carefully considering the types of laws that shall be deemed as borrowing sources, the amount and degree that foreign laws shall be borrowed, and whether there are other appropriate or supplementary options beneficial to the reform.

When updating and amending her copyright protection system under the digital network environment, China has mainly borrowed from the DMCA of the United States. Lawmaking in the United States around copyright legislations has always been made through the compromising of different stakeholders after intensive debates. The DMCA is "the fruit of intensive lobbying by a wide range of interest groups of copyright owners, on the one hand, and, particularly, users, on the other" [15, p. 137]. In the absence of negotiation processes by different parties and different customs, it is difficult to tell how wise China has been to incorporate a substantial amount of the DMCA and how effective this legislative model suits China's national situations. Furthermore, the DMCA was enacted in the late 1990s when information on the development of digital network technologies was limited. Almost 10 years later, China has nearly completely transplanted the principal norms with regard to ISP liability and anti-circumvention of technological measures from the DMCA into its 2006 Regulation. If the borrowing of foreign laws is inevitable, China could consider the modeling based on other jurisdictions, where the laws are more recent and appropriate, such as the United Kingdom, Australia, Hong Kong, Japan, or the European continental countries.

The anti-circumvention rules in the 2006 Regulation and the Modified Drafts prohibit circumvention of both access and copy-control technological measures and trafficking of devices that facilitate such circumvention. Moreover, specific exceptions to the circumvention and trafficking of devices are much more restricted than the corresponding provisions in the DMCA. Under the anti-circumvention rules, access to information is seriously restricted. In the case of the safe harbor provision for ISP liability, the 2006 Regulation and the Modified Drafts have adopted the notice and takedown requirement as in the DMCA which demands ISPs to immediately remove the alleged infringement material upon receiving notifications from the copyright owners. The copyright owners may arbitrarily send notifications of such infringement without further investigation and may even outsource the task of sending notifications to third parties who depend on automatic processing and are compensated based on the number of notifications already sent. False notifications will cause the ISPs to wrongfully remove subscriber materials, and thus, lose customers. In contrast, the ISPs cannot carefully monitor the activities of its subscribers because knowledge of suspected infringement activity may result in the loss of safe harbor privileges. Although the 2006 Regulation also embodies a counter-notification procedure which allows the recovery of material that has been wrongfully taken down, it cannot entirely compensate for the loss caused by an immediate takedown. In addition, ISPs are more likely to side with copyright owners to secure their own statutory immunity. Hence, correction mechanisms need to be introduced to restore a balance between copyright protection and information access and dissemination by amending and re-reforming current legal systems.

The next concern is then whether appropriate options and supplementary mechanisms can be introduced to carry out a reform in digital copyright law. First, neither the Copyright Law nor other regulations in China have expanded the copyright limitations and exceptions. China has not introduced a broad fair use doctrine which could have several guiding factors for courts to consider fair use case by case. Instead, the Copyright Law embodies a short list of exceptions that range from private study, teaching and research, and report of current events to the preservation of works in nonprofit organizations and translation of works into minority languages or Braille. Although the statute attempts to include all occasions that can be anticipated so far, the short list of exemptions can hardly contain all possible uses that may be deemed fair especially in an era when ways of creation rapidly change due to the development in digital technologies. This exclusive list of exceptions neglects some of the emerging popular issues generated from the remix culture such as the treatment of user-generated contents and fan fictions. The narrowness of the exceptions in the Chinese copyright system can no longer balance the interests of users against the requests of copyright owners for more protection, thus constraining many harmless and reasonable uses and leaving newly emerging issues in a grey area. The range of the copyright limitation can be widened by introducing a flexible fair use doctrine and the establishment of non-exclusive detailed cases would broaden the scope of permissible uses, appropriately address the remix works, cultivate a creative atmosphere, and attract investment in the area of digital network technologies and industries.

Aside from appropriate options in the copyright legal system, supplementary mechanisms should also be taken into consideration to assist public access and free flow of information. One feasible supplementary mechanism is open access projects based on voluntary licensing schemes. Examples include Open Source Software, the Creative Commons, the Open Audio and Publication License, and other open content initiatives. As one of the popular open access projects, the Creative Commons was formally launched in Mainland China in March 2006 under the lead of the Renmin University of China Law School in response to the copyright reform. Under the Creative Commons licensing scheme, creators can select any of the six licenses for application to their works, reserving part of the exclusive rights such as attribution and waiving other rights for wider distribution of the works. Users are to make use of the works in compliance with the license terms. Although the Creative Commons licenses do not have sufficient enforceability, such voluntary licensing schemes based on contract law would facilitate flow of information, spur creative ideas and promote the growth of small or medium creative enterprises. The introduction of such voluntary licensing schemes could also induce policymakers to rethink about an optional systematic design that may help restore a balance of interest between right holders and users by guaranteeing copyright protection on the one hand and broadening public access to works on the other hand. Policymakers and educational institutes in China should further consider the adopting of more open access initiatives based on the Creative Commons licensing scheme, such as open courseware for universities as implemented by the Massachusetts Institute of Technology and open digital libraries.

Legal transplant is not only an imitative process in which one country follows a more developed country, but there is also the opportunity that the recipient country could explore development in its own way through experimenting and improvements. As scholars have commented, legal transplant provides a fine opportunity for the recipient society to become a donor in turn [16]. The developing countries can consider two avenues to develop their copyright protection systems. One way is to adhere to time-tested solutions led by their developed counterparts with relatively greater exceptions and limitations that are recognized in international legal frameworks [17]. The other way is to embark on "a more innovative and even experimental path," by addressing and resolving problems that developed countries have found difficult [17, p. 1126]. Although the former may reduce the internal debates and costs of the recipient countries, it will also bring in problems of imbalance of interest and overprotection of copyright that source countries have failed to resolve. Furthermore, pure imitation without any localization and innovation will reduce the problem-solving capability and governance skills of developing countries [17]. The latter will inspire developing countries to better amend foreign laws so that they are adapted to domestic situations and initiate legal reforms that can better solve new problems.

India is a developing country with rapidly improving digital network technologies and has launched a new series of copyright reforms by drafting their Copyright (Amendment) Bills of 2010 and 2012 in response to digital network challenges [18, 19]. The Copyright (Amendment) Act 2012 came into force on June 21, 2012, which made amendments to the existing provisions of the Copyright Act 1957.[99] Correspondingly, the Copyright Rules 2013, the implementation regulations for the Copyright Act, was introduced to replace the Copyright Rules 1958 on March 14, 2013.[100] In the lawmaking process, India has given much attention to renewing its copyright protection system to comply with the WIPO Internet Treaties on the one hand and guarantee revisions that would be applicable to the local context, economy, and culture on the other hand.[101] The amendments put certain endeavors on maintaining balance between proprietary control and public access to information. For example, in the case of fair dealing, the amendments were expanded to cover private and personal uses with regard to all kinds of copyright works [18]. Fair dealing is utilized to assist establishing noncommercial digital library by covering the storing of a work by electronic means by a noncommercial public library for preservation if the library already possesses a non-digital copy of the work.[102] The fair dealing and compulsory license were particularly reinforced to guarantee the benefit for the disabled. The new clause (zb) was inserted into Section 52 (1) to facilitate the adaptation, reproduction, issue of copies, or communication to the public of any work in any accessible format for the disabled people's private or personal use, research, and use for educational purpose.[103] In cases where fair dealing does not apply, compulsory license was provided by the amendments for the access to and use of copyright works by the disabled. The Copyright Board should dispose the compulsory license application from people working for the benefit of the disabled within 2 months from the date of receipt of the application.[104] If the Copyright Board approves the compulsory

[99] Copyright Rules 2013 (Mar 19, 2013), available at http://www.lawyersclubindia.com/news/Copyright-Rules-2013-14404.asp (visited Apr 22, 2013).

[100] Ibid.

[101] The Copyright (Amendment) Act 2012 of India, available at http://ibnlive.in.com/news/full-text-the-copyright-amendment-bill-2012/260333-53.html (visited May 17, 2014).

[102] The Copyright (Amendment) Act 2012 of India, paragraph 32(iii), s 52(1)(n).

[103] The Copyright (Amendment) Act 2012 of India, paragraph 32(vii), s 52(1)(zb).

[104] The Copyright (Amendment) Act 2012 of India, paragraph 18, s 31B.

license after inquiry about the credentials of the applicant, the compulsory license should be granted with specification of the means and formats of publication, the period during which the compulsory license may be exercised, and the number of copies that may be issued and the royalty.[105] In the case of anti-circumvention of technological measures, the updated provisions contain two main user-favored features that cannot be found in other jurisdictions. First, the trafficking of technologies, devices, or services that facilitate circumvention of technological measures is not prohibited by law [20]. Secondly, the law protects the person who facilitates circumvention of technological measures by another person, as long as the former maintains "a complete record of such other person including his name, address and all relevant particulars necessary to identify him and the purpose for which he has been facilitated."[106] These reforms make Indian copyright protection on technological measures less draconian and more balanced and fair. In addition, the amendments of India, different from other jurisdictions, clearly addressed the problem of relinquishing copyright. The copyright owners can relinquish copyright either by notifying the Registrar of Copyrights or by way of public notice.[107] The facilitation of relinquishment of copyright puts digital commons projects, such as the Creative Commons, on a more stable footing in India.

It is time for China to rethink and amend its copyright system so as to restore a robust public domain where existing information and data can be used to produce future intellectual assets. The copyright reform should avoid the overprotecting of proprietary rights at the expense of the public domain so that future creations and innovations will not be hampered and the flourishing of creative and technological industries will not be restricted. By freely exploiting the flexibilities that are permitted under international conventional frameworks, China could expand the limitations and exceptions of its copyright law in full consideration of the interests of the information disseminators and public users in general and with the appropriate incorporation of safe harbors for ISP liability and permitted circumvention of technological measures in particular. The limitations and exceptions should be reasonably used to foster creation, research, education, and cultivation of quality at the national level. Access to knowledge and educational materials should not be overridden simply by digital locks or contracts imposed by right holders.

1.5 Conclusion

To respond to the challenges brought on by digital network technologies and resolve the copyright protection issues in the new era, countries are striving to look for feasible solutions by reforming their existing copyright protection

[105] Ibid.

[106] The Copyright (Amendment) Act 2012 of India, paragraph 37, s 65A(2)(a).

[107] The Copyright (Amendment) Act 2012 of India, paragraph 11, s 21.

systems at the domestic level and coordinating with their counterparts to update uniform conventional standards at the international level.

The establishment of the WIPO Internet Treaties compelled copyright protection to take into consideration the digital network environment by expanding protected subject matters, increasing the exclusive rights of copyright owners, establishing liability for ISPs, and introducing protection on technological measures and rights management information. These international provisions have imposed significant influence on the updating and development of national copyright systems in both developed and developing countries. Both the DMCA of the United States and the Information Society Directive of the European Union have well-implemented international conventions and treaties and developed certain mechanisms that safeguard ISP liability and protect technological measures and rights management information.

By following the international obligations and experience of developed countries, developing countries such as China have reformed their intellectual property and copyright protection regime from various angles, including reforms at the legislative, policy, administrative, and judicial levels as well as others. A series of changes in the Chinese intellectual property protection system demonstrate that China has established mechanisms with their own characteristics to enforce intellectual property and copyright protection and help resolve copyright issues in the digital network age. However, this does not mean that China has reached an optimal level of digital copyright protection. On the contrary, this is merely the first step that China has taken to deal with such issues. In the process of enforcement, China will face more challenges than ever before. Therefore, only by improving the copyright protection mechanisms based on changing situations will China be able to establish a balanced system in the digital network age.

References

1. World Intellectual Property Organization. (2000). WIPO guide to intellectual property worldwide. Available at http://books.google.co.za/books/about/WIPO_guide_to_intellectual_property_worl.html?id=LiI0BXyPlF8C. Visited 17 Oct 2011.
2. Merges, R. P., Menell, P. S., & Lemley, M. A. (2010). *Intellectual property in the new technology age* (5th ed.). New York: Aspen Publishers.
3. Tian, Y. (2009). *Re-thinking intellectual property: The political economy of copyright protection in the digital era*. London: Routledge-Cavendish.
4. Stokes, S. (2009). *Digital copyright law and practice* (3rd ed.). Oxford: Hart Publishing.
5. Ricketson, S., & Ginsburg, J. C. (2006). *International copyright and neighbouring rights: The Berne Convention and beyond* (2nd ed., Vol. I). Oxford: Oxford University Press.
6. Barbosa, R. G. (2006). *International copyright law and litigation: A mechanism for improvement*. Ann Arbor: ProQuest Information and Learning Company.
7. McCullagh, D. Senate bill amounts to death penalty for web sites. *CNET* (12 May 2011). Available at http://news.cnet.com/8301-31921_3-20062398-281.html. Visited 13 July 2012.
8. Mick, J. Wikileaks airs U.S. plans to kill Pirate Bay, monitor ISPs with multinational ACTA proposal (23 May 2008). Available at http://www.dailytech.com/article.aspx?newsid=11870. Visited 12 July 2012.

9. Wang, C. (2011, September 28–29). Function of legal transplant in Chinese social transition and legal development. In *Presentation at 2011 annual general conference of the European China Law Studies Association* organized by Science Po, Paris, France.
10. Liu, G. (1999). The ins and outs of China's accession to international copyright conventions. Available at http://www.gapp.gov.cn/chinacopyright/contents/537/20672.html. Visited 17 May 2014 (in Chinese).
11. Kong, Q. (2005). *WTO, internationalization and the intellectual property rights regime in China*. Singapore: Marshall Cavendish Academic Singapore.
12. Shan, H. (2008). *The protection of trade secrets in China*. Alphen aan den Rijn: Kluwer Law International.
13. Ganea, P., & Pattloch, T. (2005). *Intellectual property law in China*. The Hague: Kluwer Law International.
14. Xue, H., & Zheng, C. (2002). *Chinese intellectual property law in the 21st century*. Hong Kong: Sweet and Maxwell Asia.
15. Ginsburg, J. C. (1999). Copyright legislation for the 'digital millennium'. *Columbia-VLA Journal of Law & the Arts, 23*, 137.
16. Yu, P. K. (2010). Digital copyright reform and legal transplants in Hong Kong. *University of Louisville Law Review, 48*, 693–770.
17. Reichman, J. H. (2009). Intellectual property in the twenty-first century: Will the developing countries lead or follow? *Houston Law Review, 46*, 1115–1185.
18. Geist, M. India introduces Major Copyright Reform Bill (22 Apr 2010). Available at http://www.michaelgeist.ca/content/view/4974/196/. Visited 4 Nov 2011.
19. Pandey, A. Development in India IP Law: The Copyright (Amendment) Act 2012 (22 Jan 2013). Available at http://www.ip-watch.org/2013/01/22/development-in-indian-ip-law-the-copyright-amendment-act-2012/. Visited 23 Apr 2013.
20. Spicy IP. DRMs in the draft Copyright Amendments (29 Mar 2010). Available at http://spicyipindia.blogspot.com/2010/03/drms-in-draft-copyright-amendments.html. Visited 4 Nov 2011.

[illegible]

Chapter 2
Balance of Interest in Copyright Systems and Imbalances Under Digital Network Environments

2.1 Introduction

The development of copyright laws has often been affected by two divergent views, one that hold copyrights as private property and the other that consider them as a public policy issue. Scholars who subscribe to the former deem copyright as the natural property right of the author. Authors have a private proprietary interest in the works that they have originally created, which are the fruits of their efforts. Once creation is completed, they have exclusive rights in controlling the use and exploitation of the works so that they can gain from potential markets. A user who intends to use a copyright work must first obtain authorization from the author and pay the appropriate remunerations. The notion of copyright works as private property puts more emphasis on the acknowledgment of the intelligence and talent of the author with the purpose of encouraging further efforts and contributions from him/her and applying them to the original creation.

Scholars who support copyrights as a public policy issue, on the contrary, highlight the importance of public welfare in the accessing and using of copyright work. The supporters of a public policy notion consider that works are not created out of thin air and most of them are actualized by borrowing from former works and materials. Absolute monopolization is not a good way to encourage authors, but rather, it suffocates the sources of creative inspiration. Copyright systems were developed and designed as a balancing act in that the interests of authors to gain commercial benefits are weighed against the welfare of the public in accessing and using copyright works. The public policy stance advocates that only a limited monopoly should be granted to authors for a certain period of time so that works that fall within exceptions and the public domain will be free for public use. The foremost purpose of copyright systems under a public policy stance is to promote the progress of culture and useful arts.

These two divergent views have coexisted throughout the development of copyright laws. Copyright laws have developed in such a way that they adapt to the

J.J. Hua, *Toward A More Balanced Approach: Rethinking and Readjusting Copyright Systems in the Digital Network Era*, DOI 10.1007/978-3-662-43517-5_2,

changes brought on by the advancement of technologies. Copyright reforms are initiated by the lobbying of the relevant industries and concerns of governments with regard to serious economic and social problems caused by piracy. Governments are continually changing copyright laws to comply with industrial requirements for strengthening the protection of intellectual property on the one hand and carefully maintaining public interests in accessing knowledge and enjoying freedom of speech by including limited exceptions on the other hand. The digital network technologies make reproducing and disseminating information much more convenient and almost costless. In the meanwhile, copyright protection is strengthened due to the pressure imposed by copyright industries and the determination of governments to resolve rampant piracy. The strengthening of copyright protection has been supported by advocates who deem copyright works as private property and anticipate that digital network technologies would help copyright holders and relevant industries collect royalties and control the access and use of copyright works. The supporters of copyright work as a public policy issue are concerned that more and stronger protection for copyright work will threaten the free flow of information and freedom of speech. In their view, digital network technologies should promote knowledge and information sharing as well as cultural diversity rather than impede transformative borrowing and competitive innovation.

The conflicting views of copyright work as private property or a public policy issue have often been the driving force of copyright reform. The balancing of the interests that are in conflict is always the goal of legislators and copyright scholars, but this is difficult to achieve. Each time that this subtle balance of interest is violated, there would be advocates who would call for copyright reforms and revision of the law. The two conflicting views have intensified in the digital network age. An overview of the international intellectual property treaties and the tendencies of domestic copyright legislations worldwide indicate that the notion of copyright works as private property currently prevails in many aspects such as denouncing temporary reproduction as infringement, protecting the DRM and TPMs that control access and use of copyright works, curtailing copyright limitations and exceptions of DRM-protected works, increasing the liability of ISPs, and criminalizing end users who violate copyright laws. In light of the continual trends in strengthening copyright protection, many scholars have pointed out that current copyright systems should be reformed to counterattack the restrictive protectionism of copyright works as private property and restore and maintain a subtle balance of interest that existed in the predigital age.

This chapter intends to analyze the current state of imbalance in copyright legislations and the protection and reconstruction of a balance of interest in copyright under the digital network environment. The second part of the chapter will explore the interplay between copyright as private property and a public policy issue, and the balance of interest analyzed under several different perspectives, including a philosophical and economic analysis of intellectual property systems, the origin and development of copyright systems and the dual-goals of copyright protection. A historical and theoretical analysis from different angles will clearly demonstrate the design of intellectual property in general and copyright in particular and provide interpretation of the social and economic importance of maintaining a balance of interest in the intellectual property regime. The third part of the chapter will analyze the justification for copyright expansion, determine the key aspects for maintaining a balance of interest and explain the current situations of imbalance caused by continual strengthening of copyright protection and increased sanctions against digital copyright infringement. The continued strengthening of copyright protection is principally reflected in these following aspects: an extended duration of protection, expanded scope of protection, restrictive copyright limitations, protection of technological measures, aggravated liability of ISPs, and expanding monopolization of copyright industries. These hinder appropriate access and dissemination of copyright works. The final part of the chapter will suggest the restoration of the balance of interest by reforming copyright laws, including the redefining of the scope of copyright limitations and exceptions, reutilizing moderate protection on technological measures, establishing safe harbors for ISPs, mitigating the liability of end users, and introducing alternative schemes, such as open source software and the Creative Commons. These problems and proposals will be further examined and elaborated in the subsequent chapters.

2.2 Balance of Interest in Copyright Systems

The balance of interest scheme is the fundamental basis of copyright law and the driving power of copyright development and reform. The balancing game can be reflected by many aspects, such as the philosophical and economic analyses of intellectual property systems, including copyright, the origin and growth of copyright law as well as the dual goals of copyright protection systems.

2.2.1 Philosophical Analysis of Intellectual Property Systems

Intellectual property is not merely a simple legal issue based on industrial designs and norms, but also a theoretical issue that requires the examining and analysis of philosophical components. Philosophers and intellectual property scholars have contributed with their theoretical views on the right of property which could work as the fundamental basis for the notion and system of intellectual property.

Jean Jacques Rousseau, a famous Enlightenment thinker in the eighteenth century, provided his view of property in his book, *The Social Contract*. The right of property is built on social contracts and the social general will. Rousseau described the property system in a civil society as a social contract in which there are losses and gains; to gain something, one must lose something else: "what man loses by the social contract is his natural liberty and an unlimited right to everything he tries to get and succeeds in getting; what he gains is civil liberty and the proprietorship of all he possesses" [1]. Here, Rousseau differentiated natural freedom and rights with civil liberty and rights. The former is naturally given and the latter is protected by law. To own a property right that is protected by law, one must submit to the general will; therefore, the loss of natural freedom is in exchange for civil rights. Therefore, one "must clearly distinguish natural liberty, which is bounded only by the strength of the individual, from civil liberty, which is limited by the general will; and possession, which is merely the effect of force or the right of the first occupier, from property, which can be founded only on a positive title" [1].

In addition to the advocating adherence to the general will, Rousseau also proposed a theory with regard to the justice of property rights. First, Rousseau advocated the reciprocity of property rights and obligations. The effort of connecting justice with property rights aimed to establish a norm in that every individual in society respects the property rights of others. As Rousseau said, "every man has naturally a right to everything he needs; but the positive act which makes him proprietor of one thing excludes him from everything else. Having his share, he ought to keep to it, and can have no further right against the community" [2]. In Rousseau's philosophy on justice, social order means property rights which command respect and are protected in compliance with justice. Secondly, Rousseau advocated for the equality of rights. The equality does not mean that "the degrees of power and riches are to be absolutely identical for everybody" [3]. By equality, Rousseau meant limitations on individual ownership in order to subject to the general will. He pointed out that the system of property rights was based on a social contract which "sets up among the citizens an equality of such a kind, that they all bind themselves to observe the same conditions and should therefore all enjoy the same rights. Every authentic act of the general will, binds or favors all the citizens equally" [4]. In *The Social Contract*, Rousseau repeatedly favored the use of particular phrases that have a communal nature, such as "common interest", "general good" and "general will". The driving force for the communal nature of ownership is that, "what makes the will general is less the number of voters than the common interest uniting them; for, under this system, each necessarily submits to the conditions he imposes on others". Rousseau hence concluded that "the general will, to be really such, must be general in its object as well as its essence; that it must both come from all and apply to all; and that it loses its natural rectitude when it is directed to some particular and determinate object" [4].

Although Rousseau's philosophy on property rights primarily deals with tangible assets such as land, it could also be used to explain systems that regulate intangible assets. The philosophy of the social contract has greatly influenced the contract theory of patents in modern society with which patent scholars explain the relationship between information publication and exclusive proprietary rights as consideration or contract. Rousseau's analysis of the connection of general will, property rights and justice can theoretically support many balance of interest issues in intellectual property systems, including the protection and constraint of rights, dissemination of knowledge information and exploitation of exclusive rights, and public interest in intellectual property.

In addition to philosophical influence on the notions and functions of intangible property provided by the early modern philosophers, modern intellectual property scholars also contribute with their own philosophical opinions. Professor Peter Drahos proposed the theory of abstract objects for intellectual assets in his book, *A Philosophy of Intellectual Property,* based on a discussion of the origin and development of property systems and analytic property theory. According to Drahos, "intellectual property law posits rights in abstract objects" [5, p. 1]. The word "abstract objects" that Drahos uses in his philosophical analysis of intellectual property originates from the term "incorporeal things" in classical Roman law. Roman law divided everything into corporeal and incorporeal; the former is related to tangible things such as land, a slave, a garment, gold, silver and countless other things, and the latter is related to intangible things that only exist in law, such as an inheritance, a usufruct, or obligations contracted [5, p. 16]. The Roman law of incorporeal things was heavily influenced by Stoicism. In the Stoic notion of incorporeality, four things, namely, time, space, the void and *lekta* (the meaning of words or sentences) are incorporeal. "Incorporeal things were not existent, but rather subsistent. They subsisted by virtue of human mental life. They were things superimposed by the mind onto the corporeal world" [5, p. 17]. Incorporeal rights are related abstract objects; these also form the relations between individual actors [5, p. 153]. Before property rights are attached to an abstract object, some sort of "corporealization" of the abstract object is required [5, p. 153]. The process of corporealization can be formal, such as registration for patent protection, or informal, such as creating information subjected to protection by copyrighting or as a trade secret [5, p. 17]. Corporealization generates "the physical representations" and "an entity with specific meaning which amounts to the creation of an expressible" [5, pp. 17–18]. "Once the abstract object attains corporeality by becoming embodied belief, it can play a causal role in the social and productive relations of people" [5, p. 18].

In Drahos' philosophical analysis of intellectual property, abstract objects are a form of capital which has controlling power over both the product and productive means [5, p. 157]. Drahos argued that "abstract objects function as gateways to valuable physical objects. These physical objects may be the capital items important in the processes of production, or they may be the end result of such processes" [5, p. 157]. Once abstract objects control the access of valuable resources, "a formal, legally constituted person-dependent relationship" is established in addition to the resource-dependent relationship [5, p. 159]. According to Drahos, not all abstract objects have a power-creating effect and thus create a resource-dependent relationship [5, p. 158]. The creation of literary and artistic works protected by copyright will hardly increase the power base of the author [5, p. 158]. Resources such as "genes, seeds, chemical compounds or forms of medical treatment" protected by patents or new forms of legislatively created abstract objects like plant variety right are more likely to increase the power effect of the right holder and strengthen the collective dependence. However, to my understanding, copyright not only protects literary and artistic works, but also scientific works which are the key resources for the means and processes of production. In addition, the establishment of private ownership on resources of literary and artistic objects could also affect future authors who would like to borrow and create based on existing resources. Thus, the power-creating effect and a person-dependent relationship exist among all abstract objects, although different forms of abstract objects may generate different levels of personal dependence.

Drahos used an example to explain the person-dependent relationship generated by abstract objects. A farmer who wants to plant crops depends on having seeds to plant. This is an object-dependent relationship. If the seeds are protected by a patent or plant variety right, the farmer requires permission from the right holder to obtain access to the seeds. A person-dependent relationship is thus added to the object-dependent relationship [5, p. 159]. Once a dependent relationship exists between two persons, one person may face a coercion claim from the other. The theories of coercion agree that threats are coercive [5, p. 159]. Drahos made a plausible claim that "relationships of dependence create the conditions necessary for the making of credible threats", thus, making "coercion claims feasible" [5, p. 159].

Drahos then concluded on two consequences in the distribution of power. First, where abstract objects are related to resources that many people are dependent upon, the scope of the threat power of these abstract objects will be extensive and the range of power will be potentially global [5, p. 160]. Secondly, the extensive amount of power is likely to be unevenly distributed within social systems and will become increasingly so [5, p. 160]. Newly generated technology requires a large amount of investment which is costly and capital flows to high-tech production which attracts investment. In important and promising areas of science, ownership of relevant abstract objects may be controlled by a small number of well-resourced people [5, p. 161]. These individuals have significant threat power if the abstract objects are related to significant resources. That is to say in Drahos' words: "extensive, possibly global, power will probably be concentrated in the hands of those who, through their scientific/technological capabilities and superior capital resources, are able to capture, through the property mechanism for abstract objects, resources upon which there is a universal reliance" [5, p. 161].

The philosophical analysis of abstract objects and intellectual property by Drahos provides a new perspective to realize the social function and effect of intellectual property systems. Although Drahos did not deny the necessity of the existence of intellectual property systems, he placed more emphasis on the dangers of potential threat power and uneven distribution of power generated by intellectual property. The possible danger foreseen by Drahos helps us to reconsider the situation of intellectual property protection and reestablish a balanced approach, as well as readdress public interest in the intellectual property system.

One of the important purposes of intellectual property systems is to address public interest and welfare. Yet this should not deny the proprietary rights of intangible property, but rather emphasize the importance of a balance between individual exclusive rights and social public interest. Philosophers have provided different explanations and justifications which support public interest. Rousseau embodied justice into his philosophy on property. In his point of view, acknowledgement of property rights is founded on the establishment of social order which respects and protects property. Property systems should have a fair social contract that satisfies the general will so as to maintain justice in the system. Drahos analyzed the threat that intellectual property systems posed to the distribution of resources. Although

Drahos acknowledged that there is justification for the existence of intellectual property, he was concerned that the establishment of such a system in an imperfect society would enhance person-dependent relationships and powerful person-dependent relationships would create an imbalance in the distribution of resources, thus enriching a small group of people and impoverishing the majority. The warning given by Drahos undoubtedly embodies the maintaining of a balance with the public interest kept in mind in intellectual property systems.

2.2.2 Economical Analysis of Intellectual Property Systems

The economic philosophy of intellectual property systems is primarily based on guaranteeing the economic gains of creators and in turn, advancing public welfare, as the United States Supreme court clarified in the *Mazer v. Stein* case, "the economic philosophy behind the clause empowering congress to grant patents and copyrights is the conviction that encouragement of individual effort by personal gains is the best way to advance public welfare".[1] As aforementioned, the private property and the public policy views have different perspectives as to the scope and strength of intellectual property protection. The supporters of the former claim that creators should collect all economic gains from potential markets of intellectual products, while the advocates of the latter argue that the exclusive ownership of creators should be limited to a certain degree so that public welfare will not be diminished due to the high cost of obtaining intellectual products.

Intellectual products have features that are different from tangible property. Paul Samuelson differentiated private and public goods in an economic sense by taking apples and street lamps as examples [6, p. 171]. According to Samuelson, private goods refer to goods in which the use by one person precludes that of another [7, p. 100]. For example, "when one person eats an apple, others cannot eat it; a pair of pants can be worn only by one person at a time; a car cannot go two different directions simultaneously, and so forth" [7, p. 100]. These examples illustrate that "there is rivalry in the consumption of private goods" [7, p. 100]. On the contrary, there is no rivalry in the consumption of public goods. In the use of public goods, the use by one person does not exclude that of another. For example, a street lamp can simultaneously illuminate onto different pedestrians, and a bus can take many passengers.

Economists consider that intellectual products are a special type of goods, which share common characteristics with public goods. First, the consumption of intellectual goods is nonexclusive. Authors cannot exclude others from accessing and using their intellectual achievements unless their works are kept as a secret. However, if authors keep the works to themselves, their creation will not be known and acknowledged by society. Secondly, the consumption of intellectual goods is non-rivaling, because one person's use of a work does not affect another's use of the

[1] *Mazer v Stein*, 347 U.S. 201 (1954).

same work. Numerous people can simultaneously consume one single intellectual good. Thirdly, intellectual goods are non-exhaustive. In contrast to tangible public goods, intellectual goods cannot be depleted by use. On the contrary, the use of intellectual goods is more likely to increase the volume of intangible sources and generate social benefits because of the sharing and borrowing of information. This phenomenon may mean that authors will find it difficult to be adequately compensated. Thus, legislations that address the unauthorized use of intellectual goods need to be promulgated. Fourthly, intellectual goods are expensive to create, but cheap to reproduce. The development of technology makes reproduction much cheaper and easier. The emergence of printing and photocopying machines, videocassette recorders, computers and the Internet has largely decreased the cost and time that are required to reproduce a work. Once an author sells the intellectual good to a certain consumer, the consumer will become a potential competitor with the original author, or other consumers will become free riders without paying any remuneration. Therefore, protection of intellectual goods against piracy is necessary especially under the digital network environment.

As for the strength of intellectual property protection, there are discrepancies among the advocates of the private property and public policy views. The supporters of the former regard the property rights of authors of intellectual goods to be similar as tangible property rights. The establishment of private ownership over intellectual goods is important to guarantee the benefits and incentives for creations and avoid the "tragedy of the commons" in tangible goods. The "tragedy of the commons" refers to the overuse and underinvestment of property caused by public ownership [8]. Strong private property rights could provide incentives for large-scale investments, allow control over exploitation and ensure that resources are put to their most efficient use [9, p. 35]. The private property view advocates that strong property rights should also be put into place in the protection of intangible property.

On the contrary, supporters of the public policy view argue that the economic benefits of authors should be weighed against the access costs of users so as to better the entire society. William Landes and Richard Posner proposed an access-incentive paradigm in which the incentive to create justifies the legal protection of works against unauthorized reproduction [10]. Nevertheless, legal protection for the purpose of encouraging incentive to create in turn will increase the access costs of potential authors in their use and exploitation of earlier copyright works, because these authors often need to pay to access preexisting works and reasonably borrow from original works so as to avoid the expense of potential infringement litigation caused by substantial similarities. In economic analysis, producers of intellectual goods have endowment of creativity. They are likely to use their monopoly generated from their strong property rights to acquire different kinds of economic rent, especially under the circumstances where spiritual products are in shortage. Producers of intellectual goods who aim to maximize their benefits may ignore the needs of society as a whole for proper culture and advanced technology development. On the other hand, consumers of information and intellectual goods may maximize their utilization of those products based on their personal needs, thus negatively affecting the economic gains of information producers. Advocates of the public policy view continuously endeavor to find the optimal point which balances the interests of the producers of intellectual goods and public consumers.

The establishment of an intellectual property system means that the producers of intellectual goods publish their works or inventions to inform and educate the public in exchange for public acknowledgement that these producers have a monopoly over the use and exploitation of their own intellectual goods for a limited period of time. Intellectual goods are public, but intellectual property is monopolistic. Economists indicate that once property owners realize that there is scale economy in property, different interest parties will attempt to reach an agreement on establishing a government which acknowledges and protects property rights [6, p. 176]. The principle purposes of intellectual property systems are to define property rights, protect the intellectual achievements of creators, regulate property transactions and promote the dissemination of information. On the one hand, it is difficult for a new creator to recover the expenses of creation and production in an unregulated market. Monopolization is the driving power for creators to produce new works or inventions. On the other hand, the establishment of high prices by monopolists will impede the use of intellectual products. If consumers cannot afford the high costs of acquiring products, the optimum beneficial gains of resource deployment cannot be achieved. In this dilemma, inadequate intellectual goods will be produced without legal monopolies, but with monopolies, little information can be found for consumption. The solution to the dilemma is to establish reasonable restrictions on monopolistic rights to ensure that the public will find it convenient enough to use information in compliance with different rules and regulations.

The realm of intellectual property rights is generally divided into exclusive rights and free use, with a small amount of intellectual assets that fall between the two. Most intellectual goods have exclusive rights in which the use of intellectual goods must be authorized by the creator and compensation must be paid. The existence of exclusive rights compensates creators and maintains their passion and creativity. Some intellectual goods are recognized as having free use where neither consent nor compensation is required. Free use promotes information dissemination and encourages creative activity from the public. In a society where all information and intellectual goods fall within exclusive ownership rights, consumers will either refuse to use information because they cannot attain authorization by paying the monopolistic price, or will spend large amounts of money to search for information, conduct negotiations and implement transactions. This will be an inefficient and defeated society. The establishment of intellectual property systems should not only guarantee a just allocation of resources, benefits, rights, and liability, but also increase the total amount of spiritual wealth in society and strengthen the efficiency of resource exploitation.

In the realm of copyrights, Richard Posner explained in his economic analysis the reason that the scope and duration of "intellectual property rights represents the striking of a balance between the interests of the creators and of the users of intellectual property" is because "the creators themselves may benefit from the limiting of those rights" [11, p. 47]. He supposed that most of the literary and artistic works build heavily on earlier creative works. The large scope of copyright protection of earlier works will increase the costs of making subsequent works. Although an increase in the scope of copyright protection enhances the expected revenues of the authors from the sale or licensing of his/her own copyrights, it will also increase his/her costs of creating the works that s/he has copyrighted [11, p. 47]. Perpetual or unlimited copyrights will further increase the costs of the author because under such circumstances, "no earlier works were in the public domain and thus available to be used in the creation of new works without copyright expense" [11, p. 47]. Posner further argued that if the subsequent work is complementary rather than replace the earlier work, the author of the earlier work will even gain from the limitations on the scope of copyright protection. According to economists, there is a distinction between complements and substitutes, "a product is a complement of another product if a fall in its price will cause the quantity demanded of the other product to rise, and the product is a substitute if a fall in its price will cause the quantity demanded of the other product to fall" [11, p. 49]. For example, a book review may be the complement of a book so that readers of the book review may wish to buy the book; a public performance may be the complement of a song so that the audience in the performance may wish to purchase a phonographic copy of the song.

2.2.3 Origin and Development of Copyright Laws

The nascent concept of modern copyright existed in ancient Greek and Jewish laws, and in the Roman publishing system [12]. The early literary and artistic works in Greece were oral and anonymous. Due to the nature of spoken dialogue and limitations in human memory, few works were able to be recorded and preserved. In addition, authors in ancient Greece regarded their creation as collective achievements and indivisible possession of a school or group rather than personal work which could be exclusively owned by the creator [13]. The earliest concept of intellectual property emerged when individual creation began to appear in all cultural fields in sixth century B.C. Athens [13]. Ancient Jewish law linked with modern universal copyright when those who contributed with new principles to civil and religious laws were required to be identified [12]. The effort in recognizing contributions to oral cultures pushed forward the preservation of authorship and formation of the concept of nascent copyright, although the recognition of authorship was concerned more about the accurate recording of oral cultures rather than the introduction of private property rights. Ancient Roman law did not contain copyright laws either, but evidence indicates that some authors reached publishing contracts with book traders [12]. The book trade in Rome created the conditions for the birth of the notion of copyright. Although there were book sales in ancient Rome, most of the literary and artistic creative practices were controlled by the Roman Catholic Church through centralized production and dissemination. Monasteries established libraries that loaned manuscripts in exchange for land, cattle or money [14]. Although the practice of loaning did not have any connections with individual author ownership rights, it was the one of the earliest attempt to make the copying of literary works available in exchange for some sort of remuneration. However, the concept of authorship and intellectual property did not formally emerge until the religious structure and cultural unity in the Middle Ages disintegrated, as people in medieval societies saw their intellectual achievements as collective endeavors, not individual efforts.

The emergence of printing technology and capitalism spurred the birth of modern copyright laws. In the Middle Ages, the secular trade of books was initiated in European cities by stationers. Stationers organized the reproduction of texts by hand and provided copies upon the request of buyers who asked for certain titles. After printing technology was invented, these stationers invested their accumulated capital in developing the technology and transformed their book business into a capitalistic mass production. In Venice of Italy, which was regarded as the origin of capitalism according to Marxist political economists, the Venetian Collegio granted John of Speyer, who brought the printing press to Venice in the fifteenth century, exclusive printing privileges for 5 years [14], because the government intended to encourage the importation of new technology and advancement of relevant industries by granting such exclusive privileges. Similar laws with regard to printing privileges spread to many European countries at the beginning of the sixteenth century. In Germany, both imperial and municipal privileges for property rights were granted to publishers in order to encourage the growth of the book publishing industry [14]. Besides governmental granted privileges, the leading publishers also adopted noninterference agreements to protect their businesses against piracy and competition [14]. A similar situation also emerged in the Netherlands where publishers reached agreements among themselves to protect the commercial investment of their literary property interests [15]. When international book trades became more frequent and domestic publishing industries turned international, the industry agreements and state-authorized publishing privileges were gradually replaced by national and international copyright laws. The United Kingdom was deemed by copyright historians as the first country to promulgate the modern copyright law. The evolution of the copyright regime in the United Kingdom was precipitated by both the cooperation of publishers and governmental intervention [14].

At the beginning of the importation of the printing press, the British government gave book publishers who organized the Stationers' Company the exclusive right to control the reproduction and copying of books through censorship laws, such as the Licensing Act of 1662 [16]. The right to control book reproduction was once perpetual, but ended due to the expiration of the Licensing Act of 1662 in 1694. Stationers attempted to restore censorship laws at first, but when their attempts failed, they transformed their lobbying from guaranteeing the monopolization of the market for themselves to protecting the legal rights of authors. The industry lobbying led to the passing of the Statute of Anne which was proclaimed as "An Act for the Encouragement of Learning, by vesting the copies of printed books in the authors or purchasers of such copies, during the times therein mentioned" in April 1710 [14]. Under the statute, copyright protection for existing works in the Stationers Register was 21 years and the protection term for new works finished after the statute became effective was 14 years upon expiration with another 14 years of protection granted afterwards. The Statute of Anne focused only on property rights, and did not mention the moral right of authors. To fully enjoy the rewards of having property rights, an author had to assign his/her copyright to the stationers.

The history of the preconditions and development of copyright shows that copyright principally emerged for the economic benefits of publishers who monopolistically controlled the printing and distribution of individual or classes of works. Before the release of the Statute of Anne, only the economic rights of stationers could be protected and economic remunerations generated by book production and sales all went to the publishers, printers and booksellers. Nothing in the law catered to the protection of the rights of the authors for their original creations. The legislators of the Statute of Anne took on a public policy view to restrict the market monopolization on commoditization of literature by granting authors with a limited time of exclusive rights with the purpose of encouraging learning. In the face of the loss of market monopolization, the stationers attempted to regain their perpetual right on printing and publishing. They took on a private property stance by claiming that the authors should deserve a common law copyright in their original works and stationers could own a common law copyright through transfers by the authors [16]. By proposing a common law copyright, the stationers aimed to restore their perpetual control on publishing outside the scope of the Statute of Anne.

The supporters of the private property view used John Locke's labor theory of property as justification. Locke indicated that people had the natural right to owning their bodies [16]. Since every individual owned his/her own body, "the labor of his body and the work of his hands, are properly his. Whatsoever then he removes out of the state that nature hath provided and left it in, he hath mixed his labor with, and joined to it something that is his own, and thereby makes it his property" [17, p. 134]. Locke justified the private appropriation of the common wealth of nature [14]. However, Locke obviously did not extend this private appropriation and labor theory of property to the area of intangible assets, such as literary and artistic works. Supporters of the private property view have thus used Locke's labor theory of property and extended the notions in the realm of tangible goods to intangible goods.

Based on the notion of natural property rights, stationers insisted on pursuing for exclusive rights on publishing through lawsuits for nearly 40 years. The judicial efforts made by the stationers were known as the "battle of the booksellers." The first case in which the publishers sought to regain their infinite monopoly was *Millar v. Taylor*.[2] Andrew Millar was a bookseller who purchased the copyright of a popular epic poem, *The Seasons,* from its author, James Thomson. Upon the expiration of the statutory copyright of the poem, another bookseller, Robert Taylor, who did not belong to the Stationer's Company, published a competing and less expensive edition. Millar sued Taylor by alleging that the defendant committed infringement against the perpetual common law copyright transferred from the author. The Court of King's Bench confirmed the existence of a common law copyright and concluded that the Statute of Anne provided additional protection after the publication of a work. The statute did not substitute the common law right or limit its term. The decision affirmed the

[2] *Millar v Taylor* (1769) 98 Eng. Rep. 201.

author's right to reap pecuniary profits from his/her own ingenuity and labor as well as supported the infinite copyright held by the publishers. However, Justice Joseph Yates dissented with the opinion that the authors should be rewarded for their labor but the reward should not be infinite.[3] When the case was appealed to the House of Lords, the booksellers reached a settlement. This case could be seen as a victory of the publishers and supporters of the private property view.

The same issue was brought up again in the second case, *Donaldson v. Beckett*,[4] in which the legitimate publisher of *The Seasons,* Thomas Beckett, sued an unauthorized rival bookseller, Alexander Donaldson, for copyright infringement. The injunction was at first granted against Donaldson by the Chancery, but in an appeal later, the House of Lords overturned the injunction. Although the final decision recognized the common law copyright, it concluded that the Statute of Anne had a supplement with a statutory right. Once a work was published, its copyright protection was limited by the statutory term. The decision of *Donaldson v. Beckett* again abolished the market monopolization of publishers and booksellers, and returned to support a public policy stance. Sir John Dalrymple once questioned: "what property can a man have in ideas? While he keeps them to himself they are his own, when he publishes them they are his no longer" [18, p. 39]. Lord Camden also pointed out that "knowledge has no value or use for the solitary owner: to be enjoyed it must be communicated. What situations would the public be in with regard to literature, if there were no means of compelling a second impression of a useful work to be put forth? All our learning will be locked upon in the hands of the Tonsons and the Lintons[5] of the age, who will set what price upon it their avarice chuses to demand, till the public become as much their slaves, as their own hackney compilers are".[6]

Although the private property and public policy views coexisted in the early development of copyrights with constant conflict between the two of them, the public policy stance prevailed after *Donaldson v. Beckett.* Influenced by the United Kingdom, copyright origination and development in the United States modeled the copyright history in the United Kingdom. The first recorded copyright was initiated by a bookseller, John Usher, in the Massachusetts Bay Colony to protect his exclusive right to publish a revised edition of *The General Laws and Liberties of the Massachusetts Colony*. Between 1783 and 1786, 12 original states issued copyright laws with language and form modeled after the Statute of Anne [14]. The goals of these copyright statutes were to protect the rights of the authors, encourage learning, establish order in book sales and restrict market monopolization [12].

Due to the separate state registries for copyright works and weak enforcement of state copyright statutes, a uniform national copyright system was essential for regulating national publishing and book trade. The Constitution of the United States first put into place, a copyright and patent clause which stated that "the Congress shall

---

[3] Ibid.

[4] *Donaldson v Beckett* (1774) 1 Eng. Rep. 837.

[5] Tonsons and Lintons were the names of two large London booksellers and publishers in the seventeenth and eighteenth centuries.

[6] *Donaldson v Beckett* (1813) 17 Cobbett's Parl. Hist. 953.

have the power to promote the Progress of Science and useful Arts, by securing for Limited Times to Authors and Inventors the exclusive Right to their respective Writings and Discoveries".[7] Following the constitutional copyright clause, Congress then passed the first federal copyright law in 1790. The Copyright Act of 1790 granted copyright protection to American authors for a statutory term of 14 years which could be renewed once. During this term of protection, authors enjoyed exclusive rights to print, reprint, publish and sell their works. However, the Copyright Act did not mention whether the common law copyright was substituted by the statutory right after the passing of the act.

Similar to the publishers who sought a common law copyright in the United Kingdom, authors in the United States also attempted to acquire infinite copyright protection in common law through lawsuits. In *Wheaton v. Peters*,[8] Richard Peters, the fourth Reporter of Decisions of the Supreme Court, published an abridged six-volume edition based on a 24 volume version of his predecessors', in which 75 % was from that of Henry Wheaton, the third Reporter of Decisions. Wheaton sued Peters for copyright infringement under both the Copyright Act and common law, by asserting that common law copyright shall not be supplanted by the federal statute. Heavily influenced by *Donaldson v Beckett*, the Supreme Court rejected Wheaton's argument and concluded that copyright was a statutory right granted by Congress and secured by the formalities of registration, notice and deposit.[9] Justice John McLean refused to recognize the common law copyright by opining that when a work became the subject of controversy, it was decided by the highest judicial court in England, and that the right of the authors could not be asserted as common law, but under the Statute of Anne.[10] An author only remains under common law copyright when his/her work was not published. Once published, the work was protected by the statute. Upon the expiration of the term of protection, the work would enter into the public domain. By making this decision, the court avoided the issue of an infinite monopoly supported by the natural common law right and protected the public welfare in obtaining access to literary and artistic works.

Although the private property stance still exists based on the Lockean idea that individuals have natural rights to the achievements of their labor, it is the public policy view that determined the theme and tendency of future copyright legislation and development. The importance of the *Donaldson* and *Wheaton* case not only impelled lawmakers in the United Kingdom and the United States to be more concerned about public welfare but encouraged a worldwide trend in establishing a copyright system that focused more on granting a limited monopoly to authors and securing access by the public rather than merely focusing on copyright protection as an infinite right in natural law.

The concept of intellectual property was introduced into South and East Asian societies much later behind the emergence of copyright in the United States. China

---

[7] The United States Constitution, Art 1, s 8, Clause 8.

[8] *Wheaton v Peters* 33 U.S. 591 (1834).

[9] Ibid.

[10] *Wheaton* (n 8 above).

did not pass its copyright law until 1991. By enacting the first copyright law of the People's Republic of China, lawmakers obviously incorporated a balanced approach and the primary purpose of public welfare and cultural prosperity in Article 1 of the law: "this law is enacted for the purposes of protecting the copyright of authors in their literary, artistic and scientific works and the copyright-related rights and interests, of encouraging the creation and dissemination of works which would contribute to the construction of socialist spiritual and material civilization, and of promoting the development and prosperity of socialist culture and science".

2.2.4 Dual Goals of Copyright Systems

The onset and development of copyright laws clearly illustrates the dual goals embodied in the copyright system, namely, protecting creations and intellectual labor on the one hand and promoting advancement of knowledge, learning, culture and art on the other hand.

One of the foremost purposes of establishing copyright systems was to holistically protect the interest of the authors. According to Locke, "people are entitled to hold, as property, whatever they produce by their own initiative, intelligence, and industry" [19]. The original author should be entitled to a series of exclusive rights to control the use and distribution of his/her work which has been concocted by his/her own mental labor and sweat, and represents his/her personality. Without adequate protection and reward for the intellectual effort, the incentive to create will be hampered. Monetary remunerations not only acknowledge the endeavors and contribution to society, but also guarantee that material needs are met for subsequent creations. Although some, especially scholars in the academia, do not expect monetary rewards, and rather prefer a wide distribution of their works to establish their reputations, it should be noted that copyrights not only protect the economic rights of their authors, but also moral rights, such as the right of attribution and the right of integrity to the work against any unauthorized alterations, mutilations and distortions. Regardless whether the purpose of the author is to earn remuneration or not, s/he does not hope that others will take advantage of his/her skills, labor and money spent by tampering with the expression of his/her written product and authorship. Judicial decisions in copyright disputes also confirm that one of the purposes of copyrighting is to reward the author for his/her creation. In *Harper & Row v. Nation Enterprises*,[11] the Supreme Court of the United States reinforced that the function of the scheme established by the Copyright Act is to promote the original works that provide the seed and substance to the harvest of knowledge. "The rights conferred by copyright are designed to assure contributors to the store of knowledge a fair return for their labors".[12]

---

[11] *Harper & Row v Nation Enterprises* 471 U.S. 539 (1985).

[12] Ibid.

However, the protection of the interests of the authors is not the sole purpose of establishing copyright systems. More importantly, copyright laws should be made to safeguard public interest by promoting advancement of knowledge and learning, preserving public domain and forming a democratic civil society. First, copyright systems should serve to promote the advancement of knowledge and learning and the development of science and culture. These goals have been clearly stipulated in constitutions and copyright laws. The Constitution of the United States empowers Congress to "promote the Progress of Science and useful Arts, by securing for Limited Times to Authors and Inventors the exclusive Right to their respective Writings and Discoveries".[13] The Report of the Register of Copyrights on the General Revision of the U.S. Copyright Law also explained that the ultimate purpose of copyright is to "foster the growth of learning and culture for the public welfare". The Copyright Law of China underlines the ultimate purpose of making this law in its Article 1 as promoting the development and prosperity of socialist culture and science. In order to achieve this final end, the Copyright Law shall protect the copyright of authors in their works and encourage the creation and dissemination of works. The ultimate purpose of copyright systems is also illustrated by court decisions. In *Mazer v. Stein*,[14] the court stated that "the economic philosophy behind the clause empowering Congress to grant patents and copyrights is the conviction that encouragement of individual effort by personal gain is the best way to advance public welfare through the talents of authors and inventors in 'Science and useful Arts'". In *Twentieth Century Music Corp. v. Aiken*,[15] the court again stated that "the immediate effect of our copyright law is to secure a fair return for an 'author's' creative labor. But the ultimate aim is, by this incentive, to stimulate artistic creativity for the general public good. The sole interest of the United States and the primary object in conferring the monopoly lie(s) in the general benefits derived by the public from the labors of authors".

Secondly, copyright systems should serve to preserve the public domain. Preservation of the public domain means that the protection of copyrights is restricted to a certain period of time and within a certain scope. In doing so, the owners are able to fully enforce their exclusive rights. However, outside the scope, public users are allowed to use the works for free. The designing of a limited term for copyright protection, the idea-expression dichotomy, and fair use/fair dealing are major principles that limit copyright monopolization and preserve the public domain. In preserving the interest of the public domain, this provides the source for future creations and promotes storage of knowledge and learning.

Thirdly, copyright systems should have a role in the formation of a democratic civil society. Copyright functions as an engine for creative and free expression. The stimulation of expressions on various topics including political, economic, cultural, and recreational issues lays the foundation for the establishment of a democratic civil society. Moreover, the creative activity supported by copyright systems not

---

[13] *See* n 7 above.

[14] *Mazer* (n 1 above).

[15] *Twentieth Century Music Corp. v Aiken* 422 U.S. 151 (1975).

only relies on national and governmental subsidies and patronage [20], but prospers because of commercial benefit, personal desire to expand reputation, personal interests, and educational purposes. Moving away from governmental support would further encourage free expression, thus, moving society toward having a democratic and civic culture.

2.3 Current Imbalance of Interest in Copyright Systems

2.3.1 Borderline of Balance of Interests: Accessibility of Copyright Works

In order to fulfill the dual purposes of copyright systems, which are to encourage creations on the one hand and to advance knowledge and learning on the other hand, the design of copyright systems must guarantee public accessibility to copyright works. Accessibility plays a central role in copyright systems to achieve the ultimate goal and create balance between copyright holders and public users. Without appropriate accessibility, copyright works cannot be reproduced and disseminated. Thus, the goal of promoting knowledge and learning cannot be well achieved.

Accessibility to copyright works could be explained in two ways: First, the public must be able to access copyright works so as to access the ideas of the works [21]. Under the idea-expression dichotomy, the use and borrowing of ideas are free from copyright infringement as long as the user does not copy the expressions without the authorization of the owner. Second, the public who has accessibility comprises two groups of people [21]. There are the users, such as readers who cannot learn and absorb knowledge without access to different works. Then there are the potential authors who cannot create new works without access to previous works and borrowing ideas from them. Although the works created by these potential authors may compete with the original works, the competing works provide different means for the public to learn and appreciate, thus enriching cultural and social life. Access to copyright works is important to realize the purposes of copyright systems and achieve a balance of interests, because the development of culture and science is based on the fact that ideas and knowledge act as gateways for others [5]. Ideas and creations are inspired and generated from previous existing ideas. Every piece of work, in some sense, can be regarded as the "joint product of human intellectual history" [19, p. 34]. In addition, permission to access different works promptly guarantees the distribution of ideas and expressions, thus avoiding the waste of the social value of information, because certain ideas, expressions and informative knowledge are most valuable when they are communicated, disseminated and absorbed in time.

The core of copyright systems is *quid pro quo* [21]. An author gains through commercializing his/her work, while the public benefits by accessing the work. If access to commercialized work is not available, the author unfairly receives monetary rewards without contributing to society. The ultimate goal of advancing knowledge and learning will not be well served either. Under the balanced notion of *quid pro quo*, an author obtains economic gains by commercializing the work and allowing appropriate public access to the work. If the author does not permit any access to his/her work, such as restricting access through diaries, letters, and unpublished work, s/he cannot acquire any economic rewards for his/her efforts to create the work. Consequently, the *quid pro quo* notion becomes imbalanced. In the situation that the author gains, but refuses to allow public access to the work, limitations and exceptions such as fair use/fair dealing and compulsory licensing should be introduced into copyright systems so as to maintain a balance. In cases where access to the work is available to the public but the author does not gain anything, s/he can control and decide whether s/he would like to commercialize the work so as to restore a balance [21]. The interests of copyright owners and the public cannot always peacefully coincide together in copyright systems. When they conflict, balance should be sought and restored by amendment and revision of laws.

2.3.2 *Justification of Expanding Copyrights*

The expansion of copyright systems has been influenced by technology development. New technology induces new kinds of works based on new media and significantly decreases the cost of reproducing and disseminating works. Such technological advancement changes the interests of copyright owners and public users. The users are exposed to more opportunities brought on by digital network technology to obtain access and exploit copyrightable works. For example, a user who surfs the Internet can easily listen to a song online, download the file and transmit the clip to his/her friends through email, online instant messaging or by uploading onto other websites. Furthermore, the user can produce a derivative song based on the tune of the original song by using arrangement software. If copyright laws do not expand the protected subject matters and categories of exclusive rights, the authors cannot be adequately compensated under the digital network environment. Copyright laws can no longer function as incentive for creation, if there is a lack of revision and appropriate expansion. Hence, copyright laws have extended protection to new subject matters, such as computer programs and databases, granted right holders new kinds of rights, such as right of rental and right to network dissemination of information, established indirect infringement liability of ISPs and expanded protection to technological measures. These measures are adopted to mitigate the threats posed by the increasing opportunities of users to access and exploit works. When the growing benefits of users overweigh the compensation for the intellectual endeavors of authors, certain weight shall be added to the side of the authors and copyright owners in the event that this balance of interest is affected.

However, copyright expansion should not be unlimited and should cease when appropriate access to work and future creations is at risk. The expansion of copyright protection is only justified when access and use of works from the public threaten the incentive for creation and recovery of economic rewards. Overexpansion of copyright protection would again disrupt the balance of interests if access to works is narrowly restricted. Overprotection of copyrights will not only negatively affect access to the original works but will also impede future creations that are based on the originals. Therefore, limitations and exceptions on copyright systems should also be developed to respond to copyright expansion so that the ultimate goal of copyright systems will not be neglected. If users are not taken into consideration in the progress of copyright expansion in the digital network era, overly strong protection given to the work of authors and copyright owners will result in monopolization of existing works and be detrimental to the advancement of knowledge and learning.

2.3.3 Current Imbalance of Interests in Copyright Systems

The conflict between the private property and the public policy stances has reached a climax under the digital network environment, as technologies and the Internet facilitate the reproduction and dissemination of copyright works. Copies have almost the same quality as the originals. Authors face a situation in which the works that they have spent months or years to create are reproduced without their authorization by a mere simple click of the computer mouse in seconds by someone else. Thus, the supporters of the private property stance have called in favor of the widening of the scope of copyrights and strengthening of copyright protection to the copyright industries. Otherwise, these authors will suffer serious financial loss and the copyright industries will perish.

Some scholars support that the strong protection bestowed to private property of tangible goods should also be used for intangible goods in cyberspace, as there is no difference between the property rights of intangible goods under the digital network environment and the property rights of traditional intangible or tangible goods [22, 23]. Some scholars advocate for the application of digital technology to supervise the use of copyright works and collect royalties. Copyright owners and industries are concerned about the serious problem of the unauthorized use of their copyright works and online piracy. According to the Recording Industry Association of America (RIAA), revenues from the album sales of the music industry have declined from 1999 to 2002 because of peer-to-peer file sharing [24]. The RIAA has filed litigations against individuals who were engaged in directly downloading MP3 files, manufacturers of the machines used to play MP3 files, operators of websites that upload pirated works, and intermediaries which facilitate users to locate and download MP3 files, such as Napster [24]. Requests for stronger copyright protection and penalizations on infringement are also invoked by other industries, such as the motion picture industry. Besides pursuing legal remedies, copyright industries universally adopt software or digital technology to control the access and copying of their copyright works.

Governments in many countries tend to promulgate new legislations and regulations that deal with piracy issues under the digital network environment. Influenced by the lobbying of copyright owners and industries, these legislations adopt the private property stance and strong protection of copyrights. Such legislative tendencies appeared in the Copyright Term Extension Act (CTEA) and the DMCA of the United States, Information Society Directive of the European Union, Communication and the Green Paper on Copyright in the Knowledge Economy and the Digital Economy Act of the United Kingdom, graduated response scheme of France, and the 2006 Regulation of China. These laws and regulations extend the duration of copyright protection, expand the scope of copyright protection to include databases and TPMs, aggravate the infringement liability of technological intermediaries and potentially restrict the limitations that are possible under traditional copyright regimes. The expansion of copyright protection safeguards the interests of copyright owners, but to a certain degree, restricts the privacy and freedom of consumers.

The advocates of the public policy view have called for a restoring of the balance of interest between copyright owners and public users. They regard digital technology and the Internet as exceptional means to facilitate the exchange of knowledge and freedom of expression. In their points of view, technologies should enrich individual creativity, global communication and the public domain rather than hinder access to information. The Internet has changed the way that information is published and disseminated by decentralizing production and distribution which are traditionally under the centralized control of large publishing companies. Thanks to the Internet, individuals and small enterprises can also participate by forming their own cultural communities and environments. The supporters of the public policy stance fear that strong copyright protection could suffocate innovation and creativity because of the following problems.

2.3.3.1 Extended Duration of Copyright Protection

At the beginning of the promulgation of copyright laws, the duration of protection was 14 years which could be renewed by the copyright owner for an additional 14 years. The original protection time period was included in the United States Copyright Act of 1790. In 1831, Congress extended the initial term of 14 years to 28 years. In 1909, the Copyright Act again added another 28 years upon renewal, reaching a maximum of 56 years. The Copyright Act of 1976 again made revisions and changed the duration of the copyright protection to the author's life plus 50 years. The duration of copyright protection complies with the requirement in international conventions and copyright laws of most countries. However, the United States has not ceased the extension of the term for copyright protection. Following the Information Society Directive of the European Union which extended the duration of copyright protection of literary and artistic works to the author's life plus 70 years, the United States enacted the CTEA in 1998, also extending the copyright protection period by another 20 years and applying the revision retrospectively to existing works.

To sum up the continuous trend in extending the duration of copyrights, Professor Lawrence Lessig commented that "the average term of copyrights was just 32.2 years in 1973, because copyrights had to be renewed after twenty-eight years and eighty-five percent of copyrighted works were never renewed" [25]. The Copyright Act of 1976 and the CTEA largely increased the average term, as "the average term for corporate works such as Disney movies has tripled in the last thirty years" [25]. Professor Neil W. Netanel indicated that the two decades that the CTEA added onto the already lengthy copyright term did not provide additional economic incentives for authors to make new creations [26, p. 58], nor did the extension enhance the continued dissemination and availability of old works [26, p. 58]. Due to the 20-year extension, "much of the literature, art, film, and music that serves as the wellspring for further creative expression, is subject to copyright holders' proprietary control" [26, p. 58]. Although the extension of the duration of copyrights does not specifically respond to the challenges brought upon by digital network technology, it in fact postpones the time for a large number of copyright works to enter the public domain. These copyright works comprise works based on both traditional media and digital technology media.

2.3.3.2 Expansive Scope of Copyright Protection and Restricted Copyright Limitations

The history of the continuous revisions of the Berne Conventions witnessed the expansion of subject matters that have copyright protection. The Berne Convention of 1886 only included half of the current types of works, such as "books, pamphlets and other writings; dramatic or dramatic-musical works; musical compositions with or without words; works of drawing, painting, sculpture, engraving and lithography; illustrations, plans, sketches relative to geography, topography, architecture or science; and translations" [27, p. 125]. The 1908 Berlin Act added other categories, such as "choreographic works and pantomime, works of architecture, photographic works and works of applied art"; the 1928 Rome Act included "lectures and other oral works," and the 1948 Brussels Act added "cinematographic works" [27, p. 125]. The TRIPS Agreement and WIPO Internet Treaties followed this trend in widening the scope of protection to include computer programs and databases,[16] especially in the face of drastic changes brought on by technology development and strong lobbying from technology-related industries.

Similar to the increase of subject matters that fall under copyright protection, the scope of the exclusive rights enjoyed by copyright owners is also under expansion to deal with the challenges brought on by the digital network technology. Some of the exclusive rights originally existed in the Berne Convention, but were increased to cover more situations outlined in the TRIPS Agreement and the WIPO Internet

[16] TRIPS Agreement, Art 10; WIPO Copyright Treaty, Arts 4–5.

Treaties, such as reproduction and distribution rights.[17] Some exclusive rights were later acknowledged and introduced into international treaties because copyright industries advocated for them, such as the right of rental and the right of communication to the public.[18]

At the national level, the first copyright act of the United States, the Copyright Act of 1790, only protected the reproduction and distribution rights of copyright owners over maps, charts, and books. It did not prohibit users from making derivative works or translations based on the original work. Even in the nineteenth century, authors were free to publish their new works by borrowing from earlier works as long as the new works did not take the place of the original work in the market and had substantial contributions. In the landmark case, *Stowe v. Thomas*,[19] Harriet Beecher Stowe, the writer of *Uncle Tom's Cabin,* claimed that there was a copyright infringement by a German translator who made an unauthorized translation of the novel. The court ruled in favor of the defendant by concluding that translation is a new work and does not infringe on the original author's copyright. Subsequent copyright statutes gradually expanded the scope of copyright protection and diversity of exclusive rights. In the Copyright Act of 1976, copyright owners have a broad exclusive right to prepare derivative works based on the original work, including translations, arrangements, versions in other media forms and any other form in which a work may be recast, transformed, or adapted.[20]

However, all creations are based on preexisting works. Authors borrow from plots, stories, scenes, tunes, and characters in earlier works to write new novels, plays, songs and works in the form of motion pictures. Digital and network technology exacerbates the phenomenon of borrowing and recreation, especially in the making of audio-visual works, as technology facilitates reproduction, editing, synthesis and publication. Although there are doctrines such as the idea-expression dichotomy and fair use/fair dealing in the traditional copyright regime to ameliorate the tension between the exclusive rights of authors and free speech, the intensified protection of the interests of copyright owners restores the tension by latently narrowing down the scope of copyright limitations and judicially supporting infringement lawsuits against similarities in ideas.

Copyright systems allow authors to create based on ideas and information conveyed by former works. Copyright infringement only exists when the expression of the subsequent work is substantially similar to that of the earlier work. In addition, upon complying with certain conditions, authors are privileged to criticize, comment, translate, or research on previous works, which would otherwise be an infringement of copyright. The conditions are four factors that are dependent on case-by-case analysis in the United States or a list of detailed situations in common law jurisdictions such as the United Kingdom and Canada, and civil law jurisdictions such as Germany and China. However, the trend of imposing strong

[17] WIPO Copyright Treaty, Art 6.

[18] TRIPS Agreement, Art 11; WIPO Copyright Treaty, Arts 7–8.

[19] *Stowe v Thomas*, 23 F. Cas. 201 (C.C.E.D. Pa. 1853).

[20] The United States Copyright Act of 1976, Art 106 (2).

copyright protection based on substantial similarities is more likely to make the once permissible remix and reformulation of ideas or fair use become copyright infringements. In a series of cases, courts have restricted fair use to instances that would not negatively affect the potential market of the copyrighted work [26, p. 64]. Furthermore, courts have determined fair use as an affirmative defense, thus placing the burden of proof on the party who claimed fair use [26]. Thus, users in litigation must prove that the use in question will not damage the potential market of the copyrighted work, even the potential market of derivative works that copyright owners may not wish to exploit [26]. In the opinions of the courts, not only will evidence of potential market harm deny a fair use defense, lack of evidence that proves fair use could also result in the decision of copyright infringement. As Lawrence Lessig commented, the privilege of fair use has become the right to hire a lawyer to defend the right to free speech of users in costly and time-consuming litigations [26, p. 66].

In addition, restrictions on copyright limitations have been settled by laws by protecting technological measures that control access and copying of copyright works. As there are no general exceptions for permitted use under the protection of technological measures, users who circumvent technological measures to make permissible use are likely to commit copyright infringement. By benefiting from legislative protection, copyright industries have widely adopted technological measures such as digital encryption to impede unauthorized access and reproduction. Besides technological measures, the terms of use on websites and online standard contracts are also adopted by industries to further supervise the access and use of copyright works and contents. Due to the extensive adoption of technological measures and compulsory contracts, the exclusive rights of copyright owners have expanded to the right of access which is not traditionally included in copyright systems. The DMCA 2005 Supplement calls these controls a "paracopyright" regime which is already recognized by the law.[21]

2.3.3.3 Newly Added Protection on Technological Measures

The development of digital network technology expedites the reproduction, distribution, and making available of works by public users. In order to reduce the unauthorized use of works, copyright owners employ technological measures such as encryption or other similar means that block unauthorized access and reproduction of copyright works. However, technology alone cannot effectively guarantee protection of works, as users who master decryption skills and technology such as hackers may easily circumvent technological measures and make use of the works. Therefore, copyright holders and industries advocate the introducing of an additional layer of protection on technological measures and prohibiting circumvention acts. The rationale of the anti-circumvention of technological measures is as such: copyright and neighboring rights provide the first layer of

[21] The Digital Millennium Copyright Act: 2005 Supplement, p. 91.

protection to copyright works from a legal aspect; technological measures work as a second layer of protection from a technical aspect; and the anti-circumvention rules offer the third layer of protection which introduces legal remedies against circumventing acts of technological measures that protect copyright and neighboring rights [27].

The WIPO Internet Treaties for the first time granted protection to technological measures and rights management information at a multinational level. Although some countries have adopted legislations that prohibit the unauthorized decoding of technological protections before the reach of the WIPO Internet Treaties, their scope of protection was quite limited. The WIPO Internet Treaties widened the scope to protect all effective measures that are used to control the access and copying of copyright works. They do not enforce contracting parties to mandatorily adopt the technological measures and rights management information, but rather create a leeway for contracting members to decide whether to use such digital measures and the situations to use them.

Rights management information is defined by the WCT and WPPT as information that identifies subject matters under copyright and neighboring right protection, the right holders, terms and conditions of the use, and any numbers or codes that represent such information.[22] Such information is protected when it is attached to copies of works, fixed performance, or phonograms or appears in connection with communication or making available to the public.[23] The WIPO Internet Treaties provide legal remedies against two kinds of acts that will "induce, enable, facilitate or conceal an infringement" of copyright or neighbouring rights[24]: alteration or removal of rights management information without authorization, and distribution or communication to the public of protected subject matters or their copies with the knowledge that the rights management information attached to these subject matters or copies has been altered or removed. In order to stem direct and indirect infringements on rights management information, the WCT and the WPPT have urged member countries to enforce adequate and effective legal remedies against any person who has conducted the aforementioned wrongful alterations or distribution subject to different knowledge requirement.[25]

The DMCA of the United States includes provisions that protect technological measures that control access and use of copyrighted works.[26] Unauthorized circumvention of technological measures is deemed as infringement under the law. Furthermore, the DMCA also prohibits the manufacture and dissemination of devices which facilitate the circumvention of access and copying controls.[27] The legislative model of the United States has influenced many jurisdictions to establish a technological measure protection system. The European Union, Australia, and

[22] WIPO Copyright Treaty, Art 12(2); WIPO Performances and Phonograms Treaty, Art 19(2).

[23] Ibid.

[24] WIPO Copyright Treaty, Art 12(1); WIPO Performances and Phonograms Treaty, Art 19(1).

[25] Ibid. Von Lewinski [27].

[26] The United States Copyright Act of 1976, s 1201.

[27] Ibid.

Asian countries such as Japan and China, all have laws and regulations with regard to the anti-circumvention of technological measures. As scholars have commented, nowadays, it is not the court that enforces copyright laws and determines whether the use is fair. It is the technology, software, and digital codes that control how users can access and use the protected works. Even if the technology is not powerful enough, legislatures have passed laws that support any technology that effectively controls copyrighted content [25].

The anticircumvention rules expand copyright protection by providing copyright owners with the exclusive right of controlling access to their works. Traditional copyright concerns only the use of copyright works, leaving access issues to be regulated by other laws, such as contract, tort or criminal law. For example, one can freely read a book without the author's permission when s/he finds the book in a public library, buys the book at a bookstore, or even steals the book from someone else. As long as the person does not reproduce, modify, translate, or prepare derivatives based on the work, s/he has not committed infringement of copyright, although s/he may be punished by tort or criminal law due to the act of theft. However, under the situation where there is wide deployment of technological measures by industries and anti-circumvention rules imposed by the DMCA and laws in other jurisdictions, users no longer have the same freedom to read a book, listen to music or watch a video as in the traditional copyright regime. More seriously, the tendency that industries use technology to control access to non-copyrighted material expands the industrial monopolization to the public domain and further hinders the freedom of the public in knowledge exchange and speech.

2.3.3.4 Aggravated Liability on Internet Service Providers

The emergence of digital technology and new media changes the traditional model of the distribution of works into a more convenient, costless, and efficient way. Prior to the ubiquitous availability of computers and the Internet, the production and distribution of popular creative works were funded and monopolized only by media conglomerates. The Internet has given the public the capability to create their popular and core value cultures. Today, works distributed through the Internet reach mass audiences to an unexpected degree. As a result, copyright industries which own a large number of copyrights find it hard to control the distribution by intermediaries of their copyright works or derivatives based on their works. These intermediaries range from music file-sharing and downloading technology and websites such as Napster, Grokster, and Baidu to audio-visual webcasters such as YouTube and Youku. In the face of numerous unauthorized distributions via new media, copyright owners and industries have launched a series of litigations against ISPs for indirect liability of the copyright infringement acts of their online users.

In these litigations, the courts have explained the indirect copyright liability of the intermediaries as one that distributes the product with the objective of promoting its use to infringe copyright, as shown by clear expression or other affirmative steps taken to foster infringement, and should be liable for the resulting acts of infringement by third parties.[28] The claim of indirect copyright liability had been used by copyright industries especially the music and motion picture industries to prohibit the distribution of unauthorized online copyright files facilitated by many of the large ISPs, such as Napster, MP3.com, and Grokster. The industries are concerned about the threat that technology and intermediaries has imposed on facilitating copyright infringement, arguing that copyrights are not designed for consumer convenience but rather to cater to the property interests of the copyright owners.[29]

The continuing lawsuits against new media and strategic lobbying of the copyright industries have prompted governments to regulate the copyright infringement liability of ISPs. The ISP liability laws range from the DMCA of the United States, Digital Economic Act of the United Kingdom, graduated response policy of France, and the 2006 Regulation of China. Such laws respond to the calling and lobbying by copyright industries for expansive copyright protection in order to maintain their market dominance. Although the granting of intermediaries with freedom to distribute copyright works regardless whether they have authorization or not may affect the incentive of authors in producing new expressions, strict restraints on access and distribution of current works by new media will suffocate the investments on new digital technologies and promotion of such, and stifle new ways of propagating expressions.

In recognizing that the support for copyright industries to deter the development of new content distribution technology will indulge industrial monopolization over the market, lawmakers and courts have resorted to safe harbors that limit the indirect copyright liability of ISPs or compulsory licenses which require new media to pay reasonable fees in turn for the privilege of using copyright works so as to ameliorate the conflict between content providers and distribution intermediaries. In the *Sony* case of 1984, the United States Supreme Court provided safe harbors for new technology by guaranteeing that suppliers of staple articles of commerce shall not be liable for the copyright infringement of third parties even though they know users are likely to use the articles for infringement, as long as the article is produced for the purpose of substantial non-infringing use.[30] The judicial decision in the *Sony* case aimed to achieve a balance of the interests between technology developers and industries, fostering research and development in digital technologies on the one hand, and stimulating incentives for creations on the other hand. The DMCA included safe harbors for the copyright liability of ISPs, establishing a list of disclaimer conditions such as the notice and takedown regime.

Nevertheless, the balance of interests has been recently disrupted due to the new legal trend and judicial practices on implementing severe punishment over the indirect copyright liability of ISPs. Several influential cases, such as Napster, MP3.com, and Grokster, have witnessed this trend of stifling technology. Technological intermediaries were all held liable for actively inducing Internet users to commit copyright infringement, if they had knowledge of the direct infringement, obtained direct

[28] *Metro-Goldwyn-Mayer Studios Inc. v Grokster Ltd.* 545 U.S. 913 (2005).

[29] *UMG Recording Inc. v MP3.com Inc.* 92 F. Supp. 2nd 349 (S.D.N.Y. 2000).

[30] Netanel [26, p. 78]. *Also see Sony Corp. v University City Studios Inc.* 464 U.S. 417 (1984).

financial benefits from the infringer, or had the ability to control the infringement activity.[31] These judicial decisions gave copyright industries the support to address any new media that facilitated Internet users to reproduce and disseminate copyright works. In addition, the graduated response policy issued by the French government exacerbates the weak position of new media. Under the graduated response policy, the administrative authority can warn ISPs to stop the infringement activity of users in question after receiving complaints from copyright owners [28]. This policy has also spread to other jurisdictions, such as the United Kingdom, South Korea and Ireland. The adoption of the graduated response policy has aggravated ISP liability by increasing additional conditions in the safe harbors. Moreover, although the DMCA permits compulsory licensing for online transmissions, it replaces the new media's required payment based on fair return with the payment based on the market rate [26]. Without providing new media with reasonable and fair royalties, the market rate will reduce incentive and investment in new digital technology and media.

2.3.3.5 Media Concentration and Restricted Freedom of User-Generated Creations

Copyrights did not originally grant many monopolies, but nowadays, copyrights are controlled by a few entertainment conglomerates due to media concentration. As Professor Lawrence Lessig summarized, the concentration of media is drastically different from what it was 20 years ago [25]. Nowadays, "eighty percent of the music distributed in the world is distributed by five companies; seventy percent of the radio market is controlled by just four firms. Eighty percent of television and cable in the United States is controlled by six firms...... This is a concentrated form of control producing a kind of homogeneous culture, a culture which is increasingly tailored to this vision of a certain mainstream market and, therefore, protects that market against different kinds of creativity" [25].

The media concentration has constrained the creative freedom that people used to enjoy in life. Before copyright industries monopolized the market and endeavored to counter infringement, the public was free to view the existing information, borrow from existing material, create, and comment on works by others as they felt appropriate. The birth of the Internet has just enriched such personal freedom. Millions of individual Internet users have embraced the new ways of expression and communication by writing novels, blogging their ideas and daily experiences, composing songs, clipping and editing videos or producing short movies. People usually engage in these types of creative activities by working on their personal computers or accessing the Internet at home or in private places. As long as people do not use their creations based on copyright works for commercial purposes, their activities are like private or face-to-face communications in ordinary life, which impose no

[31] Examples of legislations include the United States Copyright Act, s 512 and the Regulation on the Protection of the Right to Network Dissemination of Information of China, Arts 22–23.

harm on the interests of the copyright owners. Furthermore, such individual creativity forms part of the marginalized and mass culture. The imposing of excessive liability and restrictions on personal use will negatively affect privacy, personal freedom and free expression.

However, as Professor Jane Ginsburg commented, prior to the advent of digital technology, "video recorders and photocopiers, individuals' practical ability to engage in personal copying was exceedingly limited and posed no threat to copyright markets or incentives" [29]. That digital technology and the Internet make reproduction and distribution much easier for users does not mean that copyright laws should step aside and not interfere with the potential negative effects brought on by infringement activities that erode incentives for creativity [26]. Similarly, that digital technology gives copyright industries the potential power to control access and copying of information does not mean that copyright laws should grant such access rights to industries by sacrificing user privacy and right of free speech. Therefore, as Professor Neil Netanel concluded, "adapting copyright doctrine to digital technology requires that we recalibrate copyright's balance to reflect, not stifle, digital technology's empowerment of individual speakers. Just as copyright need not countenance massive uncompensated copying of copyrighted works simply because file swappers perceive that activity to be a personal liberty, neither should we aim to give copyright holders the broad legal and technological control to re-create the predigital market structure and mass-media-to-passive-consumer model of public disclosure in the digital environment" [26, p. 75].

2.4 Conclusion

The establishment of intellectual property and copyright systems is not only for the protection of proprietary rights, but also to promote public interest and socioeconomic development as more important purposes. The philosophical and economic theories on intangible property illustrate the important function of intellectual property systems in meeting public interests and attaining social justice. Intellectual property systems should be well designed to balance the interests of right holders and public users of intellectual assets.

Copyright was developed under such ideals by granting authors with exclusive rights over their works on the one hand and setting limitations and exceptions on the other hand. However, the continuous expansion of copyright protection has disrupted the balance of interests that originally existed in the pre-digital copyright system by extending the duration of protection, expanding the subject matters and exclusive rights under protection, controlling copyright limitations, granting protection to technological measures which control access and copying of copyright works, aggravating indirect liability of technological intermediaries, and strengthening market monopolization of copyright industries. An imbalance of interests in copyright systems overprotects the exclusive rights of right owners by sacrificing the legitimate access and exploitation of the copyright works by public users and information in the public domain. The impediments in using preexisting knowledge and information will in turn suffocate future creations and innovations. Therefore, it is time for policymakers to consider revising and amending their copyright systems to adapt to the new environment and restore a balance of interest.

The key to restoring balance is to guarantee necessary and appropriate access to copyright works. Proposals that will reestablish a balance of interest include readopting moderate protection on technological measures, establishing reasonable safe harbors for ISPs, redefining the scope of copyright limitations and exceptions, and introducing alternative schemes such as projects of digital commons as supplements to copyright reforms. Such proposals are intended to appropriately alleviate the protection of copyright owners, reasonably allocate the liability of intermediaries, and moderately enrich the privileges of end users. By gradually shifting the focus, the goal of copyright systems to promote social progress and justice will be achieved. The subsequent chapters will discuss each issue and proposal in detail.

References

1. Rousseau, J. J. (1762). *Social contract* "Book I 8. The civil state". Available at http://www.constitution.org/jjr/socon_01.htm. Visited 24 Mar 2011.
2. Rousseau, J. J. (1762). *Social contract* "Book I 9. Real property". Available at http://www.constitution.org/jjr/socon_01.htm. Visited 24 Mar 2011.
3. Rousseau, J. J. (1762). *Social contract* "Book II 11. The various systems of legislation". Available at http://www.constitution.org/jjr/socon_02.htm. Visited 24 Mar 2011.
4. Rousseau, J. J. (1762). *Social contract* "Book II 4. The limits of the sovereign power". Available at http://www.constitution.org/jjr/socon_02.htm. Visited 24 Mar 2011.
5. Drahos, P. (1996). *A philosophy of intellectual property*. Aldershot: Dartmouth Publishing Company.
6. Wu, H. (2008). *Multidimensional interpretation of intellectual property (in Chinese)*. Beijing: Peking University Press.
7. Cooter, R., & Ulen, T. (1997). *Law and economics* (2nd ed.). Reading: Addison-Wesley Educational Publishers Inc.
8. Hardin, G. (1968). The tragedy of the commons. *Sciences, 162*, 1243. Available at http://www.sciencemag.org/content/162/3859/1243.full. Visited 15 Apr 2013.
9. Boyle, J. (2003). The second enclosure movement and the construction of the public domain. *Law and Contemporary Problems, 66*, 33–74.
10. Landes, W., & Posner, R. (1989). An economic analysis of copyright law. *Journal of Legal Studies, 18*, 325–363.
11. Posner, R. A. (1998). *Economic analysis of law* (5th ed.). New York: Aspen Law & Business.
12. Ploman, E., & Hamilton, L. C. (1980). *Copyright: Intellectual property in the information age*. London: Routledge & Kegan Paul.
13. Hauser, A. (1952). *The social history of art*. New York: Knopf.
14. Bettig, R. V. (1997). *Copyrighting culture: The political economy of intellectual property*. Boulder: Westview Press.
15. Bugbee, B. W. (1967). *The genesis of American patent and copyright law*. Washington, DC: Public Affairs Press.
16. Kim, M. (2005). *An analysis of the creative commons as a solution for copyright protection in the digital era*. Ann Arbor: ProQuest Information and Learning Company.
17. Locke, J. (1974). *Two treaties of civil government*. New York: Hafner.

18. Goldstein, P. (2003). *Copyright's highway: From Gutenberg to the celestial jukebox* (2nd ed.). Stanford: Stanford Law and Politics.
19. Craig, C. J. (2002). Locke, labour and limiting the author's right: A warning against a Lockean approach to copyright law. *Queen's Law Journal, 28*, 1–60.
20. Netanel, N. W. (1996). Copyright and a democratic civil society. *Yale Law Journal, 106*, 283–387.
21. Kreiss, R. A. (1995). Accessibility and commercialization in copyright theory. *UCLA Law Review, 43*, 1–76.
22. Hardy, T. (1996). *Property (and copyright) in cyberspace*. Chicago: The University of Chicago Legal Forum.
23. Hardy, T. (2001). Not so different: Tangible, intangible, digital, and analog works and their comparison for copyright purposes. *University of Dayton Law Review, 26*, 211–245.
24. Fisher, W. (2000). Digital music: Problems and possibilities. Available at http://www.law.harvard.edu/faculty/tfisher/Music.html. Visited 9 Apr 2011.
25. Lessig, L. (2004). Commentary: The creative commons. *Montana Law Review, 65*, 1–13.
26. Netanel, N. W. (2008). *Copyright paradox*. Oxford: Oxford University Press.
27. von Lewinski, S. (2008). *International copyright law and policy*. Oxford: Oxford University Press.
28. Haber, E. (2010). The French revolution 2.0: Copyright and the three strikes policy. *Journal of Sports and Entertainment Law, 2*, 297–339.
29. Ginsburg, J. (2003). From having copies to experiencing works: The development of an access right in U.S. copyright law. *Journal of the Copyright Society of the USA, 50*, 113–131.

Chapter 3
Toward a More Balanced Model: Revision of Anti-circumvention Rules

3.1 Introduction

The development of digital network technologies simplifies and speeds reproduction and distribution of copyright works. Anyone who has access to computers, mobile phones, and the Internet can simply obtain, exploit, and disseminate information without copyright owners' authorizations. Rampant piracy, however, has made copyright owners distrust the effectiveness and enforcement of the original copyright legal regime that was born and developed in a paper and analog technology age. Copyright owners began to widely adopt DRM and TPMs to impede access to and use of their works without their authorizations. These self-help measures did effectively stem piracy at the beginning, but as hacking technologies and devices were developed to circumvent or undermine original DRM, such self-help measures were no longer able to perfectly protect copyright works. The same copyright owners who once sat back and relaxed, trusting in self-help DRM technologies, again had to lobby their governments to enact new legislation which could protect the existing technological measures against circumvention. Anti-circumvention law was thus promulgated to satisfy copyright owners' interests for strong copyright protection in the digital network era. The protection of DRM and TPMs, then, is related to, but quite different from, copyright protection. Copyright law is the first layer that protects copyright owners' exclusive rights from the legal aspect; DRM and TPMs are the second layer of protection from the technological aspect; and, finally, anti-circumvention law is the third layer that protects the DRM technologies.

Private self-help measures often interact with public remedies in areas of law to better achieve objectives, provided that the private remedies do not exceed the necessary scope and force of public initiatives. The adoption of DRM technologies by copyright owners just conforms to the legal trend and brings copyright law into the fold [1]. Although the adoption of DRM by copyright owners as a self-help alternative is reasonable, the proliferation of strong legislation on the protection of

J.J. Hua, *Toward A More Balanced Approach: Rethinking and Readjusting Copyright Systems in the Digital Network Era*, DOI 10.1007/978-3-662-43517-5_3,

DRM will negatively influence many issues, such as exceptions and limitations to copyright, access to information, consumers' interests in using copyright products, and protection of privacy. Current anti-circumvention law faces challenges and criticism resulting from its overprotection of DRM and TPMs, which subverts the balance between copyright owners and public users under copyright law. The legislative process leading to the anti-circumvention rule pushed by the United States at both the domestic and international levels has been called out by Professor Peter Yu as "backdoor lawmaking," and "a process of outsourcing the legislative process to an international forum of unselected representatives in an effort to create laws that the domestic legislature would not have otherwise enacted" [2, pp. 54–55].

As early as 1995, the "White Paper on Intellectual Property and the National Information Infrastructure" issued by the Clinton Administration acknowledged copyright owners' substantial investment in the adoption of DRM technologies which could better protect their copyright works from serious piracy. As well, it supported the issuing of new laws that could prohibit the manufacturing and distribution of technologies whose primary purpose was to circumvent DRM and TPMs. At the same time, the United States went to the international forum, the diplomatic conference held by the WIPO in 1996, to propose that the anti-circumvention rule be included in a draft international treaty on copyright protections [3]. After receiving strong domestic opposition against the White-Paper-proposed anti-circumvention rule, the United States turned to support a more neutral law, later adopted by the WCT, that required member countries to provide adequate protection and effective remedies for DRM and TPMs [3]. This was the first "backdoor" called out by Professor Peter Yu, under which international standards were created "based on laws that its domestic legislature was reluctant to enact" [2, p. 55]. The results of the international conference and treaty were then taken back to the United States as legal obligations that required its compliance. The enactment of the DMCA in 1998, therefore, was the response of the United States to its domestic implementation of the WCT.

In the enactment process of the DMCA, opponents from technological intermediaries such as ISPs focused on alleviating the strict liability for their subscribers' infringing activity. They spent the majority of their energy in negotiating with copyright industries to incorporate a safe harbor rule. This was to ensure that they would not have to worry about being indirectly liable for their users' copyright infringement as long as they immediately took down the alleged infringing material upon having knowledge of the infringement. After reaching a compromise with the copyright industries on a safe harbor for ISP liability, technological intermediaries made little effort to redress the overprotection of TPMs granted by the anti-circumvention rule, even though this meant that some big companies with encryption research groups, such as AT&T, would be negatively affected by the anti-circumvention rule [3]. The anti-circumvention rule in the DMCA thus remains in a form that principally reflects copyright industries' interests.

In addition to the domestic lawmaking on the anti-circumvention rule, the United States exported its legislative model through bilateral or multilateral free trade agreements to prompt the adoption of similar DMCA-like anti-circumvention laws by other countries. This is the "second backdoor" noted by Professor Peter Yu [2, p. 55]. Through these free trade agreements, many jurisdictions incorporated their own anti-circumvention laws in the legislative model of the United States. These countries include Australia, Bahrain, Chile, Costa Rica, the Dominican Republic, El Salvador, Guatemala, Honduras, Jordan, Morocco, Nicaragua, Oman, and Singapore. Even without bilateral or multilateral free trade agreements with the United States, some countries such as China assimilated the DMCA model to create anti-circumvention laws through legal transplant in order to fulfill the obligatory requirements from the WIPO Internet Treaties. Pushed by these contractual obligations from bilateral agreements or international conventions, the domestic anti-circumvention legislation of the United States has become international. The imbalance hidden in the DMCA anti-circumvention rule has now widely spread to developing countries where access to information is perhaps more important and urgent than for their developed counterparts.

This chapter aims to explore an appropriate way to revise the anti-circumvention rules in order to restore the balance of interest between copyright owners and public users in general, as well as guarantee access to information and knowledge in less developed countries, with a particular focus on China. The second part of this chapter will introduce a basic understanding of protection of DRM and TPMs. Relevant provisions in the WIPO Internet Treaties and domestic legislations will be examined in order to demonstrate the concept, scope, and conditions of legal protection of DRM and TPMs in general. The third part will specifically analyze the anti-circumvention rule under the United States DMCA, as it represents the typical legislative model regarding TPM protection adopted by many jurisdictions. The analysis of the limitations and exceptions of the anti-circumvention rule and its existing problems that negatively influence the interests of public users points out the need to address the drawbacks embodied in current anti-circumvention law. The fourth part of this chapter then will suggest solutions for the shortcomings of current anti-circumvention legal design from a diverse range of aspects, including technological improvements for setting up minimum use of technologically protected material, legislative revision of anti-circumvention rules, and the development of judicial discretions in TPM-circumvention cases. These suggestions will be provided for revising the DMCA model anti-circumvention law, in general, and for recovering appropriate access to copyright information in developing countries such as China.

3.2 Basic Understanding of Protection of Digital Rights Management and Technological Protection Measures

The WIPO Internet Treaties are the main international conventions that address the issue of the protection of TPMs and DRM information. Articles 11 and 12 of the WCT obligate member states to provide effective protection to technological measures and DRM information used by authors in their copyright works. Similarly, Articles 18 and 19 of the WPPT oblige member states to effectively protect technological measures and DRM information used by performers and phonogram producers in their performances and phonograms. The following introduction and analysis will use provisions in the WCT to illustrate the international obligations of supplying protection on TPMs and DRM information, note the difference between TPMs and DRM information, and highlight the key factors that need to be stressed in the international obligations.

3.2.1 Conventional Protection of Technological Measures and Rights Management Information

As to the obligatory protection on technological measures, Article 11 of the WCT clearly expresses that "contracting parties shall provide adequate legal protection and effective legal remedies against the circumvention of effective technological measures that are used by authors in connection with the exercise of their rights under this Treaty or the Berne Convention and that restrict acts, in respect of their works, which are not authorized by the authors concerned or permitted by law."

As to the obligatory protection on DRM information, Article 12 of the WCT targets two kinds of actions done by any person with knowledge or having reasonable grounds to know that these actions will induce or facilitate infringement of any right covered by this Treaty or the Berne Convention: removal or altering DRM information without authority and the dissemination of works or their copies knowing that DRM information has been removed or altered without authority. Although Article 12 of the WCT provides a definition of DRM information as information that identifies works and ownership, DRM has much broader functions than merely providing identification information.

According to Professor Peter Yu, one must distinguish DRM from TPM, as "the latter focuses narrowly on mechanisms used to protect copyrighted contents, such as passwords, encryption, digital watermarking, and other protection techniques," while "the former includes a large set of technological tools that not only protect the content, but also monitor consumer behavior and facilitate payment for content usage" [2, p. 61]. By distinguishing between DRM and TPM, Professor Yu anticipated that DRM should not only protect copyrighted works against unauthorized use but should also properly serve the interests of consumers and users [2]. If properly designed, the DRM system can encompass the rights enjoyed by both copyright owners and public users.

Professor Yu's differentiation between the protection on DRM information and TPM illustrates that the serious imbalance of rights between copyright owners and public users due to the installation of technological tools is principally due to the overemphasis on developing TPMs by electronic technology industries and the legislative protection of TPMs against unauthorized circumvention. Designing DRM systems in the future to reflect both copyright owners' and consumers' rights is a promising way to recover the balance of interest in the copyright regime through technological assistance, but the current priority in weakening strong TPM protection is to readjust the current anti-circumvention law through legislative revision. Therefore, the following discussion on the substantial elements of convention obligations will focus on the relevant provisions of TPMs protections in order to further clarify the subject matter and scope of anti-circumvention laws.

3.2.2 Key Terms in the Protection of Technological Protection Measures

It is important to understand the key terms in the TPM protection provisions under the international conventions in order to acknowledge the implementation of anti-circumvention rule in domestic laws. According to the WCT Article 11, protected TPMs are adopted by "authors." "Authors" in the conventional provision should not be interpreted as the only creators who directly apply TPMs to their works. More expansive situations, such as complete or partial copyright assignment, should be taken into consideration so that "authors" include successors, assignees, licensees, agents, or other intermediaries on behalf of the original authors. After fully understanding the subject of using TPMs, let us now examine the scope of protection of TPMs and international anti-circumvention rules through the analysis of the key terms and phrases.

Firstly, Article 11 of the WCT requires that technological measures adopted by authors should be "effective." This article of the WCT, however, does not provide any definition of effective technological measures because it was difficult for the WCT drafters to decide whether they should choose a specific or general definition to cover TPMs. Thus, the drafters changed their emphasis on the purpose and effect that TPMs would be used to achieve, finally providing no definition at all. In fact, the principal purpose when copyright owners use TPMs is to control the free access and use of their works without authorization. The definition of TPMs in the European Union Information Society Directive indicates such a fact of the copyright owners' intention. In the directive, a TPM is considered effective "where the use of a protected work or other subject-matter is controlled by the rightholders through application of an access control or protection process, such as encryption, scrambling or other transformation of the work or other subject-matter or a copy control mechanism, which achieves the protection objective."[1] Therefore, TPMs will not be deemed effective if they can neither control access to nor the copying of copyright works.

To evaluate the effectiveness of TPMs, it makes better sense to take an integrated consideration of the unauthorized parties' ability to conduct circumvention, the intent of copyright holders, the specific TPMs installed, and the actual effect of the TPMs [4, pp. 287–398]. For example, if an ordinary user can circumvent a TPM

[1] Information Society Directive of European Union, Art 6(3).

through his common skill without any assistance from any specific technological tool, such a TPM cannot be deemed effective. For example, in the case where a CD-protection technology manufacturing company, SunnComm, attempted to sue a student for his online paper explaining a simple method of circumventing SunnComm's technology by clicking the shift key when loading a CD into a computer [5], the CD-protection technology against unauthorized copying could not be regarded as effective.

Secondly, the effective TPMs are used by authors "in connection with the exercise of their rights under the WCT or the Berne Convention." This phrase indicates the important connection between TPM protection and copyright protection. The adoption of TPMs should guarantee the protection of copyright owners' exclusive rights embodied in the WCT and the Berne Convention. For example, the act of circumventing TPMs which restrict unauthorized reproduction of copyright works is prohibited by the WCT, but circumvention of TPMs which protect public domain material is not banned, because the latter TPMs are not used to protect any copyright interest given by the international copyright conventions. Thus, the requirement of intensive connection between anti-circumvention and copyright protection closely relates to the justification for access-control TPMs. As the WCT does not intend to create any new intellectual property right, and the expression of Article 11 relates to the exclusive rights in other provisions under the WCT, the WCT does not provide an access right for copyright owners to prohibit circumvention of access-control TPMs per se. As to whether Article 11 includes access-control TPMs, the article does not draw a clear line but leaves the problem for member states to determine on their own.

Thirdly, Article 11 prohibits acts of "circumvention" of TPMs and the "restrict[ion of] acts, in respect of their works, which are not authorized by the authors concerned or permitted by law." "Circumvention" acts in the WCT generally mean acts of removing, breaking, bypassing, or otherwise interfering with the function of a TPM [4, pp. 287–398]. However not all circumvention acts are prohibited by the WCT, as the prohibited acts cannot be authorized by authors or permitted by law. Hence, users can engage in circumventions that are authorized by copyright owners, used to exploit public domain material, or for the purpose of achieving limitations and exceptions to copyright protection for the interest of public users.

Problems arise when determining whether circumvention and restricted acts should not only include the circumventing act itself but should also cover preparatory acts such as manufacturing and providing technology and devices that could facilitate circumvention, because one cannot simply determine copyright infringements without knowing the end use of the circumvention-facilitated technology and devices. On the one hand, circumvention technology and devices can be used for legitimate purposes. Broad bans on the supply of circumvention technology and devices could impede legitimate use of these tools and stifle the development of useful new technologies. On the other hand, if the provision is narrowly interpreted as merely prohibiting the circumvention act itself, or allowing supply of technology and devices as long as they have non-infringing uses, the protection of TPMs cannot be deemed sufficient and effective, because controlling the supply of circumvention tools is an important and costless way to stem the circumvention of TPMs. Therefore, the WCT did not expressly name circumvention devices at all, leaving room for member states to decide the scope of prohibited acts in domestic laws.

Fourthly, Article 11 requires member states to provide "adequate legal protection and effective legal remedies" against the circumvention of TPMs. As discussed above, although some commentators argue that without the prohibition on the manufacturing and dissemination of circumvention tools, the protection of TPMs cannot be deemed as adequate and effective, the WCT did not require contracting parties to totally outlaw the trafficking of circumvention tools. More alleviative measures could be introduced to compensate copyright owners without having to absolutely ban the distribution of tools that can be used to circumvent TPMs.

In addition to these concerns, there are still two other issues that need to be addressed in this discussion. Firstly, the WCT does not mandate member states to incorporate anti-circumvention rules into their copyright laws. No explicit requirement is included to compel member states to implement anti-circumvention rules through amending domestic copyright statutes. Instead, more general laws could be used to grant protection to TPMs, such as sui generis law or competition law. Secondly, the WCT does not oblige member states to install mandatory TPMs on consumer equipment. Member states have the freedom to determine whether they would like to impose mandatory installation of TPMs as part of their anti-circumvention law.

Because of the flexibility embodied in WCT Article 11, the concern over whether the balance of interests between copyright owners and public users can be maintained under the environment of TPM protection relies on the implementation of anti-circumvention rules introduced by different jurisdictions in their domestic legal systems. Despite the accomplishment of the international conventions, it remains to be seen how legislative protection for TPMs through national implementation can effectively prevent unauthorized access and use of copyright works on the one hand and guarantee the free flow of digital information on the other. Since the United States' legislative model of the DMCA broadly influences a large number of jurisdictions, including less developed countries such as China, examination of the anti-circumvention rules of the DMCA can illustrate whether current anti-circumvention law achieves the proper balance of interests between right holders and consumers, and, if not, what problems exist in the current legal design.

3.3 Balanced or Unbalanced: Anti-circumvention Rules of Digital Millennium Copyright Act

Anti-circumvention rules were incorporated into the United States Copyright Act through the enactment of the DMCA in 1998. Specifically, the new Chapter 12 deals with the issue of copyright protection and information management systems in the digital network environment. Section 1201 was designed to address the issue of anti-circumvention of technological measures with the purpose of fulfilling the international obligations compelled by Article 11 of the WCT.

3.3.1 Contents of DMCA Anti-circumvention Rule

Section 1201 divides technological measures into two categories: measures that prevent unauthorized access to a copyrighted work and measures that prevent unauthorized copying of a copyrighted work [6]. Generally speaking, there are three major principles prohibiting circumvention of technological measures that control access and protect the exclusive rights of copyright owners. Section 1201(a)(1) prevents the acts of circumventing technological measures that control access to a protected work. Section 1201(a)(2) prohibits the production and distribution of any technology, service, or device that is primarily used to circumvent the technological measures controlling access to a protected work. Section 1201(b) forbids the production and distribution of any technology, service, or device that is primarily used to circumvent the technological measures protecting exclusive rights of copyright owners in a copyrighted work.

Specifically, Section 1201(a)(1) protects technological measures that effectively control access to a copyrighted work. Under Section 1201(a), acts of circumvention of a technological measure include descrambling a scrambled work, decrypting an encrypted work, or otherwise avoiding, bypassing, removing, deactivating, or impairing a technological measure without the authority of the copyright owner.[2] An effective access-control technological measure should in its ordinary operation require "the application of information, or a process or a treatment, with the authority of the copyright owner, to gain access to the work."[3]

Sections 1201(a)(2) and 1201(b) are so-called anti-device provisions, as they stipulate that "no person shall manufacture, import, offer to the public, provide, or otherwise traffic in any technology, product, service, device, component, or part thereof" that controls the access to or copying of a protected work.[4] The devices that are prohibited are primarily designed for circumventing effective access or copy control technological measures, have limited commercially significant purpose other than circumvention use, or are marketed with the producer or distributor's knowledge of their circumvention use.[5] According to the statutory explanation for Section 1201(b), technological measures that effectively protect rights of a copyright owner are measures that, in their ordinary operation, prevent, restrict, or otherwise limit the exercise of the rights of a copyright owner.[6] Therefore, Section 1201(b) applies to infringers who may lawfully get access to the copyrighted works

[2] The United States Copyright Act of 1976, s 1201(a)(3)(A).

[3] The United States Copyright Act of 1976, s 1201(a)(3)(B).

[4] The United States Copyright Act of 1976, ss 1201(a)(2) and 1201(b).

[5] Ibid.

[6] The United States Copyright Act of 1976, s 1201(b)(2)(B).

but thereafter aid in the circumvention of copy-control technological measures embodied in the protected works. Some commentators hence refer to Section 1201(b) as the "post-access copyright control" anti-circumvention rule [7, p. 221].

The enactment of anti-device provisions was pushed forward by a lobby of powerful copyright owners. From the viewpoints of copyright owners, circumvention technologies, even though they can be used for non-infringing purposes or for other public interests, still pose great danger to copyright protection in the digital environment. In addition, it is difficult and costly to investigate every circumvention act conducted by individuals. Instead, banning the trafficking of circumvention devices is a more practical and less costly way for copyright owners to enforce their rights. Introducing anti-device provisions into national law is necessary to control the rampant piracy caused by convenient hacking of technological measures.

Confronted with the copyright owners' self-interest, individuals, educational and research institutions, as well as certain nonprofit organizations realized the danger that the anti-circumvention law poses to the fair or non-infringing use of copyrighted material, free access to information in the public domain, fair competition, and online privacy rights. However, these concerns were not given much attention by legislators, because, on the one hand, these organizations did not have lobbying power as strong as the ISPs, and on the other hand, technology developers were no longer motivated to persuade the government to make further changes after successfully introducing safe harbor for their indirect liability for online copyright infringement.

3.3.2 Balanced Designs: Exceptions Under the Anti-circumvention Rule

Despite the weak lobbying from technology developers and individual consumers, the government was still concerned about maintaining the balance of interests between different stakeholders. There are several system designs in the DMCA anti-circumvention rule that reflect such concerns, but whether these designs adequately offset the negative effects of the anti-circumvention rules remains to be seen.

First, as to the prohibition on the act of circumvention, the provisions only prevent circumventing access-control technological measures, not the copy controls. One of the reasons for this distinction is that unauthorized circumvention of copy controls will in many cases violate copyright law. It is therefore not necessary to include such a superfluous prohibition into anti-circumvention law. A more significant reason for this provision is that the legislators intended to leave room for the public to make fair or otherwise non-infringing use of the protected work, because the public sometimes can copy protected works without the right owners' authorization under the copyright limitations and exceptions.

Second, there is a more general provision in Section 1201, stipulating that "nothing in this section shall affect rights, remedies, limitations, or defenses to copyright infringement, including fair use, under this title."[7] Some commentators believe that this provision is the saving clause that could guarantee the fair use or other exceptions in the TPM environment. Additionally, a "no mandate" provision is included to ensure that equipment manufacturers will not be obliged to produce designs or components that comply with any particular technological measure.[8]

Third, Section 1201 contains a list of specific exceptions to the prohibition on circumvention and the trafficking of circumvention devices. The seven exceptions include (1) exemption for nonprofit libraries, archives, and educational institutions; (2) law enforcement, intelligence, and other government activities; (3) reverse engineering; (4) encryption research; (5) prevention access of minors to certain material on the Internet; (6) collection or dissemination of personally identifying information; and (7) security testing.[9] All seven exceptions apply to the prohibition on circumvention of access controls regulated under Section 1201(a)(1). These exceptions are narrowly tailored in regard to the anti-device provisions [4, pp. 287–398]. Some of them are applicable to one kind of anti-circumvention rule, but not to others. The exceptions for law enforcement and reverse engineering apply to the prohibition on trafficking of devices that facilitate circumvention of both access controls and copy controls. The exceptions for encryption research and security testing only apply to the prohibition on trafficking of devices that can circumvent access controls. The coverage of these exceptions attaches to specific circumstances prescribed in the provision. Circumventors or traffickers cannot be immunized from infringing liability if copyright infringement is involved in the acts of circumvention or trafficking of circumvention devices.

Finally, the United States Congress established an on-going administrative rulemaking proceeding to evaluate the impact of the prohibition against the act of circumventing access-control measures.[10] The anti-circumvention rule for protection of access controls is subject to exceptions for users of a particular class of works, who are, or are likely to be, adversely affected in their ability to make non-infringing uses of the works by virtue of such anti-circumvention rules.[11] Such exceptions are determined through a triennial rulemaking by the Librarian of Congress (LOC).[12] Up until now, the LOC has already had five sessions of rulemaking that resulted in five different sets of exceptions. There were two exceptions in the 2000 Rulemaking,[13]

---

[7] The United States Copyright Act of 1976, s 1201(c)(1).

[8] The United States Copyright Act of 1976, s 1201(c)(3).

[9] The United States Copyright Act of 1976, ss 1201(d)–(j).

[10] *See* [6].

[11] The United States Copyright Act of 1976, s 1201(a)(1)(B).

[12] The United States Copyright Act of 1976, ss 1201(a)(1)(C)–(E).

[13] DMCA Rulemaking (2000), available at http://www.copyright.gov/1201/anticirc.html (visited Oct 2, 2011). The two exceptions are (1) compilations consisting of lists of websites blocked by filtering software applications and (2) literary works, including computer programs and databases, protected by access-control mechanisms that fail to permit access because of malfunction, damage, or obsoleteness.

four exceptions in the 2003 Rulemaking,[14] six exceptions in the 2006 Rulemaking,[15] six exceptions in the 2009 Rulemaking,[16] and five exceptions in the 2012 Rulemaking.[17] Each rulemaking issued exceptions, valid for a certain period, to

[14]DMCA Rulemaking (2003), available at http://www.copyright.gov/1201/2003/index.html (visited Oct 2, 2011). The four exceptions are (1) compilations consisting of lists of Internet locations blocked by commercially marketed filtering software applications that are intended to prevent access to domains, websites, or portions of websites, but not including lists of Internet locations blocked by software applications that operate exclusively to protect against damage to a computer or computer network or lists of Internet locations blocked by software applications that operate exclusively to prevent receipt of email; (2) computer programs protected by dongles that prevent access due to malfunction or damage and which are obsolete; (3) computer programs and video games distributed in formats that have become obsolete and which require the original media or hardware as a condition of access; and (4) literary works distributed in ebook format when all existing ebook editions of the work (including digital text editions made available by authorized entities) contain access controls that prevent the enabling of the ebook's read-aloud function and that prevent the enabling of screen readers to render the text into a specialized format.

[15]DMCA Rulemaking (2006), available at http://www.copyright.gov/1201/2006/index.html (visited Oct 2, 2011). In addition to the three exceptions that are the same with the category (2)–(4) of the 2003 Rulemaking, the rest three exceptions are (1) audiovisual works included in the educational library of a college or university's film or media studies department, when circumvention is accomplished for the purpose of making compilations of portions of those works for educational use in the classroom by media studies or film professors; (2) computer programs in the form of filmware that enable wireless telephone handsets to connect to a wireless telephone communication network, when circumvention is accomplished for the sole purpose of lawfully connecting to a wireless telephone communication network; and (3) sound recordings and audiovisual works associated with those sound recordings, distributed in compact disc format and protected by TPMs that control access to lawfully purchased works and create or exploit security flaws or vulnerabilities that compromise the security of personal computers, when circumvention is accomplished solely for the purpose of good faith testing, investigating, or correcting such security flaws or vulnerabilities.

[16]DMCA Rulemaking (2010), available at http://www.copyright.gov/1201/2010/ (visited May 17, 2014). In addition to the four exceptions that are the same with the category (2) and (4) of the 2003 Rulemaking and the category (2) and (3) of the 2006 Rulemaking, the rest two exceptions are (1) motion pictures on DVDs that are lawfully made and acquired and that are protected by the Content Scrambling System when circumvention is accomplished solely in order to accomplish the incorporation of short portions of motion pictures into new works for the purpose of criticism or comment, and where the person engaging in circumvention believes and has reasonable grounds for believing that circumvention is necessary to fulfill the purpose of the use in the following instances: (i) educational uses by college and university professors and by college and university film and media studies students; (ii) documentary filmmaking; (iii) noncommercial videos; and (2) computer programs that enable wireless telephone handsets to execute software applications, where circumvention is accomplished for the sole purpose of enabling interoperability of such applications, when they have been lawfully obtained, with computer programs on the telephone handset.

[17]DMCA Rulemaking (2012), available at https://www.federalregister.gov/articles/2012/10/26/2012-26308/exemption-to-prohibition-on-circumvention-of-copyright-protection-systems-for-access-control#h-14 (visited Jun 25, 2013). The five exceptions are (1) literary works distributed electronically, to permit blind and other persons with print disabilities to use screen readers and other assistive technologies; (2) computer programs on wireless telephone handsets, to enable interoperability of software applications ("jailbreaking"); (3) computer programs on wireless telephone handsets that were acquired within 90 days of the effective date of the exemption, for the purpose of connecting to alternative networks ("unlocking"); (4) motion pictures on DVDs or

permit the circumvention of technological measures which control access to specific classes of copyrighted works.

3.3.3 *Unbalanced Designs: Existing Problems in the Anti-circumvention Rule*

Although the DMCA has established several exceptions which legitimize certain circumvention acts and trafficking of circumvention devices, such an approach to creating exceptions cannot totally eliminate the negative influence caused by the anti-circumvention rule on non-infringing uses and other personal privileges. There are two major problems embodied in Section 1201 concerning users' privileges under the traditional copyright system. One is the prohibition of circumventing access-control technological measures; another is the anti-device rule that bans trafficking of circumvention technologies and tools. Furthermore, the anti-circumvention rule may result in other problems that exist outside the spectrum of intellectual property, such as fair competition, protection of consumers' rights, and protection of privacy.

3.3.3.1 Restriction on Non-infringing Uses by Anti-circumvention on Access Controls

First of all, the DMCA prohibits circumvention of access-control technological measures. Although the legislation does not ban circumvention of copy controls with the purpose of maintaining space for fair or other non-infringing uses, one cannot reproduce a work without at first acquiring access to the work. The so-called general "savings clause" and specific exceptions are extremely narrow and restricted. Following the general "savings clause" does not mean that circumvention of access controls is generally permitted, as long as the end use is fair or for non-infringing purposes. Otherwise, the prohibition on circumvention of access-control technological measures would become meaningless. Although the seven specific exceptions allow for the circumvention of access-control technological measures upon satisfying statutory conditions, they exclude many potential fair or non-infringing uses outside the scope of the seven exceptions. The LOC rulemaking procedure is unable to address all possible users' privileges.

The analysis of Professor Jerome Reichman, Graeme Dinwoodie, and Pamela Samuelson illustrates that the LOC rulemaking "is not a sufficient safety valve" for

distributed by online services, for purpose of criticism or comment in noncommercial videos, documentary film, and nonfiction multimedia ebooks offering film analysis and for certain educational uses by college and university faculty and students and kindergarten through twelfth grade educators; and (5) motion pictures and other audiovisual works on DVDs or distributed by online services, for the purpose of research to create players capable of rendering captions and descriptive audio for persons who are blind, visually impaired, deaf, or hard of hearing.

several reasons [8, p. 1006]. According to these scholars, firstly, the valid period for each set of exceptions is short, as it only lasts 3 years. At each rulemaking, the categories of exceptions will be revised and renewed. Secondly, the rulemaking exceptions list classes of works rather than classes of uses where the latter are more relevant in determining fair or non-infringing uses. Thirdly, the burden of proof is heavily shouldered by the advocates of the new exceptions to show adverse effects from the anti-circumvention rule, not by the copyright owners or the government. This allocation of the burden of proof will exacerbate the disadvantageous situation of public users and future novice creators.

The ineffectiveness of DMCA exceptions is also shown in judicial decisions. In the cornerstone case *Universal City Studios v. Reimerdes*,[18] the plaintiff produced an encryption technology called the Content Scramble System (CSS) which protects motion pictures on the DVDs from being copied or played on non-compliant DVD players or computer drives [9]. The defendants were sued under Section 1201 of the DMCA for posting and linking to a software utility known as DeCSS which functioned to decrypt CSS [9]. The district court ruled in favor of the plaintiff, concluding that CSS was an effective access-control technological measure protected by the DMCA, because in order to gain access to the motion pictures, one needed to obtain the access-control key via a license or by the purchase of an authorized DVD player or drive. Thus, the court rejected the defendants' "weak encryption" argument, ruling that the DeCSS was a circumvention device prohibited under Section 1201(a)(2) since it was primarily designed for the purpose of circumventing CSS. According to the court, the defendants were liable for their infringing conduct under Section 1201(a)(2) on the grounds of offering the circumvention device to the public.

In this case, Judge Lewis Kaplan denied the general fair use defense by declaring that: "if Congress had meant the fair use defense to apply to actions, it would have said so. The decision not to make fair use a defense to a claim under Section 1201(a) was quite deliberate."[19] The Second Circuit also denied that Section 1201(c)(1) was a fair use "savings clause," ruling that such an interpretation was not only outside the scope of the provision, but was also clearly refuted by the statute's legislative history [8]. Upon being made aware of judicial denial of the general fair use defense, copyright owners may use permanent technological measures to control access to copyrighted works and argue for legal protection under anti-circumvention law.

3.3.3.2 Restriction on Non-infringing Uses by Anti-device Provisions

Second, the DMCA contains anti-device provisions, under which the trafficking of devices that facilitate both access-control and copy-control technological measures is prohibited. Although the specific exceptions and LOC rulemaking procedure

---

[18] *Universal City Studios v Reimerdes* 111F. Supp. 2d 294 (S.D.N.Y. 2000).

[19] *University City Studios* (n 18 above), p. 322.

legitimize circumvention of access-control technological measures under certain circumstances, users must have the adequate knowledge and skill to conduct the circumvention act by themselves. Otherwise, they cannot effectively enjoy their rights under the exceptions to anti-circumvention law, as manufacturing and providing access-control circumvention devices are unconditionally prohibited whether or not the final use is infringing.

After obtaining lawful access to the protected works, users still cannot freely reproduce works for fair use or other non-infringing uses if they lack knowledge and skill to circumvent the copy-control technological measures, as the trafficking of copy-control circumvention devices is also unconditionally disallowed. Although users who accept technological circumvention assistance are free from infringing liability, providers of those circumvention devices will violate Sections 1201(a)(2) and 1201(b). Since most circumvention devices are not available publicly, it remains very difficult for users to bypass technological measures for fair or other non-infringing uses.

Both the access-control anti-circumvention rule and anti-devices rule distort the traditional copyright principles of limited duration of protection and protectable subject matters. Under the traditional copyright system, the protection of copyright is subject to a limited duration, often 50–70 years after the authors' death. There is, however, no time limitation for protection of technological measures under the anti-circumvention law. Copyright owners thus can install technological measures to protect their works permanently, since not all users are capable enough to circumvent TPMs without technical assistance from any third party even if the work has entered into the public domain. In addition to the duration issue, copyright protection is granted to original works of authorship, not to "any idea, procedure, process, system, method of operation, concept, principle of discovery."[20] However, by using access-control technological measures, copyright owners can protect both copyrighted and non-copyrightable material. The circumvention of access controls that protect both copyrighted and public domain works, in order to use the latter, will violate the anti-circumvention law anyway. Hence, anti-circumvention law largely shrinks the scope of public domain works originally free for public use.

3.3.3.3 Restriction on Free Competition

Third, the anti-circumvention laws could badly influence free competition in the secondary market for interoperable devices by providing protection for technological measures that control access to copyrighted computer programs embodied in the products in the process of their normal operation [4, pp. 287–398]. Competitors who distribute interoperable devices that can circumvent the access controls in the original products will be held liable under the anti-circumvention law, even though they may not infringe any copyright. Cases such as *Lexmark* and *Chamberlain* in the United States and *Beijing Jingdiao* in China sufficiently illustrate this problem.

[20] The United States Copyright Act of 1976, ss 102(a)–(b).

In *Lexmark International v. Static Control Components*,[21] Lexmark, a manufacturer of computer printers and toner cartridges, claimed that its authentication sequence installed in its printers and toner cartridges was an access-control measure that made Lexmark printers function only with authorized Lexmark cartridges. Lexmark argued that Static Control's production and distribution of the chips designed for circumventing the authentication sequence, which enabled unauthorized cartridges to function with Lexmark printers, violated Section 1201(a)(2). The district court relied heavily on *Reimerdes* to find that Static Control was liable under Section 1201(a)(2) for its trafficking of devices that circumvented an access-control technological measure.[22] The Sixth Circuit reversed the trial court decision, reasoning that the DMCA applied only to technological measures that control access to the copyrighted works, not the functional aspects of the printers.[23] In the future, companies like Lexmark would not be able to use the DMCA in conjunction with copyright law to restrict competition in manufactured goods.[24]

Like Lexmark, the plaintiff in *Chamberlain Group v. Skylink Technologies*[25] also attempted to limit competition in its relevant market by filing litigation under the DMCA's anti-circumvention rule. Chamberlain claimed that Skylink's universal remote transmitter circumvented the access control on the computer program it installed in its electronic garage-door opening devices. They argued that Skylink violated Section 1201, using the support of precedents such as *Reimerdes* and the district court decision in *Lexmark*. The lower court disagreed with Chamberlain's argument and granted summary judgment to Skylink, concluding that Chamberlain authorized the circumvention of its access control due to the failure to notify consumers that the computer programs were limited to transmitters manufactured by Chamberlain only.[26] The decision of the lower court was upheld by the Federal Circuit with further interpretation of the DMCA. According to the federal court, the "statutory structure and legislative history both make clear that Section 1201 applies only to circumventions reasonably related to copyright protected rights. Defendants who traffic in devices that circumvent access controls in ways that facilitate infringement may be subject to liability under Section 1201(a)(2). Defendants whose circumvention devices do not facilitate infringement are not subject to Section 1201 liability."[27] Therefore, the court opined that the DMCA did not protect access controls per se. Unless it is proven that the circumvention devices correlate with the danger of copyright infringement, anti-circumvention liability shall not be imposed. The Federal Circuit further stated that allowing "any manufacturer of any product to add a single copyrighted sentence or software fragment to its product, wrap the copyrighted material in a trivial encryption

[21] *Lexmark International v Static Control Components* 387F. 3d 522 (6th Cir. 2004).

[22] *Lexmark International v Static Control Components* 253F. Supp. 2d 943 (E.D. Ky. 2003).

[23] *Lexmark International* (n 21 above).

[24] *Lexmark International* (n 21 above).

[25] *Chamberlain Group v Skylink Technologies* 381F. 3d 1178 (Fed. Cir. 2004).

[26] *Chamberlain Group v Skylink Technologies* 292F. Supp. 2d 1023 (N.D. Ill. 2003).

[27] *Chamberlain Group* (n 25 above) p. 1195.

scheme, and thereby gain the right to restrict consumers' rights to use its products in conjunction with competing products" would "allow virtually any company to attempt to leverage its sales into aftermarket monopolies."[28]

Similar copyright cases have also occurred in China. The most famous and earliest case regarding protection on TPMs is relevant to this discussion of the negative influence of anti-circumvention law on free competition in the second market. In *Beijing Jingdiao Company Ltd. v. Shanghai Naikai Electronic Technology Company Ltd.*, the plaintiff Beijing Jingdiao, a company specializing in manufacturing CNC engraving machines, sued Shanghai Naikai, a rival in the same market, for its circumventing acts on Beijing Jingdiao's software TPMs.[29] Beijing Jingdiao claimed copyright in the encrypted JDPaint software, one of the components of Jingdiao's self-developed CNC engraving system, which was comprised of three parts, namely, the JDPaint software, the CNC system, and the machine body. The JDPaint software was only used in Jingdiao's CNC engraving machines. In early 2006, the plaintiff found that the Ncstudio software in Shanghai Naikai's NC-1000 engraving system could read the data files in the encrypted JDPaint software. It then filed litigation against Shanghai Naikai for the manufacturing and distributing of CNC engraving machines which circumvented and destroyed the technological measure used to protect plaintiff's copyrightable software.

In its claim, the plaintiff requested the court to halt Shanghai Naikai's infringing activity and urged Shanghai Naikai to compensate for its economic loss. Shanghai Naikai, however, defended that it should not be liable for Beijing Jingdiao's economic loss, because the data file in the JDPaint software was outside of the copyright protection for computer software; thus, developing Ncstudio software which could read the unprotected data file by circumventing JDPaint software did not constitute infringement. The court therefore concentrated on the key point of whether the data file should be protected by copyright. According to the investigation of the court and the Regulation of Computer Software Protection, the data file was the outcome of the software object code after running on the computer, not the instruction sequence originally in the software, and, as such, could not be protected by copyright as computer software itself. Eventually, the lower court disagreed that the defendant's circumvention activity constituted infringement and dismissed the plaintiff's complaint. The appellate court later confirmed the decision of the lower court with further explanation that the encryption on the JDPaint software used by Beijing Jingdiao aimed to constrain the use of the software to its self-developed engraving machine and exclude the compatibility of the software with other engraving systems.[30] The high court therefore denied protection of technological measures that restrict fair competition.

---

[28] Ibid.

[29] *Beijing Jingdiao Company Ltd. v Shanghai Naikai Electronic Technology Company Ltd. (in Chinese),* Shanghai First Intermediate People's Court (2006) Hu Yi Zhong Min Wu (Zhi) Chu No. 134.

[30] *Beijing Jingdiao Company Ltd. v Shanghai Naikai Electronic Technology Company Ltd. (in Chinese),* Shanghai High People's Court (2006) Hu Gao Min San (Zhi) Zhong Zi No. 110.

In all of these cases, courts were reluctant to grant protection to TPMs that impeded free and fair competition in the marketplace for alternative technology and devices. Such uses of TPMs significantly raise the costs of equipment replacement and create inefficiency in the natural operation of the market. When technology developers file lawsuits to claim legal protection of TPMs which control access to non-copyrightable procedures or devices, the use of TPMs also increases the litigation expenses of enterprises and wastes judicial resources.

The recent 2012 Rulemaking of the LOC on the exemptions to the prohibition against circumvention of access-control TPMs, which was passed in October 2012, removed the exception that allowed mobile phone users to unlock their cell phones purchased after January 26, 2013 [10]. Such removal of exemptions to unlocking cell phones set off a firestorm on the discussion of the exacerbating impact of anti-circumvention rule on fair and free competition.

The computer program in a cell phone functions to connect the cell phone to certain telecommunication network. Unlocking a cell phone through reprogramming the computer program enables connection of the cell phone to another different telecommunication provider. Switching to another telecommunication network will often be necessary when a cell phone user travels abroad or terminates the service contract. Unlocking cell phones in order to switch telecommunication network often requires circumvention of TPMs that control access to bootloader and operating system in a cell phone, which are usually protected by copyright. Therefore, unlocking a cell phone violates the DMCA anti-circumvention rule. However, the LOC rulemaking proceedings in 2006 and 2009 once permitted unlocking of cell phones "when circumvention is accomplished for the sole purpose of lawfully connecting to a wireless telephone communication network." The 2012 Rulemaking restricted the allowance of unlocking to cell phones that were acquired "within ninety days of the effective date of the exemption." Cell phones purchased after January 26, 2013 are thus not allowed to be unlocked.

The new LOC rulemaking reflects the demand of big telecommunications companies to control the use of their cell phones by consumers and further monopolize the market. It makes the anti-circumvention rule a tool to achieve restriction of competition but not to protect copyright owners' interests in copyright works. Circumvention of TPMs that control access to certain copyrightable computer program does not reproduce, distribute, or make available to the public of the computer program, but rather reprogram the firmware, which is deemed as making adaptation of the program [11]. The Copyright Act allows the copyright owner of a computer program to make adaptation "as an essential step in the utilization of the computer program in conjunction with a machine."[31] Hence, the anti-circumvention of TPMs that prevent unlocking of cell phones has nothing to do with copyright protection, but may infringe the consumers' freedom to choose their telecommunication service providers. It gets involved into the issue that should be regulated by contract law rather than copyright law.

---

[31] The United States Copyright Act of 1976, s 117(a)(1).

In order to counterbalance the negative influence brought on by the new LOC rulemaking, three legislative bills were introduced in the Senate with different amendment approaches. The Wireless Device Independence Act proposed to include a permanent exemption in the DMCA anti-circumvention rule for unlocking cell phones and other mobile wireless Internet devices.[32] The Wireless Consumer Choice Act proposed not to change the DMCA but pushed the Federal Communications Commission to require mobile carrier providers to allow unlocking of their cell phones.[33] The Unlocking Consumer Choice and Wireless Competition Act suggested to extend the 2009 Rulemaking which exempted unlocking of wireless cell phones to 2015 when the Copyright Office is expected to reconsider the DMCA exemption.[34]

3.3.3.4 Restrictions on Consumers' Right of Notice and Privacy

Fourthly, the use of TPMs on digital works may undermine users' consumption experience through constraining the interoperability among different equipment, intentionally concealing the existence of TPMs and monitoring consumers' usage, which invades personal privacy.

After purchasing digital works, consumers often wish to make copies of the works for the purposes of time- or space-shifting or preparation of backups in case that the original copy is destroyed. For example, after people buy music CDs, they may download the sound recordings on the CDs to their personal computers or portable MP3s for their convenience. When time-shifting was determined to be fair use by courts in the *Sony* case, the increase in consumers' expectations for more convenient use of purchased copyrighted works was understandable and reasonable. Because of the flexibility and conveniences of digital network technologies, consumers not only expect to use the works in the same way as they did in the analog environment but also expect to be able to remix and recreate the works based on their ingenuity.

The installation of TPMs seriously limits consumers' ability to exploit digital copyrighted works in different ways. Unlike copyright law, which only grants copyright owners the rights to control public performances and displays of works, the legal protection on TPMs can control private performances and displays [12]. The time- and space-shifting uses and backups preparation of backups cannot be easily achieved by consumers, given the control of TPMs. The design of the iTunes Music Store (iTMS) and the iPod music player of Apple Corporation illustrates some of the consumer bafflement caused by TPMs [13]. Because of the installation of TPMs, "songs from iTMS will only play on the iPod and not on other portable digital music devices" [13]. In addition to the problem of time- and space-shifting,

---

[32] "Copyright Reform Bill Targets Anti-circumvention," available at https://www.cdt.org/blogs/andrew-mcdiarmid/1005copyright-reform-bill-targets-anti-circumvention (visited Nov 4, 2013).

[33] Ibid.

[34] "Copyright Reform Bill," (n 32 above).

TPMs are also used for regional coding which limits the authorized distribution of DVDs to a specific geographic region [13]. For example, DVDs with a European Region Code cannot be played on most United States-made DVD players, because these players are encoded to play only DVDs with the United States Region Code [13]. The region coding system is not only used to restrict access to copyrighted contents but also to limit the operation of functional equipment such as printers and printer cartridges. Thus, consumers find that their legitimately purchased DVDs or printer cartridges with region codes in one geographic area cannot function well with corresponding equipment in another region when they travel or change dwelling places.

A more serious impact to consumers' interests is the intentional concealment of the use of TPMs from copyright owners or equipment vendors. Since copyright owners are likely to know that consumers will not be fond of and willing to accept TPMs, they are inclined to conceal the existence of TPMs in their products in advance. Such intentional hidden enclosure of important information infringes consumers' right of notice and exacerbates the tensions between product vendors and consumers. The failure to disclose sufficient information and give notice of use of TPMs will decrease consumers' expectations of digital products because of the lack of interoperability.

The TPMs are also used by copyright owners to monitor the usage of their products and collect personal information from consumers. Monitoring TPMs can "aid in the detection of infringing copies of copyrighted works" and "facilitate price discrimination and profiling about customers that will allow right holders to offer new products and services to them or to sell user profiles to other firms" [13, p. 51]. Technologically unsavvy consumers often are not conscious of such monitoring and data collection. Their privacy is therefore seriously invaded because of the unexpected surveillance.

3.3.4 Conclusion: Balanced Designs Weighing Unbalanced Designs

By implementing the international obligations of the WIPO Internet Treaties, the DMCA provides much stricter protection on TPMs than the simple requirement of "adequate protection and effective remedies." Going beyond the international conventions, the DMCA explicitly prohibits circumvention of access-control technological measures and trafficking of a technology or device that is primarily designed or knowingly marketed for circumventing TPMs or that has no other commercial purposes than circumventing TPMs.

Considering the negative impact that the anti-circumvention rules may impose on public interests, the DMCA includes general exception provisions that guarantee existing limitations and defenses to copyright infringement including fair use and allows circumvention of copy-control TPMs for non-infringing uses. Specifically, the

DMCA lists seven detailed exceptions for activities such as library use, governmental law enforcement, reverse engineering, encryption research, security testing, protection of minors, as well as personally identifying information protection. Additionally, the DMCA contains a triennial rulemaking process carried out by the LOC to determine whether users' capability to make non-infringing use of a particular class of works will be adversely influenced by the anti-circumvention rule.

Despite the intricate design of exceptions and limitations, the DMCA cannot alleviate its negative influence on the public interest. As already discussed, there are more fair or non-infringing uses that cannot be covered by the DMCA exceptions because of the prohibition on circumvention of access controls and the trafficking of circumvention devices. Moreover, the anti-circumvention law brings other chilling effects, including restrictions on fair competition and the invasion of consumers' rights of notice and right of privacy. Just as one cannot restrict others' personal freedom in order to protect his property, one cannot safeguard his copyright through sacrificing others' rights of free competition, free speech, and privacy, as well as curtailing the social benefits spurred by technology and cultural development. This shows that the defective design outweighs the exceptions incorporated in the DMCA anti-circumvention law. Such defectiveness subverts the balance between copyright interest and public welfare, resulting in many unexpected and detrimental consequences.

3.4 Introduction of a More Balanced Model of Anti-circumvention Rule

Influenced by the DMCA, many countries adopted similar anti-circumvention laws that also embody the unbalanced problems of the United States original. Developing countries which have more demand for the access to knowledge and information will suffer more due to the importing of the DMCA-like anti-circumvention legal model.

Among the developing countries adopting the new legislation, China implemented the anti-circumvention rule into its domestic copyright law. In the 2006 Regulation, Article 4 stipulates that "no organization or individual may purposely avoid or break the technological measures, purposely manufacture, import or provide to the general public any device or component that is mainly applied to avoiding or breaking the technological measures, or purposely provide such technological services to any other person for the purpose of avoiding or breaking the technological measures, unless it is otherwise provided for by any law or regulation that the relevant technological measures can be avoided." "Technological measures" are generally defined by the regulation as "the effective techniques, devices and components that are applied to preventing or restricting the browse or appreciation of the works, performance and audio-visual products in the absence of the relevant owner's permission or in the provision of the work, performance and audio-visual products to the general public through the information network in the absence of the relevant owner's permission."[35] The definition and description of "technological measure" is quite vague in Chinese law, as it does not clearly express whether the technological measure is used for access control or copy control. The words "browse," "appreciation," and "provision of…to the general public through the information network" used in the definition show that the technological measures in Chinese law refer to both the measures that control access and the copying of the protected works. In addition, Chinese law does not specifically distinguish between the acts of circumvention itself and the circumvention-enabling devices. According to the general expression of the anti-circumvention provision, Chinese law prohibits circumvention of both access controls and copy controls as well as the trafficking of devices that facilitate circumvention of both access controls and copy controls. Such interpretation illustrates that the vagueness of Chinese legal expressions makes the problems inherent in the anti-circumvention rule more severe.

To take care of the public interests, Chinese law includes four specific exceptions which apply to the circumvention act itself only and not to the trafficking of circumvention devices. These four exceptions are for teaching and scientific research, provision of works for the blind, enforcement of governmental official duties, and security testing.[36] In addition, there are three general exceptions which apply to making works available through an information network generally. These general exceptions may also be regarded as limitations to anti-circumvention law. They are created to benefit nonprofit organizations such as libraries and museums, educational institutions under the national 9-year compulsory education plan, and residents in rural areas for use in their basic cultural demands.[37]

As one of the many examples of anti-circumvention laws in developing countries, the Chinese regulation model is an example of the ambiguous lawmaking that results in much stricter protection of TPMs and narrow exceptions. It incorporates all of the unbalanced problems hidden in the DMCA and is deficient in the more general exemptions that have already been incorporated into the legislative models of developed countries. Therefore, the introduction of a more balanced legislative model of anti-circumvention rule is important to overturn the current unbalanced situation and to create more opportunities for access to knowledge, as well as the advancement of technology and mass culture, in developing countries in particular.

Scholars and commentators have suggested proposals for rectifying the problems of the current anti-circumvention system, such as incorporating the anti-circumvention misuse doctrine proposed by Professor Dan Burk to regulate the abusive use of TPMs [14], establishing a reverse notice and takedown regime proposed by Professors Reichman, Dinwoodie, and Samuelson to force copyright owners to remove TPMs upon receiving users' reasonable requests [8] and Professor

---

[35] The Regulation on the Protection of the Right to Network Dissemination of Information, Art 26, Paragraph 2.

[36] The Regulation on the Protection of the Right to Network Dissemination of Information, Art 12.

[37] The Regulation on the Protection of the Right to Network Dissemination of Information, Arts 7–9.

Peter Yu's proposal of giving up the importation of anti-circumvention laws if less developed countries have not issued such legislation [2]. As many of the developing countries do not have adequate resources and expertise to introduce both an anti-circumvention regime and a follow-up correction mechanism [2], the correction proposals should not be too complex and costly for the national governments to implement. It is better to change current strict TPM protection from the readjustment of the legal mechanisms with the assistance of technological development.

My proposal for effective change is to basically amend current copyright law by inserting a general exception provision into the anti-circumvention rule, to guide judges' decision-making regarding circumvention of TPMs for non-infringing uses based on the general exception, and to import certain requirements under anti-circumvention law into the more general area of law, such as competition law. The readjustment of the existing legal mechanism could be assisted by the improvement of technology that installs automatic decoding equipment, which allows for minimum fair use, and for transferring technology so that circumvention devices are available for consumers to circumvent TPMs for non-infringing fair uses.

3.4.1 Technological Design: Guaranteeing Minimum Use

A technological mechanism could be installed into TPMs to allow users' circumvention of access controls and copy controls for minimal uses such as browsing or reproducing 5–15 % of the protected works. With such a mechanism, users only need ordinary technological knowledge and skill to partially circumvent the TPMs in order to use the authorized minimum portions of the protected works. The partially circumvented TPMs would still function in protecting against the access or copying of the remaining parts of works. The establishment of a minimalist non-infringing use clause could protect free appropriation of a small amount of expressions and decrease the transaction costs caused by license agreements between copyright owners and public users. Guarantee of minimum use by legislations which require or encourage copyright owners, in designing their TPMs, to enable certain minimum use would legalize the minimum unauthorized use of copyright works, which would not seriously impact the market for the original works and would grant more certainty of fair use to potential users and future creators.

Although technology cannot completely resolve the problem of copyright limitations and exceptions under the protection of TPMs, it can at least capture some of the fair or non-infringing use privileges. One of the possible protections of fair use is to develop technological procedures that allow users' circumvention of TPMs in order to access or copy limited parts of the protected works. Such technical design works as a starting-floor rather than limiting-ceiling to guide legitimate circumvention for fair use. Legislative and judicial mechanisms will come into play to decide whether non-infringing uses exist when portions of the protected works that have been circumvented exceed the authorized minimum portions. Therefore, the technical design to guarantee minimum use does not exclude necessary human discretion. With the development and improvement of technology, it is possible to achieve the precise circumvention of TPMs for partial access and use of copyright work without seriously undermining right holders' interests.

To design such a technological arrangement, the issue regarding the creation and invention of appropriate software is left for the technology developers and experts to resolve. Other issues regarding the definition and scope of minimum use for different kinds of copyright works could be resolved through negotiations among various stakeholders including legislatures, copyright owners, technology developers, nonprofit organizations, and consumers. As it may be not easy for copyright owners to reach a satisfactory agreement with nonprofit organizations and consumers, the participation of legislators will be necessary to help mediate interests among different stakeholders. After achieving consensus on the scope of minimum use, technological experts can then build such agreed use into TPM software. Such technical design may avoid the high expenses caused by follow-up correction mechanisms, as long as multilateral negotiation process or forum has already been incorporated in the national legislative procedure and minimum use can satisfy a number of consumers' demands.

3.4.2 Legislative Design: Inserting General Condition and Exception

The delineation of specific exceptions under current anti-circumvention laws is far from satisfying the requirement of preserving all potential non-infringing uses. The insertion of provisions into copyright statutes that restrict protection of TPMs and establish a general exception to liability is necessary and important to recover the balance of interests between copyright owners and public users. As proposed by Professor Wang Qian, the legitimacy of a prohibition on circumvention of access controls should be based on the protection of the legitimate interests of copyright owners in the copyright law [15]. To my understanding, copyright laws of developing countries in general, and of China in particular, should set up a general condition on the protection of TPMs as Professor Wang has recommended: only TPMs that guarantee copyright owners' legitimate interests in the copyright law should be under the statutory protection. In addition, a general exception should also be incorporated into copyright laws of developing countries, explicitly articulating that anti-circumvention laws will not constrain and impede limitations and exceptions to the exclusive rights of copyright owners, including fair use or fair dealing. Prohibition on trafficking of circumvention devices should only apply to devices which are primarily designed or produced for the purpose of circumventing a TPM, have only limited commercially significant purpose or use other than to circumvent, and are marketed to be used to circumvent. Provision of devices that are not primarily designed for circumvention and have commercially significant purposes other than mere circumvention should not be banned, even though these devices may be occasionally used to circumvent TPMs.

The major opinions constraining the protection of TPMs and reducing the negative influence of anti-circumvention law emphasize that copyright law should only grant protection to TPMs that are used to prevent copyright infringement. In the above-discussed cases, such as *Lexmark* and *Chamberlain* in the United States, judicial decisions have illustrated that anti-circumvention of TPMs controlling access to non-copyrighted products should not be supported by courts. Circumvention should result in legal liability only when a reasonable relationship exists between the circumvention act and the infringement of copyright.

When Australia passed the Copyright Amendment (Digital Agenda) Act (CADA) in 2000, protection of TPMs was included into the new law. In the law-making process, the definition of a TPM became the focus of multi-stakeholders' discussion. Copyright users insisted on linking TPMs to copyright infringement. In their argument, "to include access control measures in the definition of effective technological protection measure would be to extend the reach of copyright law, rather than to merely enforce it" [16]. Although the CADA finally extended the scope of protection to access control measures, it set up a strict prerequisite under which access controls must be used to prevent copyright infringement. The CADA defines a TPM as "a device, product or component that is designed to prevent or inhibit the infringement of copyright either by ensuring that access to the work or other subject-matter is available solely by use of an access code or process with the authority of the right holder or through a copy control mechanism."[38] Such definition clearly expresses the prerequisite for protection of TPMs.

In the landmark Australian case *Stevens v. Kabushiki Kaisha Sony Computer Entertainment*,[39] Sony sued Stevens for the latter's production and sale of devices that circumvented the Regional Access Codes (RACs) embedded in Sony PlayStation games.[40] Sony claimed that the RACs installed in its games are TPMs and that Steven's distribution of circumvention devices violated the Australian Copyright Act. In the first trial, Judge Sackville focused on determining whether Sony's RACs could be regarded as TPMs within the meaning of Section 10(1) of the Copyright Act. In his decision, Judge Sackville of the Federal Court of Australia decided that RACs were not TPMs, ruling that they were not designed to prevent or inhibit the infringement of copyright. It is not enough for a technology or device to qualify as a TPM when the technology or device only has "a general deterrent or discouraging effect on those who might be contemplating infringing copyright."[41] On appeal, the Full Court reversed the decision in the first trial, but the final decision, granted by the High Court, confirmed Judge Sackville's opinion and ruled that Sony's RAC

[38] Australian Copyright Amendment (Digital Agenda) Act 2000, s 10(1).

[39] *Stevens v Kabushiki Kaisha Sony Computer Entertainment and Others* [2005] HCA 58.

[40] "Stevens v. Kabushiki Kaisha Sony Computer Entertainment (2005)," available at http://en.wikipedia.org/wiki/Stevens_v_Kabushiki_Kaisha_Sony_Computer_Entertainment_(2005) (visited Oct 10, 2011).

[41] Ibid.

system could not be defined as a TPM. Therefore, Stevens was not liable for the trafficking of circumvention devices.

A large number of access-control TPMs, however, are not directly used to prevent or inhibit copyright infringement. Instead, they primarily function by limiting consumers' rights to read and use the protected works in order to collect remuneration. For example, vendors of Kindles often set up access-control TPMs in case that consumers will download digital books freely. Before payment, consumers can only browse limited pages of the book. They can only acquire the right to read the whole book within the authorization of copyright owners by submitting payment. Such TPMs merely prevent unpaid users from reading the work rather than inhibit their reproduction and dissemination through the Internet of the work. The adoption of these kinds of TPMs may generally deter potential copyright infringement, but is not primarily intended to deter infringing activities. Another example of limited rights is when copyright owners install both access-control and copy-control measures in online movies. The former TPM blocks unpaying audience members from watching the movie, while the latter forbids unauthorized downloading. The circumvention of an access-control technological measure will not result in any unauthorized downloading or distribution of the movie. Thus, there will be no copyright infringement even if circumvention takes place.

Unauthorized access to copyright works such as watching a pirated movie, listening to pirated music, or reading a pirated book does not constitute direct copyright infringement. However, this does not mean that consumers have the right to unrestrainedly carry out such activities or that copyright owners must bear these activities. In fact, copyright owners can undertake self-help measures that are not prohibited by law to decrease the possibility of unauthorized or unpaid use of copyright works. The interest in requiring consumers to pay for access to works is a justified and legitimate interest under copyright law. Therefore, protection of TPMs should better concentrate on the legitimate interests in copyright law rather than on the direct prevention of copyright infringement; otherwise copyright owners' interests and incentives will not be well protected. In the case of *MDY Industries v. Blizzard Entertainment* decided by the United States Court of Appeals for the Ninth Circuit,[42] the court refuted the argument connecting protection on access-control technological measures to prevention of copyright infringement as follows: "a linkage requirement would deprive copyright owners of an important enforcement tool, pointing to protections necessary for copyright owners who make movies or music available online, protected by an access control, in exchange for direct or indirect payment" [17].

In addition to the condition on TPM protection, copyright law in developing countries should also include a general exception article that allows for the circumvention of TPMs for non-infringing uses. The European Union, in its Information Society Directive, has required that member states should adopt mechanisms that preserve the ability of users to take advantage of certain exceptions and limitations guaranteed by copyright law notwithstanding the application

[42] *MDY Industries v Blizzard Entertainment* 629F.3d 928 (9th Cir. 2010).

of TPMs.[43] The general exception can embody all potential situations that may be deemed as fair or non-infringing uses in the digital network environment. Furthermore, it can guide judicial decision on whether the questionable acts of circumvention or the trafficking of circumvention devices violate the copyright law or not.

3.4.3 *Judicial Design: Reaching Decision Case by Case Based on Prerequisite and General Exception*

When litigation regarding circumvention issues is filed in courts, judges should decide if the use of TPMs satisfies the prerequisite of use of TPMs as protection and whether the acts of circumvention or trafficking of circumvention devices are for uses that fall within the scope of limitations and exceptions to copyright owners' exclusive rights. In countries where precedent is the legal tradition, courts can refer to the previous landmark cases to examine whether the decision should permit the acts of circumvention. In countries where precedent is not the decisive factor for judicial determinations, such as China, the Supreme Court can release judicial interpretations to specify the norms that courts should comply with when making decisions.

As to cases where the plaintiff sues the defendant for circumvention of access-control technological measures, courts should first determine whether the access-control measure installed by the plaintiff is able to protect the copyright owner's legitimate interests under copyright law. If not, the court should not support the plaintiff's argument for prohibiting and punishing the defendant's act of circumvention. If so, the court should further analyze whether the defendant's purpose and final use in circumventing the access-control measure is for fair or other non-infringing uses. If fair or non-infringing uses are found, the defendant will not be held liable for his act of circumvention. If, on the contrary, there is infringing use, then the court should rule against the defendant.

As to cases where plaintiffs file litigation against the defendant's trafficking of circumvention devices, the court should also first determine whether the adoption of TPMs by the plaintiff satisfies the prerequisite of TPMs protection or not. If not, the court should not support the plaintiff's argument against trafficking of circumvention devices. If meeting the prerequisite, the TPMs used by the plaintiff shall be protected by copyright law and the court should subsequently determine whether the circumvention devices in question are primarily designed or produced for the purpose of circumventing technological measures or have only limited commercially significant purpose other than to circumvent or are marketed as devices to be used to circumvent technological measures. If the devices provided by the defendant fall within the scope of any of the above three situations, manufacturing and distribution of such devices should be banned by law. If not, sanction should not be

[43] Information Society Directive of European Union, Art 6(4).

applied to the trafficking of such devices, even when the devices can be occasionally used to accomplish circumvention.

Under certain circumstances where users do not possess adequate knowledge and skill to circumvent TPMs for fair or other non-infringing uses, supply of circumvention devices for users is necessary to guarantee the exceptions and limitations to right holders' exclusive rights. Scholars have recommended importing a correction mechanism which allows users to notify copyright owners of their potential fair or non-infringing uses. Upon receiving users' notification, which is examined by judicial or administrative organs, copyright owners should supply circumvention devices that can facilitate consumers' fair or other non-infringing uses. This mechanism may well resolve the problem of users' lack of circumvention knowledge and skill.

Nevertheless, there will be two major difficulties in implementing the correction mechanism in developing countries. Firstly, costly expenses will be imposed upon judicial, administrative, or other special organs if these organs are required to examine every fair use notification from consumers. Secondly, it is difficult for copyright owners and third-party organizations to know users' true intentions based merely on the notifications submitted by the users themselves. In some situations, users may take advantage of the notification scheme to deceive copyright owners for the facilitation of circumventing TPMs through concealing the real purpose of the use. Therefore, taking this approach to copyright owners' provision of circumvention devices for consumers' fair or other non-infringing uses is not yet feasible or appropriate for developing countries. More suitable methods to resolve the problem of users' lacking circumvention devices may be discovered in the future.

3.4.4 Scheme Outside Intellectual Property Law: Importation of Anti-circumvention Rule into Competition Law

Apart from the approaches noted above, another way to alleviate the negative effect of the TPMs on the use of copyright material is to import anti-circumvention rule into more general laws such as competition law instead of relying on copyright law.

In the process of implementing the international obligations regarding protection of TPMs, Japan adopted a dual system to incorporate anti-circumvention rules. Copyright law only prohibits the circumvention of copy-control measures and trafficking of devices that can circumvent copy-control measures.[44] TPMs are defined under the Japanese Copyright Law as "measures to prevent or deter such acts as constitute infringements on moral rights or copyright or neighboring

[44] Yuko Noguchi, "Anti-circumvention Regulation in Japan (1): Overview," available at http://cyberlaw.stanford.edu/blogs/noguchi/archives003260.shtml (visited Mar 8, 2010); "Anti-circumvention Regulation in Japan (2): Direct Circumvention Regulation," available at http://cyberlaw.stanford.edu/blogs/noguchi/archives003261.shtml (visited Mar 8, 2010); "Anti-circumvention Regulation in Japan (3): Anti-device Regulation," available at http://cyberlaw.stanford.edu/blogs/noguchi/archives003262.shtml (visited May 17, 2014).

rights,"[45] because the Japanese government did not plan to grant copyright owners a right to control access to copyright works. As copyright owners do not have rights to control access to their works under the traditional copyright regime, a monopoly originating from the protection of access-control TPMs is avoided. In addition, the anti-device rule in Japan narrows down the scope of what technologies count as circumvention devices, as the regulations only prohibit trafficking of devices whose principal function is circumventing TPMs.[46] The regulatory prohibition only applies to the trafficking of circumvention devices to the public and not to the trafficking of devices to private persons.[47]

The banning of the trafficking of devices that facilitate circumvention of access-control technological measures is regulated under the Unfair Competition Prevention Law based on the rationale of competition law rather than copyright law.[48] The Japanese competition law also contains an anti-device provision for copy-control measures, which overlaps with the copyright law. The competition law extends the protection of copyright works to public-domain material as long as the material has commercial value for fair competition. Therefore, not only do copyright owners benefit from anti-device rule under the competition law, but so do entrepreneurs who adopt TPMs to protect their commercial intangible assets.

Inclusion of protection of access-control technological measures in competition law rather than copyright law, as enacted in Japan, does not impose restrictions on non-infringing uses of copyright works, as fair or other non-infringing uses are often for personal or private purposes that do not significantly influence the fair competition in the market and the potential benefits generated from the commercial use of the works. As explained in the report released by the Japanese TPMs protection working group in 2010, whether access-control measures that do not prevent the reproduction of copyright works should be protected under copyright law depends on whether the exclusive rights of copyright owners should be expanded so that right holders can control acts that were not covered by exclusive rights previously [15]. The issue of whether to include protection on access-control TPMs concerns the impact on the whole copyright system. It is therefore not appropriate to hastily make a conclusion on this issue.

3.4.5 Suggestions for the New Round of Reform Regarding Anti-circumvention Rules in China

In the Second Modified Draft of Chinese Copyright Law, Chapter Six contains four articles to grant protection to TPMs and DRM information. Article 64 defines TPMs and rights management information. TPMs refer to "effective technologies, devices

[45] Copyright Law of Japan, s 1, Art 2(XX), available at http://www.cric.or.jp/english/clj/cl1.html (visited May 17, 2014).

[46] Noguchi, "Anti-circumvention Regulation in Japan" (n 44 above).

[47] Noguchi, "Anti-circumvention Regulation in Japan" (n 44 above).

[48] Noguchi, "Anti-circumvention Regulation in Japan" (n 44 above).

or components used by right owners to prevent or restrict reproducing, browsing, appreciating, running or making available through information network a work, performance, phonogram product or computer program." Compared with the TPMs definition provided by the 2006 Regulation, the provision in the Modified Draft adds reproduction as one of the acts controlled by TPMs. The definition of rights management information is the same as that of the 2006 Regulation.

Article 65 is the anti-circumvention rule which prohibits intentional circumvention or sabotage of technological measures or intentional manufacturing, importing, or making available to the public, devices, or components mainly used to circumvent or sabotage technological measures or intentional providing other persons with technical devices to circumvent or sabotage technological measures. Different from the 2006 Regulation which only protects the right to network dissemination of information, the adoption of TPMs by right owners granted by the Modified Draft extends to protect all copyright and neighboring rights. Similarly, under Article 66, the prohibition of intentionally removing or altering rights management information without permission of right owners and making available to the public a work, performance, or phonogram production with knowledge or reasonable grounds to know that rights management information has been removed or altered without permission of right owners does not only restrict to works only offered through information network, but rather extend to all works available through a variety of ways.

Article 67 regulates four categories of exceptions to the circumventing acts of technological measures, including classroom teaching and scientific research, making available to the blind persons published written works for nonprofit purposes in such particular way which is perceptible to the blind, fulfillment of official duties by state organs in compliance with administrative or judicial procedure, and security testing.

Under Chapter Seven "Exercise of the Rights," in order to ban the infringing acts mentioned in Articles 65 and 66, a specific provision Article 74 offers administrative punishment such as warning, confiscating the illegal gain, or confiscating the equipment or component that is mainly used to circumvent or sabotage technological measures and, in serious circumstances, confiscating relevant material and equipment and devices, and imposing a fine, as well as criminal punishment if crimes are found.

There is no doubt that the Modified Drafts make progress in the expansion of the adoption of TPMs to protect the right to network dissemination of information to all copyright and neighboring rights, and they clearly include copying as one of the acts controlled by TPMs. The Modified Drafts, however, still seriously restrict reasonable access and exploitation of copyright works protected by TPMs. The prohibition of circumventing both access and copy controls and of the trafficking of circumvention devices severely limits the public's privilege to enjoy fair use or fair dealing. The four kinds of exceptions offered by the Modified Drafts confine the non-infringing uses to a very narrow scope and cannot contain all possible reasonable exceptions. More revision should be made to alleviate the restrictions brought by the anti-circumvention rule on fair use or fair dealing, competition and consumers' right of notice and privacy.

First, the definition of TPMs should be simplified and clarified in Chinese copyright law. TPMs should simply refer to effective technologies, devices or components used by right owners to prevent access and reproduction of copyright works without prior authorization, because a series of acts such as browsing, appreciating, running or making available through information network can be embodied in the general classification of the two categories of acts, namely, access and reproduction. In addition, such simplified language is consistent with the words defining TPMs in many other jurisdictions and will make the terminology easily understood. Emphasis should also be added to point out that TPMs under the copyright law protection are only installed to guarantee copyright owners' legitimate interests under copyright law.

Second, a general exception should be incorporated into Chinese anti-circumvention law, explicitly articulating that anti-circumvention rule will not constrain or impede limitations and exceptions to the exclusive rights of copyright owners. The general exception should be able to embody all potential situations that may be deemed fair or non-infringing under the digital network environment and guide judicial decisions on whether or not the questionable acts of circumvention or the trafficking of circumvention devices violate the copyright law. In addition, Chinese copyright law could encourage copyright owners to implement TPMs that guarantee minimum use to be installed in certain kinds of copyright works, such as literary works, so that users can access and read the table of contents and a few pages to determine whether they would like to purchase the works or not.

Third, further explanation and definition should be given to liability for circumvention devices. The prohibition on trafficking of circumvention devices should only apply to devices that are primarily designed or produced for the purpose of circumventing a TPM, have only limited commercially significant purpose or use other than to circumvent, and are marketed to be used to circumvent. Provisions of devices that are not primarily designed for circumvention and have commercially significant purposes other than mere circumvention should not be banned, even though the devices may be occasionally used to circumvent TPMs.

Finally, the judicial system and other areas of law should coordinate in establishing copyright legislation in order to alleviate the negative effects of the anti-circumvention rules. The Supreme Court of China should release relevant judicial interpretations to specify the norms that courts should comply with when making decisions in TPM circumvention cases. Moreover, China should consider whether to adopt the anti-circumvention model of Japan, regulating anti-circumvention of access controls only in competition law.

3.5 Conclusion

With the rapid growth of digital technology and right holders' desire for protecting their intellectual property against infringement, a large number of TPMs are used by copyright industries and product manufacturers to control the access and use of copyright material, office supplies, or housewares. The widespread adoption of TPMs impedes permissible use of copyright works and fair competition. The adoption of anti-circumvention rules in both international copyright conventions and domestic copyright statutes among major jurisdictions hinders the flow of information and normal operation of the market, because of the unbalanced protection of access-control technological measures and the prohibition on manufacturing and dissemination of circumvention devices. The widespread installation of TPMs and importation of anti-circumvention law result in an imbalance of interests between copyright owners and public users. It will be a disaster if the development of technology cannot appropriately accommodate the rights of users and future creators, creating an environment where the intellectual property system intercepts every unauthorized use.

Therefore, it is time to rethink current anti-circumvention laws and to revise the mechanism in a more balanced direction between copyright holder and public user. As Professor Yu has argued, "intellectual property protection is important, but not more important than how we live our daily life" [2, p. 77]. The design of new mechanism regarding DRM and TPMs protection should consider both consumers' interests and the feasibility of implementing such mechanism in less developed societies such as China. Several proposals have been suggested in this chapter with the goal of recovering the balance in the copyright system, including implementing a technical design which allows minimal uses; a legislative design that imposes prerequisites on protection of TPMs and a general exception for circumvention of TPMs; a judicial design that imposes judges' discretion on litigations regarding circumvention of TPMs case by case; and the design outside the intellectual property regime which recommends the inclusion of access-control technological measures into more general legal systems such as competition law.

References

1. Lichtman, D. G. (2006). *Defusing DRM* (John M. Olin Law & Economics Working Paper No. 282 (2nd Series)). Available at http://papers.ssrn.com/sol3/papers.cfm?abstract_id=883676. Visited 2 Oct 2011.
2. Yu, P. K. (2006–2007). Anticircumvention and anti-anticircumvention. *Denver University Law Review, 84*, 13–77.
3. Samuelson, P. (1996). Towards more sensible anti-circumvention regulations. Available at http://people.ischool.berkeley.edu/~pam/papers/fincrypt2.pdf. Visited 2 Oct 2011.
4. Efroni, Z. (2011). Anticircumvention laws. In Efroni, Z. (Ed.) *Access-right: The future of digital copyright law*. Oxford/New York: Oxford University Press.
5. Borland, J. Student faces suits over key to CD locks. *CNET News* (9 October 2003). Available at http://news.cnet.com/2100-1025-5089168.html. Visited 2 Oct 2011.
6. US Copyright Office. (1998). The Digital Millennium Copyright Act of 1998: US Copyright Office Summary. Available at http://www.copyright.gov/legislation/dmca.pdf. Visited 1 July 2011.
7. Tian, Y. (2009). *Rethinking intellectual property: The political economy of copyright protection in the digital era*. London: Routledge-Cavendish.
8. Reichman, J. H., Dinwoodie, G. B., & Samuelson, P. (2007). A reverse notice and takedown regime to enable public interest uses of technically protected copyrighted works. *Berkeley Technology Law Journal, 22*, 981–1006.

9. Besek, J. M. (2004). Anti-circumvention laws and copyright: A report from the Kernochan Center for Law, Media and Arts. *Columbia Journal of Law & Arts, 27*, 385–519.
10. Khanna, D. S. (2013). Phone unlocking made legal. Available at http://www.nationalreview.com/article/349379/phone-unlocking-made-legal. Visited 25 June 2013.
11. Band, J. (2013). Cell phone unlocking: A legal primer. Available at http://www.districtdispatch.org/wp-content/uploads/2013/03/band-cell-phone-unlocking-08mar13.pdf. Visited 4 Nov 2013.
12. Samuelson, P. (2003, April). DRM {and, or, vs.} the Law. *Communications of the ACM, 46*(4), 41–45.
13. Samuelson, P., & Schultz, J. (2007). Should copyright owners have to give notice of their use of technical protection measures? *Journal on Telecommunications and High Technology Law, 6*, 41–76.
14. Burk, D. L. (2003). Anticircumvention misuse. *UCLA Law Review, 50*, 1095–1140.
15. Wang, Q. (2011). The justification of protection on technological measures in the copyright law. *Chinese Journal of Law, 4*, 86–103 (in Chinese).
16. House of Representatives Standing Committee on Legal and Constitutional Affairs. (1999). Advisory report on Copyright Amendment (Digital Agenda) Bill 1999 (Para 4.13, p. 60). Available at http://www.aph.gov.au/parliamentary_business/committees/house_of_representatives_committees?url=/laca/digitalagenda/contents.htm. Visited 10 Oct 2011.
17. Hoffer, A. (2011, Summer). A matter of access: How bypassing DRM does not always violate the DMCA. *Washington Journal of Law, Technology & Arts, 7*(1), 13–25. Available at http://digital.law.washington.edu/dspace-law/bitstream/handle/1773.1/1049/7WJLTA013.pdf?sequence=5. Visited 10 Oct 2011.

Chapter 4
Establishing Certainty About Liability for Internet Service Providers and Safe Harbor Regulations

4.1 Introduction

Copyright works are often distributed through technological and media intermediaries. Books are commonly available to public readers because of the invention of the printing press and the establishment of publishing companies. Songs, TV programs, and movies are available to a large number of listeners and viewers because of the birth of sound recorders, radios, televisions, satellites, and movie theaters. The development of computers and digital technology and the emergence of the Internet in the late twentieth century have greatly changed how people are accessing and distributing copyright works. In the digital network world, anyone who has access to a computer and the Internet can easily make multiple perfect copies of the original copyright work in very little time and distribute either the original work or the copies by uploading them onto a website or emailing them as attachments to friends. Moreover, skilled digital technology users can easily revise, modify, and adapt copyright works by using different technological tools. When connected via the digital network, either the original or the derivative work can be easily found due to the strong searching and linking capabilities of Internet resources. Peer-to-peer file-sharing technology and portable electronic devices, such as MP3s and iPods, have further increased the reproduction and distribution of copyright works. These new technologies allow users to make works available to the public as they please. Intermediaries themselves do not distribute copyright works.

Prior to the emergence of digital network technology, it was possible for copyright owners to find and track copyright infringers as well as address piracy either through administrative or judicial procedures, because infringers in the pre-Internet world needed time and effort to produce pirated copies and find appropriate channels to sell them. They are companies or individuals whose identity can be confirmed. Due to the human and financial resources necessary for the production of counterfeit goods, the number of copyright infringers was not that large compared to the number of legal consumers of copyright works. In contrast, with the facilitation of digital network technology, any Internet surfer can easily infringe copyright

J.J. Hua, *Toward A More Balanced Approach: Rethinking and Readjusting Copyright Systems in the Digital Network Era*, DOI 10.1007/978-3-662-43517-5_4,

works by simply clicking the computer mouse and uploading or downloading copyright works, as long as their activities are not authorized by the relevant copyright owners. Peer-to-peer file-sharing technology can allow thousands of copyright works to be uploaded and downloaded simultaneously. Therefore, it will not be that convenient and easy for copyright owners to sanction and sue every individual infringer. Looking for every copyright infringer is not only costly and time-consuming, but under certain situations, it will be impossible for copyright owners to confirm the true identity of the infringer because of the anonymity in the virtual world. In order to safeguard their rights and interests, copyright owners, especially the powerful copyright industries, have begun to take action against intermediaries, mostly the ISPs that provide technologies and devices which facilitate infringement activity. They not only seek for judicial judgments that favor their standpoint but also continuously lobby legislature to enact new laws that regulate the infringing liability of intermediaries.

The United States is one such a country that reflects the continuing battle of copyright owners against the intermediaries. It established the indirect infringing liability of ISPs through a couple of influential cases and enacted the DMCA which contains a particular section on ISP liability related to material online. The indirect liability model of the United States has influenced many jurisdictions including China through legal transplant or bilateral free trade agreements. China enacted the 2006 Regulation by following the US legislative model to regulate the infringing liability of ISPs and adding provisions specific to the Chinese legal and social environment. The enactment of the regulation indirectly reflects the rapid increase of Internet use in China and the necessity of establishing the liability of Chinese ISPs.

After connection to the Internet was made possible in 1994, Internet use in China has quickly spread over the country year by year. According to the Statistical Survey Report on Internet Development in China issued by the China Internet Network Information Center (CNNIC) each year, the number of Internet users in 2000 was 22.5 million and grew to 111 million in 2005 [1, 2]. The increase in the number of Internet users remained robust in the following years. By June of 2011, the total number of Internet users reached 485 million people and the penetration rate was 36.2 % [3]. Entertainment and enjoyment of copyright contents remain as the most important use of the Internet. The number of subscribers of online music reached 382 million with a subscription rate of 78.7 %[1] [3]. The number of online video subscribers reached 301 million with a subscription rate of 62.1 %. These statistics demonstrate the necessity and importance of establishing certainty and predictability about the liability for ISPs and amending this liability to balance the interests of copyright owners and Internet users. On the one hand, lack of invigilation and legal regulation of ISP liability will induce flooding of piracy online. On the other hand, enforcing overly strict liability for ISPs will suffocate data transmission and information dissemination, thus intervening with the enjoyment of copyright contents by Internet users.

[1] *See* China Internet Network Information Center [3].

This chapter intends to provide proposals to establish certainty about liability for ISPs and alleviating current tendencies to aggravate ISP liability in general and recommend suggestions for China's digital copyright reform on ISP liability in particular by reviewing and analyzing existing copyright systems in terms of ISP liability among different jurisdictions. The second part of this chapter will examine the definition of ISPs and the importance of establishing certainty and predictability about indirect liability. The third part of this chapter will analyze the safe harbor system and contributory and vicarious liability developed through American court judgments. Certain elements in contributory and vicarious liability will be examined in detail, as these elements have been incorporated into digital copyright statutes. This part will also briefly analyze the authorization and joint tortfeasor liability developed from cases in Commonwealth jurisdictions, such as Australia and the United Kingdom, which will be compared with contributory and vicarious liability so as to conclude the consistent disciplines that are adopted to regulate ISP liability. After reviewing the rules and laws developed from common law cases, the fourth part of this chapter will examine the statutory requirements with respect to ISP liability and its limitations. The statutes will be mainly from the United States, China, and Hong Kong, as the combination of statutory regulations in these jurisdictions represents a relatively complete regime for ISP liability. The fifth part of this chapter will examine the recent development in ISP liability, including the "graduated response" policy—the new development on aggravating ISP liability by adding new conditions for safe harbors in some jurisdictions, such as France, and the ISP injunctions granted or refused by the courts in Europe. This part will argue against the graduated response policy, as it will bring about more negative influence on information dissemination and freedom of expression than its positive impact on piracy control, and will discuss the proportionality that courts should take into consideration when deciding whether to grant ISP injunctions. The final part of this chapter will provide suggestions for proposals to amend current digital copyright laws on ISP liability in general and China's digital copyright reform in particular so as to balance the interests of copyright owners, intermediaries such as ISPs and Internet users, and establish certainty about liability for ISPs.

4.2 Introduction on Internet Service Providers

4.2.1 Definition of Internet Service Providers

The first international copyright conventions that dealt with copyright challenges brought on by digital network technology are the WIPO Internet Treaties. However, these treaties do not include specific ISP liability regulations and leave room for member states to decide. Despite room to decide as pertaining to ISP liability, the WCT grants copyright owners the right of communication to the public by wire or wireless means so that "members of the public may access the works from a place and at a time individually chosen by them."[2] This provision confirms the right of control by copyright owners over the distribution of their works under a digital network environment. Any activity that allows the copyright contents to be made available to the public without authorization by the copyright owners is infringement. However, in order to avoid the overexpansion of exclusive rights enjoyed by copyright owners, and promote the development of technology, the Concerning Article 8 in the Agreed Statements Concerning the WCT particularly precludes the "provision of physical facilities for enabling or making a communication"[3] as exercise of the right of communication to the public within the meaning from the WCT or the Berne Convention. Such a provision indirectly provides safe harbors for technological intermediaries.

Among the member states of the WIPO Internet Treaties, the United States is the earliest country which enacted new copyright statutes to specifically deal with digital network challenges. Among the five titles of the DMCA, Title II, the "Online Copyright Infringement Liability Limitation Act," specifically addresses the issue of ISP liability and creates limitations on infringing liability for certain types of activities by ISPs. Title II of the DMCA has been incorporated into the US Copyright Act as Section 512, titled "Limitations on Liability Relating to Material Online." Under the definition of Section 512, the term "service provider" means "a provider of online services or network access, or the operator of facilities therefor."[4] However, there is no further definition of "online services." Thus, this definition of a "service provider" is vague. There are two possible explanations. The first explanation is that the term "online services" could mean any service offered online, including making copyrighted contents available to the public [4]. Under this interpretation, anyone who operates a website could be an ISP. The second explanation is that the term should only mean services specific to being online [4]. Under this interpretation, only companies who host websites are ISPs; those who provide contents are not, as making contents available to the public is not Internet specific. One can provide copyright works through various channels such as paper publications, radio or television broadcasting, and online video broadcasting. The Internet is one of the many media forms that can publish works, but not the sole medium.

Many defendants in ISP liability cases fall under the second definition. Both in the influential case *Sony Corp. v. Universal City Studios Inc.* and later cases that involved peer-to-peer file-sharing technology, defendants who were deemed as ISPs merely supplied consumers with the tools and technology to facilitate reproduction and distribution of copyright works. The copyright contents were provided by third parties, such as TV program companies or Internet subscribers. In a Chinese nationwide influential case, *Music Copyright Society of China (MCSC) v. NetEase Inc. and China Mobile Beijing Ltd.*, trialed by the Beijing Second Intermediate People's

[2] WIPO Copyright Treaty, Art 8.

[3] Agreed Statements Concerning the WIPO Copyright Treaty, Concerning Article 8.

[4] The US Copyright Act of 1976, s 512(k)(1)(B).

Court in 2002,[5] the first defendant NetEase was sued for providing the music works of MCSC on its website for mobile phone users to download as phone ringtones. The second defendant, China Mobile Beijing, was sued for facilitating downloading by mobile phone users. The final judgment ruled against NetEase and for China Mobile Beijing primarily based on the reason that China Mobile could not select, modify, or delete the transmitted information. As the first case in which an infrastructure service provider acted as co-defendant in an online copyright infringement issue, Chinese copyright law academia and practitioners consequently paid close attention. Judge Zhou Xiaobin of the Beijing Second Intermediate People's Court drew the conclusion from this case that Internet infrastructure service providers could be divided into three major categories, that is, Internet content provider (ICP), Internet service provider (ISP), and Internet apparatus provider (IAP). ICPs select, edit, and upload information contents; ISPs facilitate the transmission of information without selecting or editing the contents; and IAPs provide essential apparatuses for network operation. The academic classification of service providers influenced by the Chinese court judgment also demonstrates that ISPs are mostly referred to as website operators who help transmit information rather than provide contents.

Besides the statutory definition of ISPs and indication from the judgments, Section 512 of the DMCA also lists four categories of ISP conducts under which ISPs can be protected from copyright infringement liability subject to certain conditions. The four categories of ISP conducts are (1) "transitory digital network communications" which limit the liability of ISPs in circumstances where the provider merely acts as a data conduit, transmitting digital information from one point on a network to another at someone else's request; (2) "system caching" which limits the liability of ISPs that temporarily store the transmitted material made available online by a person other than the ISPs and deliver the material to the expected subscriber; (3) "storage of information on systems or networks at direction of users" which limits the liability of ISPs for infringing material on websites hosted on their systems; and (4) "information location tools" which limit the liability of ISPs that link users to a site that contains infringing material, such as search engines and online directories [5].

China has followed the US legislative model to regulate ISP liability and limitations. Under the 2006 Regulation, there are four categories of ISP conducts under liability limitations subject to certain conditions. Similar to the four categories in Section 512 of the DMCA, the four categories in the Chinese regulation are (1) ISPs which provide automatic access or automatic transmission of copyright works according to the instructions of web subscribers,[6] (2) ISPs which automatically

[5] *Music Copyright Society of China (MCSC) v. Guangzhou NetEase Inc. and China Mobile Beijing Ltd. (in Chinese)* Beijing Second Intermediate People's Court (2002) Er Zhong Min Chu Zi No. 03119.

[6] Regulation on the Protection of the Right to Network Dissemination of Information, Art 20.

store the works supplied by other ISPs and automatically transmit the works to the subscribers according to the technical arrangement with the purpose to promote network transmission efficiency,[7] (3) ISPs which provide information memory space for subscribers to supply works,[8] and (4) ISPs which provide searching or linking services to service recipients.[9] Although the expressions are different from the corresponding provisions in the DMCA, the four categories of ISP conducts in the 2006 Regulation in fact correspond to the four categories of Section 512 in the DMCA, respectively. These statutory classifications of ISP conducts from another aspect indicate that most ISPs at issue are those who merely function as data conduits for facilitating information transmission and dissemination, especially ISPs that want to argue for protection from infringement liability.

4.2.2 Importance of Establishing Certainty About Liability and Limitations for Internet Service Providers

The definition and analysis with regard to ISPs show that when ISPs are alleged to commit copyright infringement, the liability that they shoulder is secondary or indirect liability. Since ISPs do not provide copyright contents, they are liable for facilitating the direct copyright infringement of their Internet subscribers.

Why is it necessary and important to establish certainty and predictability for the indirect liability of technological intermediaries such as ISPs? There are two reasons. On the one hand, under certain circumstances, it is too costly and difficult for copyright owners to fight against direct infringers, especially when the number of direct infringers is high and direct infringers cannot be easily identified. Indirect liability becomes the only efficient and appropriate means to compensate for the losses of copyright owners. Without indirect liability, copyright owners cannot effectively enforce their exclusive rights in some situations. Therefore, it is necessary to look into the indirect liability of technological intermediaries. On the other hand, digital network technology is a double-edged sword. It can be used for both legal and illegal purposes. It is unfair to hold ISPs liable for the infringement activities of third parties if ISPs are not at fault. ISPs that are strictly held for liability will unreasonably disrupt legitimate activities in information dissemination and impede the development of new technology. Therefore, limitation of indirect liability and safe harbors should be established for ISPs so as to better balance the interests of copyright owners and technological intermediaries and protect the free flow of information.

---

[7] Regulation on the Protection of the Right to Network Dissemination of Information, Art 21.

[8] Regulation on the Protection of the Right to Network Dissemination of Information, Art 22.

[9] Regulation on the Protection of the Right to Network Dissemination of Information, Art 23.

4.3 Internet Service Provider Liability and Safe Harbor Rules Established by Common Law Cases

4.3.1 Sony Safe Harbor Rule

American cases have considerable influence on establishing ISP liability and safe harbors to protect technological intermediaries. Prior to the enactment of the DMCA, the most influential case was *Sony Corporation of America v. Universal City Studios Inc.* which established the famous safe harbor system for technological intermediaries and is still supported by many telecommunication industries and scholars today.

In this case, Universal sued Sony for indirect copyright infringement by claiming that Sony's new invention, the Betamax video cassette recorder (VCR), would result in rampant unauthorized reproduction of their copyrighted motion pictures or TV programs.[10] In 1981, the Ninth Circuit Court of Appeals reached a judgment in favor of Universal, holding that Sony was liable for contributory infringement because of its actual knowledge of the unauthorized copying of TV programs by VCR user for time-shifting purposes and the primary infringement use of VCRs.[11] In the appellate litigation of 1984, the Supreme Court reversed the decision, ruling that Sony was not liable for contributory infringement since time-shifting was fair use and the VCR could be substantially used for non-infringing purposes.[12] The final judgment of the *Sony* case borrowed a staple article of commerce rule from patent law to mitigate the holders of intellectual property and technology developers.

The US Copyright Act did not expressly render anyone liable for infringement committed by another, when the *Sony* case was carried on.[13] "If secondary liability is to be imposed on Sony, it must rest on the fact that it has sold equipment with constructive knowledge of the fact that its customers may use that equipment to make unauthorized copies of copyrighted material."[14] However, there was "no precedent in the law of copyright for the imposition of vicarious liability on such a theory" at the time.[15] The Supreme Court noticed the analogy of such a problem in patent law. The US patent law expressly regards active inducement of infringement of a patent as contributory infringement. However, contributory infringement is only applicable to "the knowing sale of a component especially made for use in connection with a particular patent."[16] The sale of a staple article or commodity of

---

[10] *Universal City Studios Inc. v. Sony Corporation of America* 659 F2d 963 (9th Cir. 1981).

[11] Ibid.

[12] *Sony Corporation of America v. Universal City Studios Inc.* 464 U.S. 417 (1984).

[13] Ibid., p. 434.

[14] *Sony Corp. of America* (n 12 above), p. 439.

[15] *Sony Corp. of America* (n 12 above).

[16] *Sony Corp. of America* (n 12 above), p. 440.

commerce suitable for substantial non-infringing use will not result in contributory infringement liability,[17] even if the seller actually knows that the article will be probably used for infringement purposes. Uses will be deemed insubstantial in patent law if they are "far-fetched, illusory, impractical, or merely experimental."[18] The courts borrowed the rule in the patent law to explain copyright indirect infringement liability and established the Sony safe harbor that technology developers or sellers should not be contributory liable if the technology will have substantial non-infringing uses. By drawing up such a conclusive rule, the court aimed to reduce the monopolies of the entertainment industry on articles of commerce that are not subjects of copyright protection.

The Sony safe harbor has been supported by scholars in the face of indirect infringement liability issues brought on by technology development. Even today, many commentators argue that the Sony safe harbor should apply to new digital technologies such as peer-to-peer file-sharing technology. As scholars of the Samuelson Law, Technology & Public Policy Clinic at the University of California, Berkeley, explained in the Interest of Amici Curiae, "the Sony safe harbor further promotes business certainty and judicial efficiency because of its simplicity, clarity, predictability, and objectivity. It does not require delving into technology developers' states of mind; it does not require extensive evidence or speculation about current and future uses of technologies and in what proportion each use exists or is likely to evolve; and it does not require courts to consider what other kinds of technologies might have been developed instead. Sony simply asks courts to determine whether the technology has or is capable of substantial non-infringing uses."[19]

4.3.2 Contributory and Vicarious Liability Rules

In a couple of cases later, technological intermediaries were sued for providing peer-to-peer file-sharing technology for Internet users to freely upload and download copyrighted music works without authorization by the copyright owners. The defendants relied on the Sony safe harbor to argue for protection from infringing liability based on the fact that peer-to-peer file-sharing technology will have substantial non-infringing uses.

In *A&M Records Inc. v. Napster Inc.*, Napster was sued for facilitating users to make available MP3 music files stored on personal computer hard drives for others to reproduce, search for music files stored in other computers of users and disseminate

---

[17] *Sony Corp. of America* (n 12 above). *Also see* 35 US Code Section 271(c).

[18] 5 Donald S. Chisum, *Chisum on Patents: A Treatise on the Law of Patentability, Validity and Infringement* Section 17.03[3] (2004).

[19] Brief of Deirdre K. Mulligan, as Amici Curiae in Support of Reversal of Stephen J. Barrett M.D., ET. AL v. Ilena Rosenthal, No. S122953 (Supreme Court of California), available at https://www.eff.org/sites/default/files/filenode/Barrett_v_Rosenthal/law_professors_amicus_brief.pdf (visited Aug 19, 2011).

copies from one computer to another via the Internet.[20] Napster defended its immunity from copyright infringement liability based on statutory limitations of ISP liability and the Sony safe harbor. The court rejected Napster's safe harbor defense and ruled against them, because Napster knew or should have known that there would be rampant unauthorized transmission of copyrighted works facilitated by its technology and system.[21] The active inducement of copyright infringement undermined the possibility of safe harbor protection for Napster despite that the peer-to-peer file-sharing technology could have been used for legal purposes.

In the *Aimster Copyright Litigation*, Aimster was also sued by the recording industry for facilitating the swapping of digital copies of music works. More indirectly than Napster, Aimster users swapped music files in an online chat room enabled by an instant messaging service.[22] However, this kind of file sharing did not shelter Aimster from infringing liability, because Aimster actually knew about the infringement activity of its users, and its business model was based on the volume of infringement uses of its technology. In addition, compared with the serious harm on the interests of the copyright owners by massive illegal file swapping, the cost of preventing the infringement activity was relatively small.[23] Aimster could not prove that eliminating or substantially reducing the infringing of its customers would be disproportionately costly.[24] Therefore, the court also ruled against Aimster despite its defense based on the safe harbor.

Although subsequent ISPs provided file-sharing technology more surreptitiously, they could not avoid being liable for the copyright infringement of their clients either. In *Metro-Goldwyn-Mayer Studio Inc. v. Grokster Ltd.*, Grokster was also sued for indirect copyright infringement due to the unauthorized file sharing of copyrighted works by their clients. In contrast to the services provided by Napster and Aimster, the software provided by Grokster enabled users to directly swap copyrighted files with each other.[25] There was not a centralized indexing system that facilitated the linking of individual users. Grokster knew about the infringing activity of its customers and financially benefited from the infringing uses. However, when examining Grokster's material contribution and supervision capability, the district court emphasized on their decentralized network system and thus ruled in favor of Grokster. In its ruling, the court also mentioned the potential non-infringing uses of Grokster technology, such as distribution of copyrighted works under authorization or of public domain works.[26] In the appellate litigation, the Ninth Circuit confirmed the decision of the district court, believing that the lack of control over the direct infringement of the users and the existence of potential non-infringing uses were sufficient enough to protect Grokster from secondary liability. Nevertheless, in the final judgment

---

[20] *A&M Records Inc. v. Napster Inc.* 239F.3d 1004 (9th Cir. 2001).

[21] Ibid.

[22] In re Aimster Copyright Litigation 334F.3d 643 (7th Cir. 2003).

[23] Ibid.

[24] *Aimster* (n 22 above).

[25] *Metro-Goldwyn-Mayer Studios Inc. v. Grokster Ltd.* 380F.3d 1154 (9th Cir. 2004).

[26] Ibid.

reached by the Supreme Court, the decisions of the lower courts were overturned. The Supreme Court ruled against Grokster, explaining that Grokster's intent of active inducement of copyright infringement could not shelter them under the safe harbor and the fact that the so-called potential non-infringing uses only accounted for 10 % of all uses also refuted Grokster's defense under the safe harbor.[27]

In all of the abovementioned cases, the courts denied the claim by ISPs to use the Sony safe harbor and relevant statutory limitations on liability and ruled in favor of the recording industries. The most important reason is that ISPs in these cases could supervise or control the consumption of their services by Internet users and actively discourage the infringing activity. In contrast, Sony was not able to supervise or control the use of their products after the Betamax VCRs were sold, although Sony could expect that such products would be used for infringing purposes. Therefore, ISPs that provide peer-to-peer file-sharing technology should be rendered liable for direct copyright infringement by their Internet users despite the potential non-infringing uses of the technology. Vicarious and contributory liability which are applicable to ISPs have been developed from these judicial decisions.

To be held liable under the contributory liability rule, three terms need to be satisfied: (1) there should be direct infringement by a primary infringer; (2) the ISP should know or have awareness of the direct infringement; and (3) the ISP should have made a material contribution to the infringement. To be held liable for vicarious infringement, there are also three terms that need to be met: (1) there should be direct infringement by a primary infringer; (2) the ISP obtained direct financial benefits from the primary infringer; and (3) the ISP has the right and ability to supervise or control the activity of the primary infringer. In the three terms, the ISPs were held either contributory or vicariously liable for the infringement of their Internet users because they all knew about the illegal reproduction and distribution of copyrighted works by their subscribers, actively endorsed and contributed to the infringement, and had the ability to cease the infringement activities. Some ISPs such as Aimster even obtain financial benefits from the infringing uses.

Although vicarious and contributory liability have developed from judicial decisions, certain factors including the knowledge of ISPs of direct infringement, obtaining direct financial benefits from the direct infringer and having the ability to supervise or control direct infringement, have been incorporated into both American and Chinese digital copyright statutes and regulations. For example, under the third and fourth categories of ISP conducts in Section 512 of the DMCA, namely, the "storage of information on systems or networks at direction of users" and "information location tools," ISPs must satisfy certain conditions in order to be safeguarded from infringing liability. These conditions are as follows: (1) the ISP does not have actual knowledge that the material or activity is infringing or, in the absence of such actual knowledge, is not aware of the fact that there is apparent infringing activity;[28] (2) the ISP does not receive any financial benefits that are directly attributable to the

[27] *Metro-Goldwyn-Mayer Studios Inc. v. Grokster Ltd.* 545 U.S. 913 (2005).

[28] The US Copyright Act of 1976, s 512(c)(1)(A) and s 512(d)(1).

infringing activity, if the ISP has the right and ability to control such activity;[29] and (3) upon receiving notification with regard to infringing activity, the ISP expeditiously removes or disables access to the alleged infringing material.[30] Similarly, in the third category of ISP conducts, the supplying of information memory space to subscribers, the 2006 Regulation of China had also established almost the same conditions for protection from liability: (1) the ISP does not know or have justifiable reasons to know about the infringing activities of the subscribers; (2) the ISP does not obtain any economic benefits from the infringing activity; and (3) the ISP removes the works in question upon receiving notice from the copyright owners.[31] Besides the requirement to expeditiously remove the alleged infringing material, other factors are a combination of vicarious and contributory liability established in American law cases. Detailed situations with regard to these factors need to be examined so as to establish certainty and predictability of ISP liability and safe harbors.

4.3.2.1 Knowledge or Awareness of Direct Infringement

Although ISPs do not have the obligation to actively monitor subscribers in the use of their services, they should not have actual knowledge or awareness of the circumstances in which infringing activity is apparent. Once they have this knowledge or awareness, the ISPs should expeditiously remove or disable access to the material. Ignorance about the infringement will definitely not safeguard the liability of ISPs. ISPs should not have an awareness of the apparent infringement either. What constitutes apparent infringement thus becomes the determinative factor on whether the liability of ISPs can be safeguarded.

Professor Jane Ginsburg concluded in her article the possible situations under which infringement is deemed apparent in a couple of cases. These possible situations that "warrant service provider's vigilance might include abnormally and disproportionately high traffic to the area of the site where the alleged infringement is located, or the appearance of terms like 'pirated' or 'bootleg' in the name of the file" [4, p. 191]. In addition, if "the file title includes the name of a motion picture, television program, or sound recording of which the person or entity posting the content is obviously not the copyright owner" and the title is the subject of "repeated section 512(c) 'take down' notices" sent by copyright owners, such files are blatant enough for ISPs to note and take action [4, p. 192]. Under Chinese regulations, these situations can also be considered as justified circumstances in which ISPs would have knowledge about the infringement.

Further explanations regarding the constructive knowledge in China were included in the Provisions on Certain Issues Related to the Application of Law in the Trial of Civil Cases Involving Disputes over Infringement of the Right to Network Dissemination of Information (thereafter, the Provisions) which was released by the

[29] The US Copyright Act of 1976, s 512(c)(1)(B) and s 512(d)(2).

[30] The US Copyright Act of 1976, s 512(c)(1)(C)and s 512(d)(3).

[31] Regulation on the Protection of the Right to Network Dissemination of Information, Art 22.

Supreme Court in November 2012 and took effect from January 1, 2013. Article 9 of the Provisions lists several factors that should be considered by courts when determining the constructive knowledge of ISPs: (1) the capability of information administration that an ISP should have based on the nature and mode of services provided by the ISP and the possibility that such services may trigger infringement; (2) type and popularity of the works, performance, and audiovisual recordings disseminated and the degree of the obviousness of the infringement; (3) whether the ISP actively selects, edits, modifies, or recommends the works, performance, and audiovisual products; (4) whether the ISP has taken positive and reasonable measures to prevent infringement; (5) whether the ISP has set up convenient procedure to receive notifications concerning infringement and respond timely and reasonably to such notifications; (6) whether the ISP has taken reasonable measures against repeated infringing acts committed by the same user; and (7) other relevant factors. Such list of factors aims to interpret constructive knowledge from multi-perspectives, including notice and takedown procedure as well as adoption of technological measures by ISPs. It would be better implementable if detailed situations discussed above are used as examples to provide supplementary explanation of the obviousness of infringement.

However, in order not to impose excessive responsibility onto the ISPs, the American court decisions also expressively emphasized that "general knowledge that infringement is ubiquitous does not impose a duty on the service provider to monitor or search its services for infringement."[32] The provisions in China also denies ISPs' fault, if they do not conduct active examination of their subscribers' infringing activities.[33] In a word, mere knowledge of the prevalence of infringing activity in general is not enough to prove that the ISPs have actual knowledge or awareness of the infringement.[34] Knowledge and awareness should be specific to particular individual circumstances.[35] In addition, if the material offered by subscribers on its surface does not clearly reveal signs of infringement, such activity is not sufficiently apparent as infringing and service providers do not need to conduct further investigations [4].

4.3.2.2 Direct Financial Benefits from Direct Infringement

As to whether ISPs obtain direct financial benefits or any economic benefits from the primary infringement, the determinative factor is based on the relationship between the infringement and benefit.

[32] *Viacom International Inc. v. YouTube, Inc.* 718F.Supp.2d 514 (2010).

[33] Provisions on Certain Issues Related to the Application of Law in the Trial of Civil Cases Involving Disputes over Infringement of the Right to Network Dissemination of Information, Art 8.

[34] *Viacom* (n 32 above).

[35] *Viacom* (n 32 above).

When the benefits that the ISPs gain are immensely associated with the infringing activity of the subscribers, it will not be difficult to determine that these are direct benefits. For example, if advertising accepted by a website targets infringing material, then the benefit is very obvious [4]. However, when the benefit is not so closely related to the infringing activity, it will be more difficult to determine whether the benefit is direct or not. Also, by using website advertising as an example again, if the rates charged do not target the infringing material, but to the popularity of the material as a whole with the advertising, it cannot be simply assessed that there is a direct benefit by assuming that the infringing material enhances the overall popularity of the website [4]. Furthermore, the need to conduct an investigation on whether the website popularity is caused by infringing material will increase ISP liability, because further investigation will clearly inform ISPs or provide them with the awareness of infringement which previously was not so obvious. Actual knowledge or awareness will eliminate the safe harbor provision that these ISPs would have originally enjoyed.

Therefore, in order to safeguard proper safe harbor protection for ISPs, benefits to service providers need to be directly associated with the infringing material. Any ambiguity between financial benefit and infringing activity will mean that there are no "direct financial benefits." If copyright owners wish to request the assistance of ISPs to cease infringement, they will need to follow statutory procedures in forwarding copyright infringement notifications to the ISPs to start the process of information removal.

4.3.2.3 Right and Ability to Supervise or Control Infringing Activity

Even if an ISP had obtained direct financial benefits from the primary infringement, they cannot be denied safe harbor protection if they do not have the right and ability to control the infringing activity. The circumstances that influence whether ISPs have control over infringement can be interpreted in various ways. The first interpretation is that ISPs have "the right and ability to control" if they can block the use of their services for infringing purposes [4]. This interpretation is supported by the common law rule of vicarious liability. The second interpretation is that the mere blocking of access to the infringing material does not indicate that the ISPs have the ability to control [4] because "[the] ability to intervene before the infringing content is placed on the website" is also required under Section 512 of the DMCA [4].

In the first interpretation, the requirement for ISPs to have "the right and ability to control" will automatically disqualify them for safe harbor protection because under the notice and takedown regime, almost all ISPs are able to subsequently block access to alleged infringing material upon receiving notifications from the copyright owners. The simple interpretation of "the right and ability to control" as taking subsequent measures to cease infringement will result in most ISPs being held liable for the infringing activities of their subscribers. The second interpretation, however, is more appropriate to define the ability to control, since the ability to intervene before the infringing material is posted online also implies that the ISP has knowledge or awareness of the infringement. Therefore, it is better to interpret "the right and ability to control" as a prerequisite to intervene with the infringement of subscribers so as to comply with the combined immunities of indirect liability and safe harbors.

4.3.3 Authorization or Joint Tortfeasor Liability of Commonwealth Jurisdictions

Similar to vicarious and contributory liability, some of the Commonwealth jurisdictions, such as Australia, the United Kingdom, and Hong Kong, have also developed indirect liability doctrines, such as those that deal with authorization or joint tortfeasor liability for technological intermediaries through various cases and statutory supplements.

4.3.3.1 Liability by Authorization

In these Commonwealth jurisdictions, the infringement of the exclusive rights of copyright owners can be realized in two ways: direct and indirect. Technological intermediaries will be regarded as directly liable if they have a role in determining the content of the communication where copyright infringement is found. Even if the technological intermediaries do not play a part in determining the contents of the communication, they are indirectly liable if they have authorized infringing activity by third parties. "Authorization" for cases in both Australia and the United Kingdom is defined by the courts with an ordinary dictionary definition of "sanction[ing], approv[ing] and countenance[ing]."[36] After they analyzed various cases, Professors Jane Ginsburg and Sam Ricketson concluded that "authorization" in the Commonwealth judicial sense not only includes specific granting of permission but should also contain implications from the surrounding circumstances that allow a suspect to carry out an infringing act [6]. The inference may be determined case by case. In order to draw the correct implication from the actions of the defendants, relevant facts in each case should be very carefully examined [6].

Since liability by authorization may increase the possibility of holding the intermediaries indirectly liable, Australian courts have developed a series of common law rules to limit broad explanations with regard to issues around authorization or permission. First, in order to be liable for the copyright infringement of a third party, the alleged authorizer must have some ability to control the use of its services. In *University of New South Wales v. Moorhouse*, the defendant or the university was not held liable for providing photocopy machines in its library for making copies,

[36] *Falcon v. Famous Players Film Co. Ltd.* [1926] 2KB 474 (CA); *University of New South Wales v. Moorhouse* (1975) 133 CLR 1.

which was deemed to be infringing, because the university did not set up control mechanisms on who could use the copiers.[37] In later cases,[38] defendants were sued for manufacturing and offering tape-recording facilities for consumers to make infringement copies of sound recordings. However, none of these defendants were charged for liability by authorization, because they did not have any control over the use of their products after the sale. Thus, providing potential opportunities to commit infringement or encouraging the act of infringement is insufficient. There needs to be some actual association between the intermediaries and direct infringers. Secondly, the alleged authorizer must have some degree of knowledge of the infringement. The courts have refused to determine liability by authorization if no action was carried out because the defendant did not know or had any reason to suspect that an infringement act may have been carried out.[39] Otherwise, it will be concluded that the defendant had authorized the infringing activity, if he/she knew or had reason to suspect that infringing activity was being carried out or likely to be carried out.[40] The third rule may be inferred from the second rule with regard to the knowledge of the intermediaries about the infringement: if a defendant anticipates that infringing activity may take place due to the facilitation of his/her services and takes reasonable measures to avoid this from happening, he/she will thus not be held liable.

These rules developed by various cases were amended and incorporated into the Australia Copyright (Digital Agenda) Amendment Act in 2000 which revised the Australian copyright regime to adapt to the digital network environment. Under Section 36(1A) of this copyright act, several factors are listed which must be taken into consideration when judging whether a defendant has authorized any act that infringes copyright: (1) the extent (if any) of the person's power to prevent the infringement, (2) the nature of any relationship that exists between the person and the direct infringer, and (3) whether the person took any reasonable steps to prevent or avoid the infringement, including whether the person complied with any relevant industry codes of practice.[41] By codifying the rules developed in the various cases, the Copyright Amendment Act 2000 aims to establish legislative certainty on liability for authorizing infringements.[42]

Despite the different expressions, the Australian cases and statutory factors make liability by authorization more closely resemble vicarious and contributory liability under the US legal system. The first and third provisions of the statute focus on the ability of the intermediaries to control infringing activity and subsequent takedown action after finding out about the infringement. The second provision, the relationship

---

[37] *Falcon* and *University of New South Wales* (n 36 above).

[38] *WEA International Inc. v. Hanimex Corporation Ltd.* (1987) 10 IPR 349; *RCA Corp v. John Fairfax & Sons Ltd* (1982) RPC 91; *Australian Tape Manufacturers Ltd. v. Commonwealth of Australia* (1993) 25 IPR 1.

[39] *Australasian Performing Right Association Ltd. v. Jain* (1990) 18 IPR 663.

[40] *University of New South Wales v. Moorhouse* (1975) 133 CLR 1.

[41] Australia Copyright (Digital Agenda) Amendment Act 2000, s 36(1A).

[42] Explanatory Memorandum to the Digital Agenda Bill, paragraph 57.

between the intermediary and the direct infringer, implies many situations that need to be taken into consideration, such as whether the intermediary knows or is aware of the direct infringement or the intermediary gains financial benefits from the suspected infringing activity. For example, in cases that involve tape-recording, the relationship between the apparatus vendor and buyer comes to an end when the apparatus has been sold. However, under the digital network environment, the relationship between the providers of peer-to-peer file-sharing technology and subscribers continues, as long as the service providers maintain the administration of the websites and offer upgrades or technical assistance. The service providers may also continue a relationship with the subscribers if they are financially benefited from advertising which targets to the hits on the online material.

4.3.3.2 Joint Tortfeasor Liability

Joint tortfeasor liability is similar to contributory liability under the US common law, as it punishes the assisting, abetting, facilitating, and inducing of the commission of infringing acts [6]. However, joint tortfeasor liability is different in that there is an additional requirement for the participation of the intermediary with the direct infringer in furthering a common design to commit infringement, which narrows the scope of acts that can be deemed as indirect infringement because it is difficult to prove common design.

Under the principle of joint tortfeasor liability, the ISPs that provide peer-to-peer file-sharing technology will not be held liable for the infringement of their subscribers. The ISPs merely supply the technology and services for facilitating data transmission and information dissemination. Such technology can be used for both legitimate and illegitimate purposes. It will be quite difficult to determine the presence of a common design between ISPs and their subscribers with the aim to upload and download copyright files. However, liability by authorization is a different matter. Even though ISPs are not joint tortfeasor liable due to the absence of a common design with their subscribers, ISPs may be liable by authorization if they have reason to know and own the ability to prevent the infringement, but did not take any reasonable measures to stop the infringement. In other words, although joint tortfeasor liability limits the possibility of holding ISPs indirectly liable, liability by authorization restores this possibility by codifying conditions developed from various cases.

4.4 Internet Service Provider Liability and Safe Harbor Rules Established by Statutes

Besides the principles of indirect infringing liability and safe harbor rules developed from common law cases, legislatures among different jurisdictions have also created statutory conditions that limit the liability of ISPs. In order to be protected from vicarious or contributory liability or liability by authorization, ISPs must follow the statutory notice and takedown regime which was first legitimized in the US legal system.

4.4.1 Notice and Takedown Regime

Upon receiving proper notification from copyright owners under the notice and takedown regime, ISPs must promptly remove or block access to alleged infringing material identified in the notification. Once the takedown requirements have been immediately satisfied, an ISP is exempted from liability.

Section 512 in the DMCA of the United States has established detailed procedures on how ISPs receive notifications, the elements of a qualified notification, and the actions taken by ISPs after receiving proper notification. First, an ISP must designate an agent to receive notifications of infringement claims. The ISP shall make available to the public both on its website and by providing to the Copyright Office the name, address, and contact information of the designated agent.[43] Secondly, the infringed party must file a qualified notification including a list of specified items to the agent that informs the ISP about the infringement. The list of items that contribute to an effective notification includes (1) the signature of the person authorized to act on behalf of the owner whose exclusive right has been allegedly infringed, (2) identifying the copyrighted works that have been infringed or a representative list of such works if multiple works are on a single website, (3) identifying the materials that have been infringed and information to permit the ISP to locate the said materials, (4) providing information for the ISP to contact the accuser, (5) providing a statement that clarifies the good faith of the accuser, and (6) a statement that verifies the accuracy of the information under the penalty of perjury.[44] A notification that fails to include these items will not be considered when determining the actual or constructive knowledge of the ISP and thus may waive the responsibility of the ISP to perform a takedown.[45] Finally, the ISP should act expeditiously to remove or disable access to the material once they receive proper notification. Regardless of the notice and takedown regime, Section 512 does not require ISPs to affirmatively monitor their services or actively disable access to the suspected infringing material in order to qualify for the statutory safe harbor protection.[46]

By assimilating Section 512 of the DMCA, China also incorporated the notice and takedown regime in its 2006 Regulation through legal transplant. If copyright owners believe that works which are accessed through the ISP services are an infringement of their right to network dissemination of information, they can file a

[43] The US Copyright Act of 1976, s 512(c)(2).

[44] The US Copyright Act of 1976, s 512(c)(3)(A).

[45] The US Copyright Act of 1976, s 512(c)(3)(B).

[46] The US Copyright Act of 1976, s 512(m).

notice to the ISP and require them to delete or block access to the works concerned.[47] The notice should contain the name and contact information of the copyright owner, names and hyperlinks of the works concerned, and preliminary evidence of infringement.[48] Once the notice has been received from the copyright owner, the ISP should immediately delete or block access to the works that are suspected of infringement and notify the subscriber involved in the infringement.[49] If the notification cannot be sent to the subscriber, the content of the notification should be published on the information network.[50]

Although other jurisdictions have not incorporated the notice and takedown regime as opposed to the United States and China, they all include relevant provisions in their statutes that prompt ISPs to expeditiously remove or disable access to materials of issue if the ISPs actually know or are aware of the illegal activity. Such provisions appear in the European Union Directive on Electronic Commerce, the Electronic Commerce Regulations 2002 of the United Kingdom, and the Copyright (Digital Agenda) Amendment Act 2000 of Australia. Australia later incorporated the notice and takedown regime after signing the Australia-United States Free Trade Agreement in 2004. The obligation of implementing the agreement led to the enactment of the Copyright Amendment Act 2006 under which ISPs are to act in accordance with the notice and takedown regime and comply with the requests of copyright owners to prevent infringement so as to safeguard themselves from liability.

The notice and takedown regime in the United States, China, and Australia and the immediate takedown provision in other jurisdictions facilitate copyright owners to effectively supervise online material and remove suspected infringing copies via cooperation with ISPs. This sort of legal system will efficiently address copyright infringement in the digital network environment at a low cost. This is especially true if the notice and takedown regime has established detailed procedures and conditions which copyright owners and ISPs can easily follow. However, immediate takedown requirements in the system will increase the risk of errors, which may result in the removal or blocked access of legitimate works. Thus, Section 512 of the DMCA has also established a "counter notification" regime which may help to remedy the losses suffered by ISPs and their subscribers due to erroneous takedowns.

4.4.2 Counter Notification Regime

The counter notification regime allows subscribers to request ISPs to recover links to their works if proven that the works in question have not committed infringement. Similar to the notice and takedown regime, several steps should also be followed.

---

[47] Regulation on the Protection of the Right to Network Dissemination of Information, Art 14.

[48] Ibid.

[49] Regulation on the Protection of the Right to Network Dissemination of Information, Art 15.

[50] Ibid.

First, the ISP shall notify the subscriber that the material has been taken down.[51] Secondly, the subscriber needs to submit a proper counter notification in order for the removed material to be reinstated. Similar to the items found in a proper notification, a counter notification also needs to satisfy several conditions, including providing the signature of the subscriber, identifying the removed material, providing a statement of the good faith of the subscriber under the penalty of perjury, and submitting the name and contact information of the subscriber.[52] Thirdly, upon receiving the counter notification, the ISP shall inform the subscriber that they will reinstate the removed material in 10 business days.[53] Finally, the ISP shall reinstate the material which has been removed or blocked in no less than 10 days and no more than 14 business days, after receiving the counter notice.[54]

The counter notification regime has also been transplanted into China but with subtle variations. The counter notification in China has the following items: name and contact information of the subscriber, name and hyperlink addresses of the works that are requested for recovery, and the preliminary evidence on non-infringement.[55] After receiving the counter notification, the ISP should immediately reinstate the deleted works or the hyperlink to the works and deliver the counter notification to the copyright owner.[56] After receiving the counter notification, the copyright owner cannot request the ISP to delete or block access to the works concerned again.[57] Furthermore, the copyright owner will be charged for compensation liability if the erroneous takedown resulted in any losses to the subscriber.[58]

The establishment of a counter notification regime balances the interests of ISPs and subscribers to a certain degree against copyright owners by providing the opportunity for suspected infringers to dispute the issue and remedy any erroneous takedowns. China even grants monetary compensation to innocent subscribers. This type of legal system is a great leap in achieving a balance of interest between copyright owners and Internet consumers. However, counter notification alone cannot entirely eliminate the negative effects brought upon by an immediate takedown, because the provisions do not give any detailed explanations with regard to the exact period of time which would constitute as "immediate." Under an immediate takedown requirement, the suspected subscriber may not have the chance to defend himself/herself before his/her material is removed or has access blocked. In addition, it will be costly for individual users to collect evidence to prove their innocence when facing censure from powerful entrepreneurial copyright holders. The immediate takedown requirement will also place ISPs in a dilemma: if they cooperate with copyright owners to expeditiously take down the alleged infringing material, they

[51] The US Copyright Act of 1976, s 512(g)(2)(A).

[52] The US Copyright Act of 1976, s 512(g)(3).

[53] The US Copyright Act of 1976, s 512(g)(2)(B).

[54] The US Copyright Act of 1976, s 512(g)(2)(C).

[55] Regulation on the Protection of the Right to Network Dissemination of Information, Art 16.

[56] Regulation on the Protection of the Right to Network Dissemination of Information, Art 17.

[57] Ibid.

[58] Regulation on the Protection of the Right to Network Dissemination of Information, Art 24.

will face the risk of losing customers; if they delay in removing suspected infringing material to protect current or potential customers, the ISPs will lose the statutory safe harbor protection.

4.4.3 Subpoena Procedure or Norwich Pharmacal Order

In addition to the notice and takedown regime and counter notification, the DMCA also includes a subpoena procedure under which the copyright owner may request a district court to issue a subpoena to an ISP to identify an alleged infringer.[59]

In order to initiate a subpoena under the DMCA, copyright owners should first file a request to the district court clerk which contains a notification, including the same items that are in the notice and takedown regime, the proposed subpoena and a sworn declaration that the information released by the clerk will only be used for copyright protection.[60] After receiving the abovementioned documents, the district court clerk will expeditiously issue and sign the subpoena and deliver the document to the ISP for disclosure of the requested information.[61] Upon receiving the subpoena, the ISP should immediately disclose the concerned information to the copyright owner.[62]

The subpoena procedure could help copyright owners collect pivotal information with regard to suspected infringers with the purpose of establishing reliable evidence, thus better addressing online copyright infringement. Nonetheless, there is negative impact in the subpoena procedure on the protection of the personal privacy of Internet users. The procedure may be abused by copyright owners to collect whatever information they want on Internet subscribers, even information that is not relevant to copyright protection.

China has not imported the American subpoena procedure. Instead, the administrative departments of copyright are empowered to demand an ISP to disclose information, such as the name, contact information, and web address of the subscriber who is suspected of infringement.[63] If the ISP does not cooperate or delays in disclosing relevant information without a justifiable reason, the administrative departments can give a warning to the ISP or, more seriously, confiscate the equipment that is used to facilitate the supply of infringing material.[64] In comparison to the

[59] The US Copyright Act of 1976, s 512(h)(1).

[60] The US Copyright Act of 1976, s 512(h)(2).

[61] The US Copyright Act of 1976, ss 512(h)(3)–(4).

[62] The US Copyright Act of 1976, s 512(h)(5).

[63] Regulation on the Protection of the Right to Network Dissemination of Information, Art 13.

[64] Regulation on the Protection of the Right to Network Dissemination of Information, Art 25.

subpoena procedure in the United States, there is less protection of the privacy of subscribers in China due to administrative power abuse.

Commonwealth jurisdictions, such as the United Kingdom and Hong Kong, have incorporated the Norwich Pharmacal judicial order in their legal system. In these jurisdictions, courts can order individuals who have information that may lead to the identification of the defendant to disclose that information.[65] In the Preliminary Proposals for Strengthening Copyright Protection in the Digital Environment released by the Hong Kong government in 2008 after launching a public consultation, Hong Kong aims to maintain the current Norwich Pharmacal discovery procedure in its copyright protection system. Under the Norwich Pharmacal procedure, copyright owners can obtain a court order that requires ISPs to disclose the source of the alleged infringing material.[66] In contrast to the subpoena procedure which allows copyright owners to request a subpoena at any time, the court will not exercise the Norwich Pharmacal procedure unless the individual who is seeking a court order has a genuine intent to commence a proceeding, and the proceeding cannot be commenced without information on the defendant.[67] Therefore, personal online privacy will be more safeguarded. Even though some have commented that the Norwich Pharmacal procedure is too slow and costly, the Hong Kong government is opposed to adopting more convenient procedures in case the personal privacy of Internet users cannot be guaranteed.

The Norwich Pharmacal discovery procedure is widely used by copyright owners to identify direct infringers in the digital network environment. In *Dish Network LLC & Others v. Zentek International Co. Ltd. & Another* judged by the Hong Kong High Court, the plaintiffs who were North American satellite broadcasters applied for the Norwich Pharmacal order against the defendant, a Hong Kong company and its director who hosted services for websites that provided pirated computer software for subscribers to use in descrambling the encrypted programs of the plaintiffs.[68] The plaintiffs sought for the Norwich Pharmacal order to compel the defendants to disclose the identity and information of the owners and subscribers of the websites so as to advance the proceeding against the primary infringers. The court finally approved the Norwich Pharmacal procedure and ordered the defendant to disclose the requested information.

---

[65] "Norwich Pharmacal Orders: A Quick Guide," available at http://ld.practicallaw.com/0-211-3137 (visited Sept 1, 2011).

[66] "Preliminary Proposals for Strengthening Copyright Protection in the Digital Environment," available at http://www.ipd.gov.hk/eng/intellectual_property/copyright/Consultation_Document_Prelim_Proposals_Eng(full).pdf (visited Sept 1, 2011).

[67] *See* n 65 above.

[68] *Dish Network LLC & Others v. Zentek International Co. Ltd. & Another* [2009] HKEC 220, available at http://www.hklii.hk/cgi-bin/sinodisp/eng/hk/cases/hkcfi/2008/887.html?stem=&synonyms=&query=title(Dish%20Network%20LLC (visited May 17, 2014).

4.5 New Development in Internet Service Provider Liability

Despite that there is the notice and takedown regime and subpoena or the Norwich Pharmacal discovery procedure, copyright industries continue to lobby governments to adopt more aggressive and strict anti-counterfeiting policies to address copyright infringement in the digital network environment. A new policy with regard to ISP liability that has been recently adopted by some jurisdictions is "three strikes and you're out" or the "graduated response" policy which allows ISPs to disconnect the Internet access of the alleged infringer after sending several warnings to the infringer about the suspected infringing activity. In addition, the courts in Europe heatedly discussed injunctions as remedies requiring ISPs to monitor or block access to third-party infringing websites.

4.5.1 New Conditions for Safe Harbors on Internet Service Provider Liability: The Graduated Response

The graduated response system was originally known as "three strikes and you're out" which originated from baseball.[69] However, the term "three strikes" could easily be misunderstood to be associated with physical assault and violence. In addition, this is erroneous with regard to the number of strikes, because the number of warnings will vary according to the legal systems in different jurisdictions. The phrase is inappropriate because of the consequence. In baseball, when a player has been struck out, he may get another chance to go to bat and can also keep playing in the field [7]. In contrast, a repeat infringer may not have another chance to go to bat. He/she may not have the opportunity to keep playing in the field. Therefore, "graduated response" is a more appropriate term to reflect the continuous and stepwise actions of ISPs against suspected infringers.

4.5.1.1 Graduated Response Approach

Under the graduated response system, an ISP can take a wide variety of actions in warning Internet users about their potential copyright infringing activity. These actions may vary among different jurisdictions, including "suspension or termination of service, capping of bandwidth, and blocking of sites, portals and protocols" [8, p. 1374]. Among these actions, suspension or termination of Internet services is the most severe sanction against the potential infringement.

The European Data Protection Supervisor summarized the graduated response approach in detail. "Under three strikes Internet disconnection policies copyright holders using automated technical means, possibly provided by third parties, would identify alleged copyright infringement by engaging in monitoring of Internet users'

---

[69] Available at http://en.wikipedia.org/wiki/Graduated_response (visited Sept 1, 2011).

activities, for example, via the surveillance of forums, blogs or by posting as file sharers in peer-to-peer networks to identify file sharers who allegedly exchange copyright material. After identifying Internet users alleged to be engaged in copyright violation by collecting their Internet Protocol addresses (IP addresses), copyright holders would send the IP addresses of those users to the relevant Internet service provider(s) who would warn the subscriber to whom the IP address belongs about his potential engagement in copyright infringement. Being warned by the ISP a certain number of times would automatically result in the ISP's termination or suspension of the subscriber's Internet connection."[70]

The graduated response system was adopted by various jurisdictions, including France, the United Kingdom, New Zealand, South Korea, and Taiwan, as legislations and by Ireland as a private ordering. Australia and Singapore assimilated the graduated response system and released their policies that copyright infringers can be disconnected from the Internet under judicial procedure [9]. Despite the widespread adoption or support, this policy was met with opposition by many jurisdictions, such as Germany, Spain, Sweden, and Hong Kong.

Among the supporting jurisdictions, France is representative of the policy. In May 2009, the French government passed a new law named *Law Promoting the Distribution and Protection of Creative Works on the Internet (Creation and Internet Act)* to implement the graduated response policy [9]. The law was initially rejected by the Constitutional Council due to its violation of a constitutional basic right, the right of communication and expression, but was later revised and thus approved by the Constitutional Council. The law became effective on January 1, 2010 [9]. The Creation and Internet Act established an administrative authority, the High Authority for the Dissemination of Works and the Protection of Rights on the Internet (HADOPI), to monitor online copyright infringement and the implementation of the graduated response policy.[71] Upon receiving a complaint from the copyright owner, including the IP addresses and infringing activity of the suspected infringing users, the HADOPI will notify the relevant ISPs and the latter will warn the alleged infringers. The first warning is sent by email which requires the subscribers to cease the infringement. Upon receiving a second complaint from the copyright owners which includes the same IP addresses within 6 months after the first complaint, the HADOPI will once again notify the ISPs, and the latter will send a second warning by regular mail. When a third complaint is received by the HADOPI which involves the same IP addresses within 1 year after the second complaint, the ISPs will send a third warning which will result in the implementation of a special judicial procedure held by a single judge against the subscribers. The judgment may enforce a fine against the subscribers or the suspension of the access of the subscribers to the Internet for 2 months and up to 1 year.

---

[70] Opinion of the European Data Protection Supervisor on the current negotiations by the European Union of an Anti-Counterfeiting Trade Agreement (ACTA), paragraphs 21 & 22, available at http://www.edps.europa.eu/EDPSWEB/webdav/site/mySite/shared/Documents/Consultation/Opinions/2010/10-02-22_ACTA_EN.pdf (visited Sept 1, 2011).

[71] "Internet Law-Developments in ISP Liability in Europe," available at http://www.ibls.com/internet_law_news_portal_view.aspx?id=2126&s=latestnews (visited Sept 1, 2011).

Although some European countries have actively adopted the graduated response system into their national laws, the European Union was reluctant to incorporate this system into the Anti-Counterfeiting Trade Agreement (ACTA), a new plurilateral treaty that improves global standards for the enforcement of intellectual property rights.[72] According to a European Commission spokesperson who was interviewed before the finalization of the ACTA, the ACTA would not demand that countries disconnect individuals from the Internet due to illegal downloads [10]. "The 'three-strike rule' or graduated response systems are not compulsory in Europe" [10]. The European Commission wanted to maintain flexibility so that different countries could adopt different approaches [10]. In the finalized version of the ACTA released in November 2010, there is no graduated response policy. In addition, in Section 5 on the enforcement of intellectual property rights in the digital environment, the provisions indicate that the enforcement procedures shall be implemented in a manner that avoids the creation of barriers to legitimate activity and preserves fundamental principles such as freedom of expression, fair process, and privacy.[73] Similarly, the Hong Kong government expressed in its copyright reform proposal for the digital environment that it is not an opportune time to consider the introduction of a graduated response system in Hong Kong, "especially when its implications are yet to be fully tested in overseas jurisdictions."[74]

The adoption of a graduated response system will have both positive and negative impacts on copyright owners, ISPs, and Internet users. Before importing the system into national legislations, a jurisdiction should carefully analyze whether the positive outweighs the negative or vice versa.

4.5.1.2 Impacts on Copyright Owners

The graduated response system was created through the endeavor of copyright industries to address rampant online copyright infringement and, thus, will greatly benefit copyright owners. First, the graduated response system can prevent repeated copyright infringement and cultivate public respect for intellectual property rights. As the Internet has already become a part of people's lives in their work, acquiring of information, entertainment, communication, and establishing of friendships, many Internet surfers, especially young people, are concerned about being disconnected from the Internet. Upon receiving the first or second warning from the ISP, a large number of Internet users may stop their infringing activity, in fear that they will be isolated from society. A test in the United Kingdom showed that 70 % of the Internet users stopped infringing after the first warning and a further 16 % stopped after the second warning [11]. This effective type of deterrence will reestablish

[72] Anti-counterfeiting Trade Agreement, available at http://trade.ec.europa.eu/doclib/docs/2011/may/tradoc_147937.pdf (visited Sept 7, 2011).

[73] Anti-Counterfeiting Trade Agreement, s 5, paragraphs 2–4, available at http://trade.ec.europa.eu/doclib/docs/2011/may/tradoc_147937.pdf (visited Sept 7, 2011).

[74] Proposals for Strengthening Copyright Protection in the Digital Environment, available at http://www.legco.gov.hk/yr09-10/english/panels/ci/papers/ci1117cb1-341-8-e.pdf (visited May 17, 2014).

respect for intellectual property law. Secondly, the graduated response system is an effective and inexpensive means to address and control rampant online copyright infringement. It can reduce a large amount of spending that has been used on massive lawsuits. Compared with imposing indirect liability on ISPs or direct liability on Internet users, the graduated response system can be economically efficient as there is a reduction in the launching of costly and time-consuming lawsuits. At the same time, the policy suffocates infringing activity by cutting off the channel that is used to facilitate infringement.

The impacts of the graduated response system on copyright owners seem to be all positive because peer-to-peer file-sharing technology facilitates the unauthorized dissemination of copyright works, thus negatively affecting the interest of copyright owners. This assumption misses the fact that file-sharing technology may benefit some authors and artists, especially starters who mainly want to establish their reputation rather than earn money. File-sharing technology can distribute works of artists quickly and cheaply, thus increasing their exposure [9]. Broader exposure will in turn increase concert ticket sales and other merchandise [9]. The deterrence brought on by the graduated response system will decrease the use of file-sharing technology and negatively affect certain authors and artists.

Although there may be some negative effects from the graduated response policy on copyright owners, the positive outweighs the negative in general. The number of authors and artists who are starting up is proportionally small in comparison to the large number of copyright owners and industries. Online piracy more often decreases the profits of copyright owners rather than increase their reputations and popularity.

4.5.1.3 Impacts on Internet Service Providers

The graduated response system can prevent ISPs from being sued for indirect infringement by establishing cooperation between copyright owners and ISPs. Upon satisfying the requirements of sending Internet users warnings and disconnecting Internet access, ISPs will not be held indirectly liable for the infringing activity of Internet users. Thus, the graduated response system saves time, labor, and costs for ISPs in otherwise dealing with civil lawsuits. ISPs have more resources to improve and maintain their services without concern about being scapegoats for infringing activity [8]. In this regard, the graduated response system plays a similar role as the safe harbor rules regulated by Section 512 of the DMCA. In addition, the graduated response system can help ISPs to resolve the problem of network traffic and congestion [8]. Since rampant online file sharing results in limited bandwidth, network congestion, and declining quality of user experience, disconnection of Internet access of infringing users can restore network flow and the quality of overall user experience. Prior to the enactment of the graduated response policy, ISPs had to monitor their subscribers in order to improve the quality of services. Deep packet monitoring may cause ISP to identify the nature and type of traffic and actual knowledge of infringement by subscribers and, thus, will render ISPs ineligible from safe harbor protection [12].

However, these advantages for ISPs are likely to be outweighed by the high expenses that they need to pay for the implementation of a graduated response system. In order to ensure the functionality of a graduated response system, ISPs must invest in surveillance, identifying subscribers, sending notifications of alleged infringement, running call centers to answer questions, developing new equipment to manage the system, maintaining data retention, and reallocating human resources.[75] These expenses will be much higher than the subscription fees that Internet users pay to the ISPs. Increase of subscription fees will negatively affect both the ISPs and Internet users. Moreover, the graduated response system may put ISPs into another dilemma: satisfying complaints from copyright owners by warning alleged Internet users and disconnecting Internet access without further investigation will reduce user experience and put ISPs at risk of losing customers. However, further investigation on determining the real activity of suspected Internet users will increase their costs and possibly render them ineligible for safe harbor protection provided by current copyright statutes.

In summary, the disadvantages brought on by a graduated response system to ISPs very likely outweigh the advantages, because the expenses that ISPs will spend on the implementation of the new system may offset or even exceed those that they spend on litigations. Although the graduated response system can maintain network flow, and thus the quality of services, the effective implementation of such a system will put ISPs at risk of losing customers, which is a greater issue if ISPs profit from Internet users.

4.5.1.4 Impacts on Internet Users

Compared with being sued by powerful copyright industries and facing unfair judgment, Internet users will feel that the graduated response policy is a better approach to sanction online copyright infringement and the outcome of such a policy is more acceptable than a large amount of compensation or imprisonment. Prior to the release of the graduated response system, the courts reached quite a number of judgments that heavily awarded the copyright industries for damage, and against individual online file sharers, which aroused public concern on the fairness between damage and harm caused by file sharing to copyright owners. In the judgments, a woman was fined 54,000 USD for infringing 24 songs,[76] a man in Hong Kong was sentenced to 3 months of imprisonment for uploading three movies by

---

[75] Michael Geist [13]. *Also see* Yu [8] and Haber [9].

[76] *Capitol Records, Inc. v. Thomas-Rasset*, Memorandum of Law & Order, Civil File No. 06-1497 (MJD/LIB), document 457 (D. Minn. 2011), available at http://ia700504.us.archive.org/21/items/gov.uscourts.mnd.82850/gov.uscourts.mnd.82850.457.0.pdf (visited Sept 7, 2011). *Also see* "Capitol Records, Inc. v. Thomas-Rasset," available at http://en.wikipedia.org/wiki/Capitol_v._Thomas (visited Sept 7, 2011). The first trial in 2007 ordered the defendant to pay $222,000 in statutory damages. The second trial in 2009 ordered $1,920,000 in statutory damages and later reduced the amount to $54,000. The third trial in 2010 resulted in an award of $1.5 million and was reduced by court in July 2011 to $54,000 or $2,250 per song.

using BitTorrent,[77] and another man was sentenced to jail for 18 months in the United States for copyright infringement by using peer-to-peer file-sharing technology.[78] Disconnection from the Internet as stipulated by the graduated response system seems to be more agreeable to Internet users than the remedies in civil and criminal litigations. Besides replacing severe remedies, the improvement of network flow as a result of the graduated response system can also benefit Internet users, especially those who never or hardly infringe copyright.

Despite their relative advantages, the graduated response system has serious negative impacts on a series of fundamental rights of Internet users, including the right of due process, freedom of expression, and right of privacy. In addition, the graduated response system may not satisfy the requirements for fairness in legal enforcement and may disrupt the balance of interests between copyright owners and public users.

First, the graduated response system deprives Internet users of due process due to the lack of verification on their suspected infringing activity. Since the complaints from copyright owners are generated by third-party companies that rely on automated web technologies and databases of digital fingerprints, alleged infringing activity will not be investigated by either the copyright owners or ISPs [14, p. 13]. The detection process of infringement based on unreliable automatic identification technology has been proven "notoriously inaccurate" through various cases which imposed sanctions on people who do not have computers or are deceased [14, p. 13]. Even though technology can be improved to improve accuracy, large copyright industries such as records and motion picture companies are inclined to outsource the task of searching for suspected infringement to third parties which are financially motivated to send as many notices as possible [14, p. 17]. If tried under judicial procedures, these alleged infringers may be proven innocent based on defenses such as fair use or errors and may be compensated if there are losses due to being wrongfully identified. However, the judicial verification and remedy process will not appear in a graduated response system which is enforced by private parties rather than judicial authorities. Copyright owners are not likely to carefully screen the suspected infringers, as their copyright works will be better protected if more end users are deterred from committing infringement. Neither will ISPs examine the facts in case they lose their current safe harbor protection. Without the inclusion of due process, Internet users cannot guarantee certain procedural rights, such as the right to be heard in trial and the right to have their complaints fully considered by courts or a neutral judge [9]. Although the French policy allows Internet users to be heard by the HADOPI, such procedure cannot fully meet the standards of due process due to the administrative nature of the HADOPI.

Secondly, the graduated response system may suffocate the freedom of expression and speech by intimidating Internet users by cutting off their access to the Internet which has already become a very important communication channel in everyday life. The freedom of expression and speech is a basic human right that

---

[77] *Chan Nai Ming v. HKSAR* [2007] 10H.K.C.F.A.R. 273 (C.F.A.).

[78] *United States v. Dove* 585F. Supp. 2d 865 (W.D. Va. 2008).

includes "freedom to hold opinions without interference and to seek, receive and impart information and ideas through any media and regardless of frontier."[79] With the development of digital network technology, the Internet has become a major medium that facilitates access to information; publishing of expressions or artistic works via digital books and journals, blogs, online chatting forums, or podcasting; and personal interaction through email or instant messaging services. Internet surfers will largely reduce their online communications due to the threat of Internet disconnection for fear that their thoughts and expressions would be monitored and, consequently, suppress their thoughts.

Thirdly, the graduated response system may undermine individual Internet privacy by imposing ISPs to monitor and retain the identity and relevant data of alleged repeat infringers. Personal data under the digital network environment including IP addresses and information about the activities linked to such addresses are usually anonymous. Upon finding suspected infringing activity, copyright owners will release the identity of alleged infringers to ISPs, thus giving intermediaries knowledge on previously anonymous personal data of the subscribers. In order to recognize repeat infringers, ISPs will retain such personal data for a long period of time or even exchange data with other ISPs in case they are not able to accomplish the task after receiving second or third notifications from copyright owners. Such data retention or exchange can jeopardize personal privacy because of monitoring and preserving information with regard to individual behaviors of users and activities carried out by private parties.

Finally, the graduated response system may lead to disproportion and imbalance in copyright systems by strengthening the power of copyright owners in addressing infringement against the interests of end users in acquiring information, recreation, and free expression. As Professor Peter Yu indicated, "taking away an individual's Internet access as a penalty for alleged copyright infringement is even worse than introducing criminal sanctions for downloading and peer-to-peer file sharing. While the criminal court system will determine whether sanctions will attach under the 'beyond a reasonable doubt' standard, a graduated response system may involve mere allegations of infringement of copyright holders or their industry group" [8, p. 1401]. The "mere allegations of infringement" also discourage opportunities for users to provide a fair use or fair dealing defense. Even downloading material for noncommercial research purposes or file sharing user-generated contents is likely to be deemed as infringement and punished by network disconnection. Some users may stop legal use after receiving the first or second warnings due to a lack of intellectual property knowledge. Both erroneous accusations by copyright owners and the misunderstanding of the users themselves will seriously narrow the scope of privileges that were originally enjoyed by the users.

To conclude the impacts of the graduated response system on Internet users, the negative factors strongly outweighs the relatively positive factors. The protection of the right of due process, freedom of expression, and right of privacy as well as maintaining a balance of interest against copyright owners is more important to Internet

[79] The Universal Declaration of Human Rights, Art 19.

users than the enjoyment of quality network services or avoiding unfair judgments. After all, few users need to pay copyright owners large statutory damages or are criminalized and imprisoned because of unfair judgments, but quite a number of consumers will be disconnected from Internet access, thus facing the risk of losing privacy, free speech, and due process under the graduated response system.

4.5.1.5 China's Reaction to the Graduated Response System

The graduated response system has not aroused public concern in China yet. The only public discussion on the new system reported by news is a conference held by the copyright administrative organ of the Hebei Province in March 2011.[80] In this conference, experts from legislatures, administrative organs, industries, and the academia discussed the strengthening of copyright protection in the digital network environment and promoting the development of content industries. The graduated response system was introduced and supported by scholars in this conference to better inhibit online copyright infringement and piracy. However, until now, there has not been any response from the state authorities on whether China should adopt the graduated response system.

Supporters of the graduated response system may argue that China is a country where copyright infringement is severe. Due to the large number of population and Internet users, the enforcement of copyright protection in the digital network environment will be quite difficult in China. Traditional copyright protection is based on licensing by copyright owners or authorized proxies, while users in the digital environment can easily obtain works through digital network technologies. The quick development of cloud computing technology which aims to achieve a unified management and scheduling of network resources further aggravates the difficulties of copyright protection enforcement.[81] Moreover, due to the previous absence of strong governmental execution and general education on intellectual property law, a culture that respects intellectual property rights has not been well formed in China yet. The importation of the graduated response system may help to effectively address copyright infringement and educate people to respect copyrights.

Opponents of the graduated response system may focus on the disadvantages discussed above to argue that China has already adopted a strict network filtering policy and should not further intensify network control. According to a filtering watchdog group, the Open Net Initiative, "China has one of the largest and most sophisticated filtering systems in the world" [15]. By establishing a complex system of regulation, licensing, and ISP liability, China can control Internet usage and

---

[80] "Hebei: the Graduated Response System May Inhibit Online Infringement and Piracy," (in Chinese), available at http://www.sipo.gov.cn/wqyz/dfxx/201104/t20110407_595456.html (visited May 17, 2014).

[81] "Investigation of Status Quo of Copyright Protection in the Network Age: Severe Burden of Proof Makes Protection of Rights Difficult," (in Chinese), available at http://www.ce.cn/xwzx/gnsz/gdxw/201104/01/t20110401_22340359_1.shtml (visited Sept 7, 2011).

touch every point of Internet access and transmission [15]. The introduction of a graduated response system will exacerbate the current situation. Under certain circumstances, the government may exploit the graduated response system to disconnect linkage to the Internet for public administration purposes rather than merely for copyright protection. Taking freedom of expression, due process, and privacy issues into consideration, China should not rashly import the graduated response policy without carefully examining whether the advantages will outweigh the disadvantages in the national situation. It is better for China to wait and observe the effect of the graduated response system that has been implemented in overseas jurisdictions and then to decide whether she should import the new policy.

Even if China intends to transplant the graduated response system to address digital copyright infringement, in the face of pressure from protecting copyright industries and maintaining an international image, several factors should be seriously considered in the reestablishment of such a new system. These factors are proposed by Professor Peter Yu, which include the introduction of "independent review" mechanisms which will avoid the wrongful identification of suspected infringers as much as possible through judicial or administrative processes; system's "educative and rehabilitative" purposes under which Internet users should easily understand the contents of the warnings and the reason why their actions are wrong; maintaining of "reasonable alternative access" to the Internet; minimization of "collateral damages"; safeguarding of "proportionality" so that protection of copyright interests would not damage the protection of free speech and privacy and "flexibility" so that alleged infringers could claim a fair use defense or lack of originality of copyright ownership; and finally, the use of "Internet disconnection as a last resort" if less severe measures such as "bandwidth reduction, monitored access, or site, port, or protocol blocking" are available [8, pp. 1419–1429].

4.5.2 Internet Service Provider Injunctions Ruled in European Courts

During the 5 years between 2006 and 2011, a couple of national courts in Europe received applications from copyright owners requiring ISPs to filter and block infringing material which was posted on third parties' platforms but was accessed by subscribers using the ISPs' services. Among the judgments, most of them granted injunctions requiring ISPs to block access to the third parties' websites or filter and block the infringing contents,[82] while a few of them refused the granting of the

[82] According to the list of judgments complied by Judge Arnold in 20th Century Fox v. BT ruled by the High Court of London in the United Kingdom, the judgments that granted injunction orders include IFPI Danmark v. Tele 2 A/S ruled by Copenhagen City Court, SABAM v. Tiscali SA ruled by Brussels Court of First Instance, IFPI Danmark v. DMT2 A/S ruled by Fredericksburg Court, sub nom Telenor v. IFPI ruled by Danish Supreme Court, Bergamo Public Prosecutor's Office v. Kolmisoppi ruled by Italian Supreme Court of Cessation, Columbia Pictures Industries Inc v. Portlane AB ruled by Swedish Court of Appeal, and Constantine Film v. UPC ruled by Commercial Court of Austria.

injunctions.[83] Two representative judgments given later on by the High Court of London of the United Kingdom in *20th Century Fox Film Corp. v. British Telecommunications plc* in July 2011 and by the Court of Justice of the European Union in *Scarlet Extended SA v. SABAM* in November 2011 reached opposite results with regard to the copyright owners' request of installing filtering and blocking mechanism in the ISPs' services. Analysis of the detailed facts and the judges' logic in the two cases may help sorting out the appropriate conditions for granting ISP injunctions.

4.5.2.1 Legislative Basis

The legal basis for ISP liability, safe harbor, and remedies is mainly provided by three European Union directives, namely, Directive 2000/31/EC of the European Parliament and of the Council of June 8, 2000, on certain legal aspects of information society service, in particular electronic commerce, in the Internal Market (Electronic Commerce Directive), Information Society Directive, and Directive 2004/48/EC of the European Parliament and of the Council of April 29, 2004, on the enforcement of intellectual property rights (IP Enforcement Directive).

Recital 40 of the Electronic Commerce Directive imposes duty on service providers to act under certain circumstances to prevent or stop illegal activities. Although Recitals 43 and 44 and Articles 12–14 of the Electronic Commerce Directive classify categories of ISPs into mere conduit, caching, and hosting and supply safe harbor protection for these ISPs subject to certain conditions, Recital 45 clarifies that safe harbor established for ISPs does not affect "the possibility of injunctions of different kinds" granted "by courts or administrative authorities requiring the termination or prevention of any infringement, including the removal of illegal information or the disabling of access to it." However, the requirement of termination or prevention of infringement does not impose a general monitoring obligation on service providers, according to Recital 47 and Article 15.

Similar provisions are also included into the Information Society Directive and IP Enforcement Directive, since these two directives shall be implemented in compliance with the Electronic Commerce Directive. Both of the two directives provide that right holders should have the possibility of applying for an injunction against an intermediary who carries a third party's infringement of a protected work or intellectual property rights.[84] The sanctions thus provided for shall be effective, proportionate, and dissuasive.[85] In addition, the IP Enforcement Directive further

[83] According to the list of judgments complied by Judge Arnold in 20th Century Fox v. BT ruled by the High Court of London in the United Kingdom, the judgments that refused injunction orders include Nordic Records Norway AS v. Telenor ASA ruled by Borgarting Court of Appeal, Stichting Bescherming Rechten Entertainment Industrie Nederland (BREIN) v. Ziggo BV ruled by District Court of the Hague, and EMI v. UPC ruled by High Court of Ireland.

[84] Information Society Directive, Recital 59 and Art 8(3); IP Enforcement Directive, Art 11.

[85] Information Society Directive, Art 8(1); IP Enforcement Directive, Art 3(2).

imposes conditions on the general service provider obligation: "those measures, procedures and remedies shall be fair and equitable and shall not be unnecessarily complicated or costly, or entail unreasonable time-limits or unwarranted delays."[86]

4.5.2.2 Representative Cases

The legislative basis for ISP injunctions embodied in the three directives was analyzed in detail with combination of the discussion of the case facts in *Scarlet Extended SA v. SABAM* and *20th Century Fox Film Corp. v. British Telecommunications plc*.

In *Scarlet Extended SA v. SABAM*, the Court of Justice of European Union (ECJ) ruled that EU law precluded an injunction made against an ISP which required it to install a system for filtering all electronic communications passing via its service, in particular those involving the use of peer-to-peer software, which applied indiscriminately to all its customers as a preventive measures exclusively at its expense and for an unlimited period and which was capable of identifying on that ISP's network the movement of electronic files containing a copyright work, with a view to blocking the transfer of files, the sharing of which infringes copyright.[87]

In this case, SABAM was a collecting society which represents author, composers, and editors of musical works. Scarlet was an ISP which provided access to the Internet. The proceeding was brought by SABAM against Scarlet before the Court of Brussels in 2004, claiming that Internet users used Scarlet's service to download works in SABAM's catalog without the latter's authorization and requiring Scarlet to take measures to terminate the infringement committed by the users. In June 2007, the Court of Brussels ordered Scarlet to terminate the infringement by making it impossible for the users to send or receive files through peer-to-peer software. Scarlet appealed to the Court of Appeal of Brussels against the decision that it was technically impossible to implement the injunction and the injunction was contrary to the European Union directives that deny imposing a general obligation on an ISP to monitor communications on its network. The Court of Appeal of Brussels referred the case to the ECJ.

The ECJ first considered the lawfulness of the injunction by examining whether the adoption of filtering system would impose general monitoring obligation on Scarlet. It found the injunction unlawful because implementation of the filtering system would require the ISP to identify the peer-to-peer files within all of the electronic communications of all its customers, identify the files in which the copyright owners claimed to hold rights, determine which of these files were shared unlawfully, and block file sharing that it considered to be unlawful.[88] Such filtering system would require the ISP to actively observe all electronic communications conducted

[86] IP Enforcement Directive, Art 3(1).

[87] Scarlet Extended SA v. SABAM (c-70/10, 2011), available at http://eur-lex.europa.eu/LexUriServ/LexUriServ.do?uri=CELEX:62010CJ0070:EN:HTML (visited Nov 2, 2013).

[88] Scarlet Extended SA v. SABAM judgment, paragraphs 38–40.

on the network, which was contrary to the directive requirement of not to impose general monitoring obligation on ISPs.

The ECJ then balanced the protection of intellectual property rights as a fundamental right to property against the protection of other fundamental rights. In particular, the ECJ emphasized the potential serious infringement of the freedom of the ISP to conduct its business because the filtering system would be complicated, costly, and permanent and would be established at the ISP's own expense.[89] The ECJ further considered that the filtering system might also infringe the fundamental rights of the ISP's customers, such as the right to protection of personal data and the right to receive or impart information, since the injunction would involve collection and identification of users' IP addresses which were protected personal data and would not distinguish adequately between unlawful contents and lawful contents, with the result that might lead to the blocking of lawful communications.[90]

Different from the ECJ judgment in *Scarlet Extended SA v. SABAM*, the UK High Court delivered an opposite judgment in *20th Century Fox Film Corp. v. British Telecommunications plc (BT)* that granted injunction order against the ISP as requested by the copyright owner, the 20th Century Fox Film Corporation. Prior to the BT case, the 20th Century Fox and other movie studios (Studios) had sought injunctions in the High Court of London against unauthorized distribution of copyright works by the website, www.newzbin.com (Newzbin1). Newzbin1 stored binary content and provided two kinds of membership, free basic membership and fee-paid premium membership, to its customers. Premium members could download binary contents and resemble them to form an entire movie or TV program. Justice Kitchin in the *20th Century Fox Film Corp. v. Newzbin* found that Newzbin1 committed copyright infringement by authoring premium subscribers to download infringing copies of movies and TV programs and thus granted injunction against Newzbin1.[91] Newzbin1 sought voluntary liquidation and ceased to operate in 2010. However, Newzbin2 resumed the same URL as Newzbin1 with hosting servers located outside the United Kingdom shortly thereafter. BT, as the largest ISP in the United Kingdom, provided communications between its customers and any third-party websites including Newzbin2. Thus, BT was sued by the Studios to block access to the Newzbin2 website and terminate the infringement. One more thing worth noticing is that BT already implemented a blocking system named "Cleanfeed" to block access to child sexual abuse content provided by certain websites identified and listed by the Internet Watch Foundation (IWF). The Studios requested BT to adopt similar measures in relation to termination of infringing copyright content against Newzbin2.

---

[89] Scarlet Extended SA v. SABAM judgment, paragraph 48.

[90] Scarlet Extended SA v. SABAM judgment, paragraphs 50–52.

[91] "The Twentieth Century Fox v. BT Decision: A New Development in the Debate About ISP Obligations to Prevent Copyright Infringement," (2011) *Communications Law Bulletin* Vol. 30(2) available at http://www.hdy.com.au/Media/docs/DOC121011-5a25b007-23a0-4ea6-a465-241cd4090c2d-0.pdf (visited Nov 2, 2013).

Similar to the European Union directives, Section 97 A of the Copyright, Designs and Patents Act 1988 (CDPA) of the United Kingdom works as the legislative basis for courts to grant injunctions against ISPs, which is read as follows: "The High Court… shall have power to grant an injunction against a service provider, where that service provider has actual knowledge of another person using their service to infringe copyright…." During the defense, BT submitted the arguments that the Court had no jurisdiction to grant the injunction based on four reasons: (1) there was no use of BT's service to infringe copyright, (2) it had no actual knowledge of the infringement, (3) the injunction was contrary to Articles 12(1) and 15(1) of the Electronic Commerce Directive, and (4) the injunction was contrary to Article 10 of the European Convention on Human Rights which protects freedom of expression.[92]

As for the first argument, Judge Arnold confirmed the BT subscribers' active downloading of content by BT's service as use of BT's service to infringe copyright, since the subscribers did not passively receive information and BT enabled the subscribers to access the Internet that was being used by a third party to infringe copyright. BT facilitated the transmission of unauthorized copies of works between subscribers and third-party websites.

As for the second argument, Section 97A implemented Article 8(3) of the Information Society Directive which states that injunction shall be granted against an ISP since ISPs are best placed to bring the infringing activities to an end. Judge Arnold held that this suggested that the requirement of actual knowledge should not be interpreted too restrictively [16]: "what must be shown is that the service provider has actual knowledge of one or more persons using its service to infringe copyright… but it is not essential to prove actual knowledge of a specific infringement of a specific copyright work by a specific individual."[93] Therefore, Judge Arnold confirmed that BT had actual knowledge of the copyright infringement which was on a large scale and a large number of copyright works were involved.

As for the third argument, Article 12(1) of the Electronic Commerce Directive provides safe harbor protection of ISPs that act as mere conduit. However, limitations to ISP liability would not preclude orders requiring the ISP to disable access to illegal information. Article 15(1) addresses the issue of not imposing general monitoring obligation on ISPs. Judge Arnold held that the order only required BT to block access to Newzbin2 website and such blocking measures were passive and automatic rather than active. Hence, the monitoring was specific rather than general and would not be in conflict with Article 15(1).

As for the fourth argument, Judge Arnold found that the injunction order was clear and precise with regard to the nature and scope of the blocking measures, since it only required BT to adopt existing technical mechanism for a specific purpose, which would not be contrary to the protection of right to freedom of expression.[94]

[92] Ibid.

[93] 20th Century Fox Film Corp. v. British Telecommunications plc [2011] EWHC 1981 (Ch) judgment, paragraph 148.

[94] Ibid.

Moreover, evidence in this case showed that there was a large scale of copyright infringement through the Newzbin2 service. The non-infringing purpose and use in the Newzbin2 service by BT subscribers were significantly diminished. In a word, protection of intellectual property rights owned by the right holders clearly outweighed the protection of the right to freedom of expression.[95] Therefore, Judge Arnold granted injunction order against BT requiring the latter to use existing technology to block access to Newzbin websites as requested by the Studios.

4.5.2.3 Conclusion: Proportionality in ISP Injunction

The rulings of the two representative judgments stress the importance of proportionality in the courts' decisions with regard to whether to grant injunction order against ISPs. First, courts will determine whether the injunction order in question complies with Article 15(1) of the Electronic Commerce Directive which requires member countries not to impose general obligation on ISPs to monitor the information stored or transmitted on their platforms. Detailed facts in each case will be analyzed by the courts so as to make decisions. Comparing the facts in *Scarlet* and *BT* cases, implementation of injunction in *Scarlet* case would require the ISP to identify all files transmitted by its subscribers using its service and the alleged infringing files, as well as to determine and block the unlawful files, while the injunction order in *BT* case only required the ISP to adopt existing automated technology to block customers' access to certain websites, namely, Newzbin1 and Newzbin2. In addition, it would be hard for Scarlet to differentiate the lawful content from the unlawful content, while injunction against BT targeted at infringing activity, so there was little chance that BT would block access to non-infringing material. Thus, the injunction against Scarlet was deemed as general monitoring obligation, but the order against BT was specific.

Second, courts will balance the protection of intellectual property rights of the right holders against other fundamental rights, such as freedom of expression, right to personal data, right to receive and impart information, and freedom of ISPs to conduct business. In *Scarlet* case, the general monitoring obligation imposed on the ISP would impede the ISP's freedom to conduct business, and identification of IP addresses of subscribers would infringe users' right to personal data and right to receive and impart information. The protection of users' right to personal data and freedom of expression and ISP's freedom to conduct business outweighed the protection of copyright owners' rights in *Scarlet* case. However, in *BT* case, the adoption of existing technical mechanism was used to block access to specific websites which facilitated a large scale of copyright infringement. The protection of copyright owners' rights in this case thus outweighed the protection of users' freedom of expression and privacy. As emphasized by Judge Arnold, the order against BT was "a narrow and targeted one and it contains safeguards in the event

[95] *See* n 93 above.

of any change of circumstances. The cost of implementation to BT would be modest and proportionate."[96]

Therefore, courts will take a couple of factors into consideration when deciding whether to grant injunction order against ISPs and balance the protection of intellectual property rights against other fundamental rights. A couple of factors shall include without limitation to the cost and time to implement the blocking and filtering technology, the targeted websites of the injunction, the impact of the injunction to the ISPs' transmission service, the scale of the infringement, and ISPs' knowledge about the infringement.

4.6 Conclusion: Recommendations for Establishing Certainty of Internet Service Provider Liability

After reviewing and analyzing the development of ISP liability and safe harbor regulations among different jurisdictions, several suggestions are made to establish the certainty of ISP liability in general and for China's digital copyright reform on ISP liability in particular.

In the new round of reforms in China, Article 69 of the Modified Drafts excludes the obligations of ISPs to review information under the circumstances that the ISPs only provide purely Internet technology services, such as storing, searching, linking, etc. It incorporates a simplified notice and takedown procedure which protects the infringing liability of ISPs if they promptly take the necessary measures to remove, hide, or disconnect the hyperlinks upon receiving notification. On the contrary, ISPs will be held joint tortfeasor liable with Internet subscribers if they know or should know about the infringing activity of their subscribers, but did not carry out any further measures. ISPs will be held contributory liable if they instigate or aid commitment of copyright infringement by third parties.

In contrast to the protection of TPMs and DRM information which is stipulated under a specific chapter, provisions for ISP liability and safe harbors are overly simplified and abstract to embody the important categories of liability immunization, key factors that determine liability and detailed procedures that concern the notice and takedown regime. Lack of specified stipulations is already found in the 2006 Regulation, and the ISP liability and safe harbor provision in the Modified Drafts can be deemed as retrogression. Therefore, these provisions need to be revised.

First, certain standards about the following factors should be settled either in common law indirect liability principles or statutory liability regulations of ISPs: the knowledge of ISPs on primary infringement, obtaining of direct financial benefits from primary infringement, and the ability to control or supervise infringing activity. In summary, in terms of the first factor, ISP knowledge shall include both

[96] 20th Century Fox Film Corp. v. British Telecommunications plc judgment, paragraph 200.

actual knowledge and awareness of apparent infringing activity. The emergence of certain situations should be deemed as apparent infringing activity, including abnormally high traffic on the network, the appearance of terms like "pirated" or "bootleg" in the file title, inclusion of names of copyright works in the file title of which the uploader is obviously not the copyright owner, and the repeated appearance of materials that have been targeted by statutory takedown notices. However, mere knowledge of the prevalence of infringing activity in general should not be deemed as awareness of apparent infringement. As for the second factor, direct financial benefits should show a very close relationship between ISPs and the alleged infringing activity. Situations such as the attraction of advertising probably by the popularity of the infringing material shall not be deemed adequate to prove a close relationship between an ISP and the alleged infringer. As for the third factor, the ability to control or supervise subscriber activities could mean ISPs' prerequisite ability to intervene in the infringing activities.

Secondly, the design of immediate takedown requirements in the notice and takedown regime increases the risk of erroneous takedowns. The notice and takedown regime can be reformed in a stepwise manner by incorporating a reasonable grace period for suspected subscribers to defend themselves and the establishment of certain exemptions by ISPs even if they fail to take down the suspected infringing material. In the first step, a reasonable grace period can be incorporated for suspected subscribers to defend themselves prior to the removal of their material by ISPs. A reasonable grace period could be around 4–5 days which is neither too short for subscribers to prove their innocence nor too long for copyright holder and ISPs to monitor the suspected subscribers and address the infringement. Under circumstances in which the suspected subscriber does not respond during the grace period after receiving a notice from the ISP, the ISP should expeditiously take down the material in case they are deemed to be liable for the infringement. The period of time within the expeditious takedown should be better defined as 24 h. In the second step, some exceptions can be established in the grace period, including special circumstances under which ISPs can immediately take down the suspected material without waiting for the end of the grace period. Examples include the circumstances where copyright owners have already suffered great losses due to the unauthorized online transmission of their works. In the third step, special exemptions can be established, which still allow ISPs to be protected by safe harbors even if they fail to take down the suspected material after the notice and the grace period. Such exemptions include circumstances where enforcement of the takedown will cause great economic loss or impose undue burden on the ISPs. In China's situation, the counter notification procedure should be maintained. The combination of "notice and takedown with a grace period" and "counter notification" will better achieve the multiple purposes of controlling digital copyright infringement, promoting ISP participation in online information dissemination and e-commerce, and protecting the interests of Internet consumers.

Thirdly, China does not include a "subpoena procedure" as found in the United States or the "Norwich Pharmacal" discovery procedure as found in Hong Kong. Instead, the administrative organ in China is allowed to disclose the personal information of subscribers. Although the administrative approach is more efficient and coercive than any other measure, the protection of the privacy of subscribers is more at risk due to the high possibility of administrative power abuse. It is understandable that the adoption of administrative procedures in information collection by the Chinese government aims to effectively supervise the suspected infringers and resolve the rampant piracy problem in China. However, the privacy of subscribers may be seriously infringed if the alleged infringer is finally proven to be innocent. The aforementioned comparative discussion between the "subpoena procedure" and "Norwich Pharmacal" discovery procedure shows that the latter places more concern on the protection of privacy because of the prerequisite in which a person who is seeking for a court order should have a genuine intent to commence a proceeding. Therefore, China could consider importing the "Norwich Pharmacal" procedure to balance the interests of different parties. On the one hand, China could grant the authority to district or intermediate courts to decide whether the information of the alleged infringers should be disclosed upon the requests made by copyright holders. On the other hand, Chinese legislations could include a provision that requires ISPs to record the information of suspected infringers when a judicial procedure is commenced.

Fourthly, countries that have not imported the graduated response policy, such as China, should not rush to adopt it without carefully examining and balancing the positive and negative factors that will impact copyright owners, ISPs, and Internet users. Even if the Chinese government intends to adopt the graduated response system, several key factors should be taken into consideration as mentioned above: an "independent review" mechanism, "educative and rehabilitative" purposes, the maintaining of "reasonable alternative access" to the Internet, minimization of "collateral damages," safeguarding of "proportionality" and "flexibility," and the use of "Internet disconnection as a last resort."

Fifthly, judicial decisions with regard to whether to grant injunctions against ISPs as requested by copyright owners should well take multi-factors into consideration and balance the protection of copyright against other fundamental rights, such as freedom of expression, right to privacy, right to receive and impart information, and technology intermediaries' freedom of conducting business. The multi-factors that determine the proportionality of the injunction shall include the cost and time to implement the blocking and filtering technology, the targeted websites of the injunction, the impact of the injunction to the ISPs' transmission service, the scale of the infringement, and ISPs' knowledge about the infringement.

Finally, heterogeneous approaches combined with legislative measures should be adopted by countries, such as China, to better achieve the certainty of ISP liability and the free flow of information. In addition to revisions to current copyright laws and regulations, China should broadly adopt various other methods, including revision of other relevant laws such as competition and privacy laws, government policy and industry guidelines, as well as introduction of public consultation and multi-party forums so as to make these mechanisms collaboratively work on the issues of ISP liability, free dissemination of information, and protection of privacy in the digital network environment. Hong Kong has already set a good example for

Mainland China by collecting opinions and comments from different stakeholders via public consultations and drafting proposals for legal reforms. In December 2006, the Hong Kong government issued a public consultation document to seek opinions from various sources on how copyright protection should be strengthened in the digital age.[97] After the public consultation, the Hong Kong government released the Preliminary Proposals for Strengthening Copyright Protection in the Digital Environment for further public engagement in April 2008.[98] After further public consultations were held in 2008 at the Tripartite Forum, the Hong Kong government released the Proposals for Strengthening Copyright Protection in the Digital Environment in 2009 as a reference source for legal reform.[99] Mainland China may thus learn from Hong Kong to obtain more feedback from the public so as to create more realistic and reliable copyright reform proposals. When applying heterogeneous approaches into digital legal reforms, it is important for China to avoid potential overlapping and conflicts between different approaches and try to merge them so that they are able to systematically and consistently resolve legal issues under the digital network environment.

References

1. China Internet Network Information Center. Semiannual survey report on development of China's Internet (January 2001). Available at http://www.cnnic.cn/hlwfzyj/hlwxzbg/200906/P020120709345368965113.pdf (in Chinese)
2. China Internet Network Information Center. 17th statistical survey report on the Internet development in China (January 2006). Available at http://www.cnic.cas.cn/qkbg/cnnictjbg/cnnic-tjfz/200601/P020090819615860278077.pdf. Visited 17 May 2014 (in Chinese).
3. China Internet Network Information Center. 28th statistical survey report on the Internet development in China (July 2011). Available at http://www1.cnnic.cn/IDR/ReportDownloads/201209/P020120904421102801754.pdf. Visited 17 May 2014.
4. Ginsburg, J. C. (2010). User-generated content sites and Section 512 of the US Copyright Act. In I. A. Stamatoudi (Ed.), *Copyright enforcement and the Internet*. Alphen aan den Rijn: Kluwer Law International.
5. US Copyright Office. (1998). The Digital Millennium Copyright Act of 1998: US Copyright Office Summary. Available at http://www.copyright.gov/legislation/dmca.pdf. Visited 17 Aug 2011.
6. Ginsburg, J., & Ricketson, S. (2006). Inducers and authorisers: A comparison of the US Supreme Court's Grokster decision and the Australian Federal Court's KaZaa ruling. *Media and Arts Law Review, 11*, 1–25.
7. Weinberg, M. (2010). Three strikes, exile, and Judge Dredd. Available at http://www.publicknowledge.org/news-blog/blogs/three-strikes-exile-and-judge-dredd. Visited 17 May 2014.
8. Yu, P. K. (2010). The graduated response. *Florida Law Review, 62*, 1373–1430.

[97] Copyright Protection in the Digital Environment, available at http://www.ipd.gov.hk/eng/intellectual_property/copyright/digital_environment.htm (visited Sept 1, 2011).

[98] Preliminary Proposals for Strengthening Copyright Protection in the Digital Environment, available at http://www.ipd.gov.hk/eng/intellectual_property/copyright/Consultation_Document_Prelim_Proposals_Eng(full).pdf (visited Sept 1, 2011).

[99] *See* n 74 above.

9. Haber, E. (2010). The French revolution 2.0: Copyright and the three strikes policy. *Journal of Sports and Entertainment Law, 2*, 297–339.
10. Meyer, D. Europe 'will not accept' three strikes in ACTA treaty. *ZDNet* (26 February 2010). Available at http://www.zdnet.co.uk/news/networking/2010/02/26/europe-will-not-accept-three-strikes-in-acta-treaty-40057434/. Visited 7 Sept 2011.
11. Sookman, B., & Glover, D. Graduated response and copyright: An idea that is right for the times (20 January 2010). Available at http://www.barrysookman.com/2010/01/20/graduated-response-and-copyright-an-idea-that-is-right-for-the-times/. Visited 7 Sept 2011.
12. Frieden, R. (2008). Internet packet sniffing and its impact on the network neutrality debate and the balance of power between intellectual property creators and consumers. *Fordham Intellectual Property Media & Entertainment Law Journal, 18*, 633–675.
13. Geist, M. Estimating the cost of a three-strikes and you're out system (26 Jan 2010). Available at http://www.michaelgeist.ca/content/view/4731/135. Visited 7 Sept 2011.
14. Patry, W. (2009). *Moral panics and the copyright wars*. Oxford: Oxford University Press.
15. Burger, J. (2009). Filtering & graduated response against online infringers. Available at http://www.dvd-and-beyond.com/features/feature.php?feature=118. Visited 14 May 2014.
16. Zavin, J. (2011). Twentieth Century Fox Film Corp. v. British Telecommunications plc. Available at http://www.lexology.com/library/detail.aspx?g=6cbbb90c-f32f-4dbe-a4ef-8ef993e1aea6. Visited 17 May 2014.

Chapter 5
Reconstruction of Copyright Limitations and Exceptions in Digital Network Age: Importation of Legal Flexibility and Certainty

5.1 Introduction

Copyright systems contain limitations and exceptions on the exclusive rights held by copyright owners. They statutorily allow copyrightable works to be exploited without permission and payment of remuneration to copyright owners. There are basically two kinds of legislative models for these limitations and exceptions. One is a flexible legislative model which includes several guiding factors for courts to make decisions, such as the four-factor test in the United States. Another is a list of exceptions which contain specific situations such as fair dealing in the United Kingdom and a list of exceptions in China.

Limitations and exceptions are indispensible mechanisms embodied in the copyright system. It is alleged as a series of exceptions in the exclusive rights of the copyright owners, mostly exerting social functions such as personal study and research, comments, social event reporting, governmental use, and library preservation. It is often used by defendants as a defense to their advantage in copyright infringement litigations.

The modern doctrine of copyright limitations and exceptions originated from the leading precedents of English copyright law in the early nineteenth century. In the leading case, *Cary v. Kearsley*,[1] the defendant was sued for the infringing reproduction of parts of the plaintiff's book in his own work. The infringement issue was discussed in the judgment by Lord Ellenborough as whether what was taken or supposedly transmitted from the plaintiff's book was fairly done with a view to compile a useful book for the benefit of the public or taken merely with the view to steal the copyright of the plaintiff. The decision made by Lord Ellenborough on distinguishing fair use from copyright infringement rested on whether the defendant productively used the plaintiff's work supported by credible evidence of good faith in promoting the benefits to the public. This basic point of view was adopted and

[1] *Cary v. Kearsley* (1802) 170 Eng. Rep. 679.

J.J. Hua, *Toward A More Balanced Approach: Rethinking and Readjusting Copyright Systems in the Digital Network Era*, DOI 10.1007/978-3-662-43517-5_5,

developed by other jurisdictions in their modern judicial and legislative law on copyright limitations and exceptions.

The United States included a fair use doctrine in its 1976 Copyright Act under Section 107 with a general preamble and a list of four factors. According to Professor Paul Goldstein on the reasons why America has adopted such a legislative style, one reason is that everyone loves a list with arithmetic orderliness; another reason is the historic origin on the factors with regard to Justice Joseph Story's decision in the classical case, *Folsom v. Marsh* [1, p. 436]. In determining whether Charles Upham, the defendant, was taking too much from a 12-volume collection of writings by George Washington by Jared Spark, the plaintiff, into his own creation of a 2-volume work called the *Life of Washington* and committing copyright infringement, Justice Story explained his thoughtful criteria on the fair use of copyrighted work that falls outside of infringement as "the nature and object of the selections made, the quantity and value of the materials used, and the degree in which the use may prejudice the sale, or diminish the profits, or supersede the objects of the original work."[2] Justice Story's consideration was much later evolved to the general criteria of fair use in the 1909 Act revision which in turn contributed to the four factors as included in Section 107 of the 1976 Copyright Act, "the purpose and character of the use; the nature of the copyrighted work; the amount and substantiality of the portion used in the work; and the effect of the use upon the potential market."[3] The American style of legislation on fair use provides a general and flexible guide, although such a legislative model is still questioned by scholars about its legal flexibility and certainty both in theory and in application.

In contrast to the flexible legislative model of the United States, Commonwealth countries, European countries, and China precisely list all foreseeable cases that are particularly suitable under the defense of copyright limitations. The circumstances under Chinese copyright limitations and exceptions include "use of a published work for the purpose of the user's own private study, research or self-entertainment; appropriate quotation from a published work for the purpose of introduction to, or comments on a work or demonstration of a point; reuse or citation of a published work in newspapers and periodicals or on radio stations or television stations for the purpose of reporting current events; reprinting by newspapers or periodicals or rebroadcasting by radio stations or television stations articles published by other relevant organizations on current issues relating to politics, economics or religion; publication in newspapers or periodicals or broadcasting by radio stations, television stations or any other media of a speech delivered at a public gathering; translation or reproduction in a small quantity of copies of a published work by teachers or researchers for classroom teaching or scientific research; use of a published work by state organs to fulfill official duties; reproduction of a work in its collection by a library, archive, memorial hall, museum, art gallery or any similar institution for the purpose of display or preservation; free-of-charge

[2] *Folsom v. Marsh* 9F. Cas. 342 (C.C.D. Mass. 1841).

[3] The US Copyright Act of 1976, s 107.

live performance of a published work; copying, drawing, photographing or video recording of an artistic work located in an outdoor public place; translation of a published work of a Chinese citizen or organization from the Han language into any minority nationality language for publication and distribution within the country; transliteration of a published work into Braille and publication of the work so transliterated."[4] The Chinese legislative model attempts to include all occasions that the legislators could consider so far, while incorporating Chinese characteristics applicable to national conditions. Compared with the general criteria in the American model, and the four-factor legislative model, the list of all exceptions in the Chinese copyright law provides more certainty to copyright work users and creators who can thus measure their actions through exceptions. Nevertheless, the list can hardly contain all possible uses that may be deemed fair especially in the era when digital network technologies develop rapidly and make recreation and remix easier and popular.

Regardless of the type of legislative model that incorporates limitations and exceptions into copyright law, the flexibility and certainty of laws have always been the key focus of scholars and commentators for a long time and should be seriously considered by legislators in different jurisdictions. In the digital network era, technologies simplify the skills and process of reproduction, adaptation, and distribution of copyright works. The worldwide remix culture turns users into creators who largely increase the quantity of creative works which may be infringing under traditional copyright laws, but have positive effects in that the original works are promoted. In light of the high risk of infringement, copyright owners utilize technological measures to block access and copying of their works, which render traditional exceptional use of copyright works difficult and impossible. To reconcile the conflict, rethinking and reconstructing copyright limitations and exceptions both in context and legislative format will address the challenges instigated by continuously updated technologies.

This chapter intends to propose feasible suggestions to amend copyright limitations and exceptions, especially laws for developing countries such as China in this spectrum. The proposal for amendment of copyright limitations and exceptions discussed in this chapter will apply not only to the exclusive rights held by right owners but also to the rights granted by law to performers, phonogram producers, and broadcasting organizations. The first part provides a brief introduction on the content and origin of copyright limitations and exceptions based on typical legislative models. The second part of this chapter will illustrate the necessity of copyright limitations and exceptions through explanations from academic arguments and international treaty obligations. The third section will propose mechanisms for the amendment and reconstruction of copyright limitations and exceptions by importing legal flexibility and certainty along with a discussion on digital challenges to copyright limitations in general and the relationship between copyright limitations and user-generated contents in particular. The fourth section will examine additional schemes that support copyright limitations such as compulsory licensing

[4] Copyright Law of the People's Republic of China (2010 Amendment), Art 22.

schemes, no action notices, and community guidelines. The aim of the importation of these schemes is to use them with fair use/fair dealing to provide more room and freedom for the public to exploit and recreate existing copyright works.

5.2 Theories of Copyright Limitations and Exceptions

5.2.1 Academic Arguments That Support Copyright Limitations and Exceptions

Copyright systems were established with the intent to well maintain a balance of interest between copyright owners and public users and protect the exclusive rights of copyright owners for the purpose of motivating creativity on the one hand and guaranteeing access and reasonable use by public users and new authors of the existing works on the other hand. Two mechanisms typically function to balance the interests; they are the idea-expression dichotomy and copyright limitations. Guided by the idea-expression dichotomy, copyright only protects expression of a work while leaving the idea of a work for free flow and borrowing. Free access and borrowing of ideas continuously contribute to creations and cultural products, from literature to music and from films to digital games. Similar to the idea-expression dichotomy, copyright limitations also contribute to the development and furthering of culture and science by providing certain privileges for teachers, researchers, journalists, commentators, and critics.

Creative practice stipulated by the legal structure of copyright laws not only depends on the market economy but also on the social framework. Monetary incentives for creative practice of authors are well protected by a series of exclusive rights granted by copyright legislation. These exclusive rights include but are not limited to the rights of reproduction, distribution, rental, exhibition, performance, broadcasting, adaptation, translation, and compilation. Different exclusive property rights guarantee full exploitation by copyright holders of works and obtaining of benefits in different markets. Examples given by Professor Randal Picker clearly illustrate this sort of market drive [2]. In the example on the right of translation, the author who creates an English novel should determine the market reaction before translating the novel into Mandarin in order to better exploit the market. If consumers do not like the English version at all, the author should not invest in the translation. By monopolizing the right of translation, the author enjoys an abundance of time to determine the market feedback and make the most reasonable decision. Otherwise, others would create the translation soon after the publication of the English version, thus dominating the Mandarin market which should be the right of the original author. The same situation is applicable to right of public performance which helps the play writer to benefit in the public performance market as opposed to the market for play readers. Undoubtedly, the maximization of benefits from different markets greatly drives the creativity and enthusiasm of authors and promotes full exploitation of existing works. However, money is not everything. People create not only because of money but also due to their desire to establish a reputation, earn recognition, and share thoughts and feelings. Exploitation and use of existing copyright material and production of new works influenced by nonmarket factors constitute fair use/fair dealing. In contrast to a market-driven incentive, fair use should be associated with social functions and framework. Teaching, scholarship, scientific research, journalism, and criticism are examples of social practices in a nonmarket framework. To conclude, exclusive rights govern market-driven exploitation of work, while fair use/fair dealing governs the social use.

Fair use/fair dealing is an indispensible mechanism embodied in copyright, but designing a general theory of fair use/fair dealing is challenging. According to Professor Paul Goldstein, a fair use/fair dealing theory should "achieve a level of abstraction that is at once sufficiently generous to encompass the various uses that courts have judged fair or not fair over the year, yet sufficiently specific to predict results in individual cases, as any working theory must" [1, p. 434], namely, maintaining "the difficult middle distance between abstract theory and minute prescription" [1]. Professor Wendy Gordon's "market failure" [3, pp. 1602–1603] discussion on fair use represents the most prominent theory that approaches the ideal status of fair use/fair dealing. According to Professor Gordon, fair use plays an important role in curing "market failure" of one sort or another. Fair use claims will be declined if the use replaces the actual or potential market for the original work; a fair use defense will be supported if the original author unlikely develops this use in his/her actual or potential market and the use supplements the original work with particular social value. There is a three-part test for granting fair use: (1) the presence of market failure, (2) the social desirability of transferring the use to the defendant, and (3) no substantial injury to the incentives of the plaintiff copyright owner upon award of fair use [4, p. 152].

Theoretical arguments proposed by other scholars also reflect the concerns about market actors, although different phrases are used to express these theories. Professor Raymond Shih Ray Ku regarded fair use/fair dealing as "a series of justifiable creative destruction of copyright markets" [5]. As long as the uncompensated use does not impair the incentive for creation, such use could be deemed fair. Similar to "market failure," the "creative destruction" theory also gives an abstract hypothesis under which fair use/fair dealing is favored on the premise that the driving force of the creative market is preserved and consumers indeed internalize the full cost of the exploitation of copyrighted works. Professor William Fisher recommended a reconstruction of fair use/fair dealing which balances the interests and incentives of copyright owners against the interests of public consumer in access and use of works in any particular case. The reconstruction of fair use/fair dealing aims to achieve "a substantive conception of a just and attractive intellectual culture" [6]. Fisher's proposal blends economic efficiency with the legal theory of fair use/fair dealing based on the balance of interest and social practice philosophies. Although many scholars realize that fair use/fair dealing should support valuable uses for social, cultural, or political interests, few have agreed as to the kinds of uses that fall under this notion. Education and research, private entertainment, news reporting, transformative uses, and noncommercial uses may represent some typical examples that can be subsidized by fair use/fair dealing.

Despite the difficulties of maintaining an appropriate distance between abstract theory and minute prescription, the designing of a legislative model for copyright limitations that can ensure flexibility, certainty, and predictability in law is necessary, especially in an era when advancement of digital network technologies could bring about potential changes to the uses of literature and artistic works at any time. Rethinking and reconstruction of copyright limitations offer opportunities for courts to adapt the doctrine to new circumstances and also to clarify in any particular case whether the defendant can rely on the doctrine.

5.2.2 International Treaty Obligations

Copyright limitations in the Berne Convention were raised for the first time in the 1967 Stockholm Conference and later adopted by the 1971 Paris Act as one of the formal provisions, namely, Article 9 Paragraph 2. Such provision aims to provide general and principal guidance for member countries to take fair practice into consideration apart from the restriction on right of reproduction based on Article 10. It is difficult to list all possible situations of fair practice and unify the scope of copyright limitations due to the discrepancies among different jurisdictions. Therefore, the establishment of a widely applicable standard is more flexible and acceptable, while granting member countries the right to decide on the specific model of legislation that they would like to adopt.

Article 9 Paragraph 2 of the Berne Convention provides a three-step test to weigh copyright limitations, stipulating that member countries shall enact laws to permit reproduction of the copyright work "in certain special cases, provided that such reproduction does not conflict with a normal exploitation of the work and does not unreasonably prejudice the legitimate interests of the author." However, the three-step test in the Berne Convention only applies to limitations and exceptions for the right of reproduction. It has not yet become the general principle of copyright limitations. The international TRIPS agreement later expanded the three-step test to limitations of all exclusive rights. Article 13 of the TRIPS agreement articulates that "members shall confine limitations or exceptions to exclusive rights to certain special cases which do not conflict with a normal exploitation of the work and do not unreasonably prejudice the legitimate interests of the right holder." Besides the expansion of limitations to all exclusive rights, the provision in the TRIPS agreement emphasizes more the confinement on limitations of rights rather than granting limitations as specified in the Berne Convention. The WIPO Internet Treaties further extended the three-step test into the digital network environment. Article 10 of the WCT requires contracting parties to provide limitations or exceptions to the copyrights granted under the Treaty or the Berne Convention in "certain special cases that do not conflict with a normal exploitation of the work and do not unreasonably prejudice the legitimate interests of the author." Article 16 of the WPPT applies the three-step test to protecting performers and phonogram producers under a digital network environment.

As for the three-step test, the WTO panel report on the EC/US copyright act dispute explains the three factors. For the first step, limitations or exceptions should be confined to certain special cases. According to WTO panel specialists, "an exception or limitation in national legislation must be clearly defined. However, there is no need to identify explicitly each and every possible situation to which the exception could apply, provided that the scope of the exception is known and particularised."[5] For the second step, limitations or exceptions to an exclusive right should not conflict with a normal exploitation of the work. An exception or limitation "rises to the level of a conflict with a normal exploitation of the work, if uses, that in principle are covered by that right but exempted under the exception or limitation, enter into economic competition with the ways that right holders normally extract economic value from that right to the work and thereby deprive them of significant or intangible commercial gains."[6] As for the third step under which the limitations or exceptions should not unreasonably prejudice the legitimate interests of the author, "prejudice to the legitimate interests of right holders reaches an unreasonable level if an exception of limitation causes or has the potential to cause an unreasonable loss of income to the copyright owner."[7] Limitations and exceptions to exclusive rights granted by national copyright laws comply with the three-step test only when they simultaneously meet all the requirements with regard to the three factors.

5.3 Reconstruction of Copyright Limitations and Exceptions

Regardless of the legislative model used to regulate copyright limitations and exceptions, legal flexibility and certainty are always the key points that should be seriously considered by policymakers. China is one of the countries that are trying to incorporate both flexibility and certainty into her copyright laws through a new round of reforms. As an example, under Chapter Four "Limitations of the Rights" of the second Modified Draft, a general limitation has been added as the second paragraph of Article 42 which stipulates that the "use of a published work without permission of the copyright owner should not influence the normal exploitation of the work and should not unreasonably infringe the legal interests of the copyright owner." In addition, the first paragraph of Article 42 generally maintains the original

[5] "United States Section 110(5) of the US Copyright Act Report of the Panel," WT/DS160/R (June 15, 2000), paragraph 6.108, available at http://www.wto.org/english/tratop_e/dispu_e/1234da.pdf (visited May 5, 2012).

[6] Ibid., paragraph 6.183.

[7] *See* n 5 above, paragraph 6.229.

list of specific exceptions but eliminates the situation of reproducing the published works of others for personal appreciation.[8]

The expression of the general exception provision in the first Modified Draft and later in the second Modified Draft as paragraph two of Article 42 is the same as the provision in the Regulation on the Implementation of the Copyright Law of People's Republic of China. This is deemed as a transformed transplant of the three-step test in the TRIPS agreement and the WIPO Internet Treaties but modifies three-steps to two steps, namely, to not influence the normal exploitation of a work and not unreasonably prejudice the legitimate interests of the copyright holder. Although the two-step test in the Chinese copyright law seems as a general exception to provide more flexibility for determining fair use, it does not clearly address whether the two-step test applies to potential situations outside the specified list of a number of exceptions in the first Modified Draft or only for the statutorily listed situations. The text "in accordance with the provisions of the law" which appears before the two-step test indicates that the two-step test may only apply to the specified circumstances already listed in the statute. Thus, general exception functions as a condition to

---

[8] Copyright Law of People's Republic of China (second Modified Draft), Art 42: In the following cases, a work may be used without permission from, and without payment of remuneration to, the copyright owner, provided that the name of the author and the title of the work are mentioned and the other rights enjoyed by the copyright owner in accordance with this Law are not prejudiced:

(1) Reproduction of another person's published work for purposes of the user's own personal study and research.
(2) Appropriate quotation from another person's published work in one's own work for the purpose of introducing or commenting a certain work or explaining a certain point. The quotation shall not constitute a major or substantial part of the published work.
(3) Unavoidable inclusion or quotation of a published work in the media, such as in a newspaper, periodical, and radio and television program, for the purpose of reporting current events.
(4) Publishing or rebroadcasting by the media, such as a newspaper, periodical, radio station, and television station, of an article published by another newspaper or periodical or broadcast by another radio station or television station, etc., on current political, economic, or religious topics, except where the author declares that such publishing or rebroadcasting is not permitted.
(5) Publishing or broadcasting by the media, such as a newspaper, periodical, radio station, and television station of a speech delivered at a public gathering, except where the author declares that such publishing or broadcasting is not permitted.
(6) Translation or reproduction in a small quantity of copies of a published work by teachers or scientific researchers for use in classroom teaching or scientific research, provided that the translation or the reproductions are not published for distribution.
(7) Use of a published work by a state organ to a justifiable extent for the purpose of fulfilling its official duties.
(8) Reproduction of a work in its collections by a library, archive, memorial hall, museum, art gallery, etc., for the purpose of display, or preservation of a copy, of the work.
(9) Gratuitous live performance of a published work, for which no fees are charged to the public, nor payments are made to the performers.
(10) Copying, drawing, photographing, or video recording of a work of art put up or displayed in an outdoor public place.
(11) Translation of a published work of a Chinese citizen, legal entity, or other organization from Han language into minority nationality languages for publication and distribution in the country.
(12) Transliteration of a published work into Braille for publication.

restrict the twelve detailed situations rather than abstractly guide the standard of judgment for all potential fair uses. The second Modified Draft later added "other situations" on the prescribed list in order to expand the exceptions. In other words, under the updated and revised version, the two-step test not only applies to the already specified situations but also to potential reasonable uses outside the prescribed scope.

The proposal to incorporate a four-factor balancing test originated from the US case law and statutes as general guidance to weigh all potential situations and the nonexclusive list of exceptions as minute prescriptions may work better to guarantee both legal flexibility and certainty.

5.3.1 Importing Flexibility and Certainty into Copyright Limitations and Exceptions

The American legislative model that uses a four-factor fair use test provides general flexible guidance as to who should receive the privilege of fair use. Derived from Justice Story's opinion in *Folsom v. Marsh*, the four-factor test that was imported into the 1976 Copyright Act has continuously played a role in adapting the fair use doctrine to new circumstances, from traditional cases on education and journalism to new technological cases that involve video recording and software reverse engineering.

It is better to incorporate the four-factor balancing test based on US copyright legislation with focus on the first and fourth factors as an abstract guide and clearly point out in the legislation that the four-factor test is used to determine both a numbered list of exceptions and potential fair uses outside the list. There are several reasons that the four-factor balancing test is more appropriate than the three-step or two-step test. First, the conditions in the three-step test are accumulatively applied when judging fair use cases. A legitimate or fair use must satisfy all three conditions in the three-step test. In contrast, the determination of fair use based on the four-factor test relies on balancing and weighing of each factor. A legitimate or fair use does need to comply with all four factors but, rather, weighed as a whole as fair and non-infringing. Under the four-factor balancing test, judges will not rule against fair use simply due to one condition that has not been satisfied, such as commercial use, but will comprehensively consider all potentials. Secondly, the expression of the three-step test is more abstract and principled than the four-factor balancing test. The explanation and analysis of each condition in the three-step test are subject to specific case and contexts. Comparatively, elements in the four-factor balancing test are detailed and easy to understand. Judges can determine whether the use in question is transformative or commercial, copyright work is fictional or factual, copies used are a substantial part of the work, and new work based on the use replaces the original work. It is more practical for judges to apply the four factors, since the capability of judges in developing countries such as China is not yet at the level of WTO specialists.

Nevertheless, the four-factor test is questioned about its clarity and accuracy in that multiple factors generate substantial uncertainty on how they shall be balanced and weighed [7, p. 574]. No guidance has been provided "as to how to measure these factors against one another, whether all must be satisfied for a finding of fair use, or how conflicts among them are to be reconciled" [8, p. 1496]. More influential elements cause more difficulties in the process of outcome prediction. In an attempt to mitigate the problem of uncertainty, Professor Joseph Liu suggested a two-factor test to determine fair use litigation which only includes the first and fourth factors of the original statutes: (1) the purpose and character of the use and (2) the effect of the use on the potential market of the copyrighted work [7]. He supposed that a shift from a complicated multifactor test to a simplified two-factor will impose more accuracy on fair use determination since the courts can directly balance one factor against another. The weighing of two considerations is more feasible. Hence, a more appropriate and effective four-factor balancing test with the focus on the first and fourth factors would be better adopted by national legislations.

To my understanding, the four-factor balancing test with a focus on the first and fourth factors could be imported into legislation as an abstract resource that guides the decision of the courts since mastering such an approach is feasible. However, the amendment of a legislative model of copyright limitations and exceptions as a four-factor balancing scheme is not enough for some developing societies, such as China, because of the significant disparities in various regions and sectors of the country. Differing economic and marketing conditions mean that there is uneven quality of judges and public education on intellectual property protection. A one-size-fits-all balancing test cannot fully guarantee the certainty of copyright limitations and exceptions, because the litigation outcome depends on the discretion of the judge, which is hard to predict in less developed regions. Therefore, it is necessary to list a series of nonexclusive exceptions that work collaboratively with the four-factor abstract test. A legislative model that combines abstract guidance and detailed prescriptions will work better for developing countries in view of their national conditions, guarantee predictability on the one hand, and incorporate flexibility on the other hand. The following paragraphs will individually analyze the four factors and explain the importance of the first and fourth factors in comparison with the rest of the other factors. Emphasis will be placed on the analysis of the transformative nature in recently popular user-generated contents and remix works. The subsequent parts will discuss that the means of exploitation of works should be integrated into the nonexclusive list of exceptions as minute prescriptions.

5.3.2 Importing Four-Factor Balancing Test as Abstract Guidance

5.3.2.1 Four-Factor Balancing Test

The four factors in the balancing test embodied in Section 107 of the US Copyright Act are the purpose and character of the use, nature of the copyrighted work, amount and substantiality of the use, and effect of use on the market. When making decisions, the courts will consider all four factors and weigh each one against the other to determine whether the use can be deemed as fair.

As for the first factor "the purpose and character of the use," the courts will analyze whether the use has a commercial nature or is for nonprofit education purposes as well as whether the use has a transformative nature or is non-transformative. Generally, if it is found that the use is transformative and for noncommercial purposes, these favor the fair use defense. Otherwise, the court is more likely to weigh the first factor against the defendant. Commercial use is presumptively considered unfair at the beginning, as explained by the judges in *Sony Corp. of America v. Universal City Studios Inc.* in which "every commercial use of copyrighted material is presumptively ... unfair."[9] However, this was later overturned by the decision in *Campbell v. Acuff-Rose Music* under which "the mere fact that a use is educational and not for profit does not insulate it from a finding of infringement, any more than the commercial character of a use bars a finding of fairness."[10] Thus, commercial nature is no longer definitely weighed against fair use. As user-generated works and the rise of the remix culture due to the assistance of digital technology, transformative nature becomes quite an important factor to weigh the fair use defense. As the court concluded in *Campbell*, "the more transformative the new work, the less will be the significance of other factors, like commercialism, that may weigh against a finding of fair use."[11] The standard to determine the transformative nature will be further discussed in subsequent parts in detail, as the transformativeness has already become the most important factor to judge the effect of use to the market so as to further decide the existence of fair use.

As for the second factor "the nature of the copyrighted work," the courts will determine whether the work is fictional or factual. More creativity in the copyrighted work means that it is more likely that the court will rule against fair use. Works under copyright protection all meet the preliminary requirement of originality. The second factor goes beyond the fundamental requirement of copyright protection, as demonstrated in *Campbell* that "some works are closer to the core of intended copyright protection than others, with the consequence that fair use is more difficult to establish when the former works are copied."[12] Accordingly, courts are more likely to rule in favor of fair use if the copyrighted work is factual, while ruling against fair use when the copyrighted work is fictional.

As for the third factor "the amount and substantiality of the use," the courts will take both quantitative and qualitative aspects into consideration. Under certain circumstances where the defendants only copy a small amount of the copyrighted works, the courts will not approve a finding of fair use if the reproduced portion is the soul of the whole works. In *Harper & Row Publishers Inc. v. National Enterprises*,[13] the Supreme Court denied the argument of fair use by National Enterprises because of the small amount of text copied from President Ford's memoirs, thus ruling that

[9] *Sony Corp. of America v. Universal City Studios Inc.* 464 U.S. 417 (1984).

[10] *Campbell v. Acuff-Rose Music* 510 U.S. 569 (1994).

[11] Ibid.

[12] *Campbell* (n 10 above).

[13] *Harper & Row Publishers Inc. v. National Enterprises* 471 U.S. 539 (1985).

the extracted 300 words by the defendant constituted the heart of the book. Under certain circumstances where the defendant reproduces the entire work, the court confirms fair use if the use is transformative. Several cases with regard to the reproduction of whole pictures for transformative use which will be examined later have proven the importance of the transformative nature of the use.

As for the fourth factor "the effect of use upon the market," the courts are more likely to reject the fair use defense if the use has actual or potential harm to the market of the original works. Uses are often deemed as having negative effect to the market if the subsequent work based on these uses replaces the original work. On the contrary, uses are regarded as fair if the later work supplements the original work. Although in certain situations where the criticism from parody may decrease the profits of the original work, the courts will not deny fair use simply because the public is reluctant to pay for the original work due to criticism. The court in *Campbell* has well explained that "when a lethal parody, like a scathing theatre review, kills demand for the original, it does not produce a harm cognizable under the Copyright Act."[14]

5.3.2.2 Concentrating on First and Fourth Factors

Although the four-factor balancing test continuously plays an essential role in judging fair use, many scholars have doubts on the certainty of the ability of the test to balance a multitude of factors. The testing of a multitude of factors for fair use is likely to mislead the courts in deciding which side has met the most factors. The test does not provide sufficient and clear guidance to potential users. The courts of the United States often consider "the totality of the four factors in an impressionistic fashion" [7, p. 575]. Professors William Fisher and Glyn Lunney also suggested that the courts should directly consider the final question of fair use and disregard the four factors [6, 9]. Opinions from American courts in several cases emphasize the first and fourth factors of the four factors, that is, they put less emphasis on the role played by the second and third factors in fair use decisions. In influential cases such as *Sony v. Universal City Studios*[15] and *Sega v. Accolade*,[16] the courts played down the importance of the creative nature of the copyrighted work and that a large amount of the work was being copied. Empirical research by Professor Barton Barbee on fair use cases also proves the reduced importance of the second and third factors [10].

As for the second factor, the nature of the work, a large volume of fair use cases show that works in question are creative with commercial value, since copyright primarily concerns originality and creativity of works. Courts often weigh this factor against the defendant, which results in futility in balancing the influence of the second factor. In addition, the nature of the work is often analyzed by the courts

[14] *Campbell* (n 10 above).

[15] *Sony Corp. of America* (n 9 above).

[16] *Sega Enterprises Ltd. v. Accolade, Inc.* 997F.2d 1510 (9th Cir. 1992).

when considering the first factor, the purpose and nature of the use. The consideration of the second factor is captured in the first factor. As for the third factor, the amount of the copyrighted work used, the courts are more likely to weigh this factor against the defendant if more parts of a copyrighted work are used. Similarly, the consideration of the third factor is also captured in the fourth factor, the effect of the use on the market of the copyrighted work, because commonly, significant use will interfere with the existing and potential markets of the original work. Furthermore, considerations of both factors may sometimes make fair use judgments confusing and complex. Due to the rapid development of digital network technologies, copying and adapting an entire piece of work requires less time and labor and does not have seriously negative impact on the market of the work. Under circumstances in which significant use does not affect the original market of the work, the resolving of the fair use litigation will become an issue.

By comparing the association of the four factors to fair use cases, the first and fourth have direct and determinative influence, but the second and third are less relevant to the ultimate decision and, under some circumstances, will even make fair use analysis more complex. As to how one and four can work together to clarify fair use arguments, the first factor, or the nature and purpose of the use, reflects the main purposes of the user and the fourth factor, or the effect of the use on the original market, reflects the influence on the creativity of the original authors. Under the four-factor balancing approach with focus on the first and fourth factors, the courts could first consider the nature and purpose of the use to examine whether the use is transformative and noncommercial with positive social values. The courts could then balance the purpose of the use against the effect on the potential market of the original work, while taking the nature of the copyright work and the amount of use into consideration. In situations where both the first and fourth factors either favor or disfavor fair use, it is not difficult for the courts to make unanimous judgments because the nature and purpose of the use and its effect on the market of the original works are more conclusive than the other two factors. However, the courts should be more meticulous in the balancing test, when either the first and fourth factor favors fair use while the other negates the fair use defense. The strength of factor one may outweigh the strength of the fourth factor, or vice versa [7, p. 579]. Factor one concentrates on the social value of the use, encouraging various social practice such as education, research, commentation, and journalism. Factor four puts more emphasis on the economics by considering negative effects on the market. Under some circumstances, the courts may find greatly positive social value of the use, despite some repercussions on the market. By focusing on the first and fourth factors, the courts can develop "intra-factor doctrines" [7] to examine how each factor is weighed for fair use or against fair use.

Discussions have recently concentrated more on how the courts determine the transformative nature and social value of the use, as well as the relationship between the transformative value of the use and the potential market of original copyright work. The change in the focus to the transformative nature and purpose of use is mainly due to the rapid growth of technology-based user-generated works, fan fictions, and remix culture.

5.3.2.3 Determining Transformativeness of Use

Although fan fictions and user-generated works have long existed in the traditional text-based paper world, the rapid development of digital network technologies greatly facilitates the expansion of fan fictions and user-generated works to new media formats, such as music and videos. These works are primarily noncommercial in nature and credit the original authors. They narrate new stories based on the characters, plots, and scenes from the original works. The transformative manifestations of fan fictions and user-generated works range from critiques, parodies, and satires to laudations. Transformative creation makes works more meaningful and appealing to the users and disseminates the understanding and attitude of the originals by users. Aided by digital network technologies, young fans have more sources and inspiration to express their creative ideas, polish their writing skills, compose videos, and establish recognition in their fan communities.

The popularity of the Harry Potter series by J. K. Rowling has caused numerous parodies and satires all over the world, in nearly every kind of media. The transformativeness of these works relies on diverse formats that range from traditional instruments, such as books, analog films, and televisions to digital network media including online films and animations, online audios, and web comics.[17] The Harry Potter series was also transformed by fan creators to create new stories, plots, and language and scenes adaptive to the culture and society of different countries. Various fan communities and fan fictions also expanded to other successful and popular copyright works, including American TV series such as CSI and Star Trek and Japanese animations such as Saint Seiya and Slam Dunk.

Fan fiction in China originated from Chinese youth followers of Japanese cartoons and animations and gradually extended to animations and TV series produced in China. With a national policy that encourages the development of the cultural industries, the production of a significant amount of quality domestic animations, films, and TV series has led to a fast generation of Chinese-based fan fictions and user-generated works. The popular 3D Chinese animated TV series, Qin's Moon, has attracted numerous adaptations created by its fans in the forms of online novels, cartoons, stage dramas, audios and videos, online radio programs, and mobile games from its broadcasting in 2007. Most of the fan works are not licensed under the authorization of Qin's Moon and do not pay remuneration to the producer. Some fans use the characters and the dynasty to narrate entirely new stories, making their beloved character become a hero, creating romantic relationships that did not previously exist between characters, and designing personalized endings that represent their own preferences and values. Other fans may not devote much creativity into their works, but simply copy screenshots from the animation and rearrange the screenshots into different chronological orders coupled with existing copyright music. Due to their noncommercial nature, fan works are more likely to be regarded as fair use and contain contents that the market will not produce or sustain [11, p. 507].

[17] "Parodies of Harry Potter," available at http://en.wikipedia.org/wiki/Parodies_of_Harry_Potter (visited Nov 17, 2011).

As for the first instance of recreated storytelling, user-generated works are more readily deemed as transformative, since transformativeness has been explained in some important cases as "adding something new, with a further purpose or different character, [thus] altering the original with new expression, meaning, or message."[18] However, the latter instance of rearrangement is less likely to be transformative, as there is little material variation in the rearranged works. Although many of the latter instances are nonprofit, the use can hardly be considered as fair when the collections of screenshots are disseminated online by the fan creators. These examples pose a key question as to how the use can be determined as transformative so that the four-factor balancing test would be mostly inclined to favor the use.

In intellectual creation, "borrower-as-creator" has long had a constant presence "both as a matter of historical description and as a central figure in copyright law fair use commentary" [12, p. 450]. The widespread user-generated contents and popular remix culture depend on borrowing-as-creation, and it in turn depends on copyright limitations [12, pp. 450–451]. Although American courts have long been discussing the nature and purpose of borrowing use, it was not until the 1990s that the courts began to address the argument in that borrowing use should be deemed fair because it situates the work into a new context. In *Campbell*, 2 Live Crew's rap song "Oh Pretty Woman" used the repeating hook and the first line of Roy Orbison's song "Pretty Woman."[19] In order to decide whether 2 Live Crew's use could qualify as fair use, the court took Justice Story's discussion into consideration by examining "whether the new work merely supersedes the objects of the original creation or instead adds something new, with a further purpose or different character, altering the first with new expression, meaning, or message; it asks, in other words, whether and to what extent the new work is transformative."[20] The second work "lies at the heart of the fair use doctrine's guarantee of breathing space within the confines of copyright, and the more transformative the new work, the less will be the significance of other factors, like commercialism, that may weigh against a finding of fair use."[21] According to the court's analysis based on Judge Pierre Leval's opinion on transformative criteria, the transformativeness of the use relies on whether it "fulfills the objective of copyright law to stimulate creativity for public illumination" [13] in general, as well as whether "it is productive and employs the quoted matter in a different manner or for a different purpose from the original" [13] in particular. In determining the transformativeness of the use, the courts have focused on the purpose of the user-as-creator.

Research by Professor R. Anthony Reese on the relationship between transformativeness and the right of derivative work of the copyright owner further confirms the judicial focus on the purpose of the use to determine transformativeness based on more than 50 circuit court cases [14]. Due to the transformative feature of most

[18] *Campbell* (n 10 above), p. 579.

[19] *Campbell* (n 10 above).

[20] *Campbell* (n 10 above).

[21] *Campbell* (n 10 above).

derivative works within the scope of the right of derivative work of copyright owners, commentators are concerned that weighing transformativeness in favor of fair use will result in negatively affecting the right of derivative work of copyright owners. Reese's comparative analysis of a large volume of cases indicated that "appellate courts have not applied fair use transformativeness in ways that significantly implicate the scope of the derivative work right" [14, p. 471]. In a conclusive review of the relation between transformativeness and fair use, Reese divided the cases into four categories: "(1) the defendant has transformed the content of the plaintiff's copyrighted work and is using it for a transformative purpose; (2) the defendant has transformed the content of the plaintiff's copyrighted work but is not using it for a transformative purpose; (3) the defendant has not transformed the content of the plaintiff's copyrighted work but is using the copyrighted work for a transformative purpose; and (4) the defendant has not transformed the content of the plaintiff's copyrighted work and is not using the copyrighted work for a transformative purpose" [14, p. 486].

It will not be difficult to anticipate the decisions of the courts in "double or nothing" situations as shown in the first and fourth categories. In the first category, the courts are expected to favor the fair use defense, since transformation is involved in both types and more transformativeness of the use means more strongly that the courts will support the fair use defense. In the fourth category, the courts are more likely to reject the fair use argument, as the defendant does not make either type of transformation and the defendant's use of the original work cannot be found as transformative. In order to determine a transformative fair use, the focus should be on "either-or" transformation in which the defendant engages in only one type of transformation.

With regard to the third situation in which the user-as-creator does not make any substantive adaptation or transformation to the content of the original work, but the use is for a different purpose, four typical cases are provided as examples to demonstrate that the courts view different purposes as transformative and weigh the purpose in support of the fair use defense. In *Nunez v. Caribbean International News Corporation*,[22] the defendant used the modeling photographs of Miss Puerto Rico Universe in conjunction with a news article and editorial commentary to discuss the controversy over whether Miss Puerto Rico Universe had engaged in conduct that was unbecoming for her position. The first circuit court decided that the newspaper's use of the photos was transformative in support of its fair use defense, because the plaintiff's photographs were originally intended to appear in modeling portfolios, but the defendant used the photos to report and comment on a news story, which transformed the original purpose of the photo production and gave them new meaning and purpose, even though the content of photos remained unchanged. In *Bill Graham Archives v. Dorling Kindersley*,[23] the defendant DK reproduced seven concert posters among over 2000 images in its biography of the musical group, the Grateful Dead. Similar to Nunez, the second circuit court ruled in favor

[22] *Nunez v. Caribbean International News Corp.* 235F.3d 18 (1st Cir. 2000).

[23] *Bill Graham Archives v. Dorling Kindersley* 448F.3d 605 (2nd Cir. 2006).

of the defendant by explaining that DK's use of the copyrighted images at issue aimed to historically document and represent the actual occurrence of Grateful Dead concert events, which was different from the plaintiff's original purpose of artistic expression and promotion of live concerts.[24] Although DK's reproduction was entirely the same as the originals, the use of the images in its biography of the Grateful Dead was transformative enough for fair use purposes. The court further emphasized that regardless how unobvious the link between image and text, the accompanied commentary or criticism was necessary to fulfill the transformative purpose in order to render fair use. In *Kelly v. Arriba Soft Corporation*[25] and *Perfect 10 v. Amazon.com*,[26] the Ninth Circuit regarded the reproduction of the plaintiffs' images by the defendants in the form of thumbnail versions in search engines as transformative, since the creation of thumbnail images in search engines transformed the original purpose of artistic expression to an entirely new purpose of improving access of web users to sources of information. Despite the exact reproduction, the court refused to adopt the judgments of earlier cases in which unchanged reproduction was not considered transformative and confirmed the transformative nature of the work as having a different purpose.

In the second situation, more than ten cases have proven that the courts did not find the use transformative in favor of fair use because the defendants did not use the original work for any transformative purpose although they altered the contents. Among these cases, the most famous is *Dr. Seuss Enterprises, L.P. v. Penguin Books*,[27] in which the defendant created a humorous book named *The Cat Not in the Hat* about the O.J. Simpson murder trial, by using characters and rhyme schemes from the popular children's book *The Cat in the Hat* by Dr. Seuss. Despite the substantial alteration of the original content, the Ninth Circuit opined that the defendant's use was not transformative in favor of fair use, in that the purpose of creating the new book was to provide a satire rather than a parody. The court carefully distinguished parody from satire based on a previous case, *Campbell*. "A parody is creation in which the copyrighted work is the target of humorous criticism; a satire, by contrast, uses the copyrighted work to make fun of some other target."[28] Since the creator of *The Cat Not in the Hat* did not intend to comment or criticize the work of Dr. Seuss, but rather targeted the O.J. Simpson murder trial, the court viewed the new creation as non-transformative without "new expression, meaning, or message."[29] In the viewpoint of the American appellate courts, the purpose of producing parody is transformative, since the parody creator transforms the purpose of the original author for literature expression and entertains readers for a different purpose to criticize and comment on the original work. In contrast, the purpose of creating satire is not transformative because the purpose of the satire author is to

---

[24] Ibid.

[25] *Kelly v. Arriba Soft Corp.* 336F.3d 811 (9th Cir. 2003).

[26] *Perfect 10 v. Amazon.com* 508F.3d 1146 (9th Cir. 2007).

[27] *Dr. Seuss Enterprises, L.P. v. Penguin Books* 109F.3d 1394 (9th Cir. 1997).

[28] Ibid., p. 1400.

[29] *Campbell* (n 10 above), pp. 569, 579.

express his/her thoughts and amuse readers, which does not differentiate the work from the original author's purpose of the creation. In other cases such as *Castle Rock Entertainment v. Carol Publishing Group*,[30] the appellate court did not regard the production of a trivia quiz book by the defendant which extracted information from the television show as transformative. In view of an evaluation of the transformative purpose of the use, the court viewed the defendant's repacking of trivia quizzes as entertaining the viewers rather than criticizing or commenting on the quizzes. Thus, the defense of a transformative purpose was denied. Similarly, in *Columbia Pictures Industries Inc. v. Miramax Films Corp.*,[31] the plaintiff sued the defendant for an advertising poster put out by the latter on a film, *The Big One*, which featured the attire and the stance of the hero in the plaintiff's advertisement of the film *Men in Black*. The defendant admitted that the alleged infringing poster made derivation of the plaintiff's work, but claimed a fair use defense for its derivative. In the ruling, the court denied the fair use defense, finding that the poster did not comment on or criticize the plaintiff's advertisement for *Men in Black*, and the making of the poster with the aim to attract audience to watch *The Big One* was not different from the plaintiff's intent of producing the original advertisement.

The representative "either-or" transformation cases illustrate that in order to garner fair use, transformation of the purpose for which the work is used is far more important than transformation of the work's content. The courts are more likely to find a fair use defense justified if the use of the work has transformative purposes even though the use does not alter the work's content. On the contrary, the courts are more inclined to reject the fair use argument if the purpose of the use is not transformative despite substantive alterations made by the defendant in the work's content. The judging of the purpose for which the work is used highly relies on judicial discretion. Due to the specifics and complexities of each case, it is not feasible to speculate a rigid standard that can be applied to all possible transformative purposes. Therefore, a judge should analyze the purpose of the use by a defendant from an ordinary person's perspective and rationale.

Although the nature and purpose of use is not the only determinative factor in fair use analysis, it plays a significant role in balancing other factors, which are the nature of the copyrighted work, amount of work being used, and the effect of the use on the market of the original work. Taking the aforementioned fan fictions of Qin's Moon, a Chinese animation as an example, the direct reproduction and editing of the clips of the screenshots in the original animation would infringe the exclusive rights of the copyright holder and cannot be considered as fair use even though these fan works are noncommercial and nonprofit, because fan creators have not used any parts of the original animation for a transformative purpose. As for other types of fan fictions which have substantively altered the original storyline of the animation, it is necessary to examine whether the purpose of creating such fan works is transformative so that the fan fictions fall into the fair use scope. An attractive Chinese

[30] *Castle Rock Entertainment v. Carol Publishing Group* 150F.3d 132 (2nd Cir. 1998).

[31] *Columbia Pictures Industries Inc. v. Miramax Films Corp.* 11F. Supp.2d 1179 (1998).

case about transformative use arouses continuous public dispute on the legitimacy of remix works in China.

In 2006, Hu Ge, a Chinese video editor and broadcaster, produced a 20-min video named *The Bloody Case That Started from a Steamed Bun* (thereafter *The Steamed Bun Bloody Case*) by using fragments of the film *The Promise* made by a famous Chinese director, Chen Kaige [15]. Due to his dislike of *The Promise*, Hu Ge edited the clips and rearranged parts of the film in conjunction with dubbing and background music to refashion the story line as an investigative TV program in a mocking and ironic manner. The publishing and distribution of this video on the Internet attracted widespread concern and thus came to the attention of Chen Kaige who threatened to file a copyright infringement and defamation lawsuit. Although Chen Kaige did not actually sue Hu Ge for his mock video creation, *The Steamed Bun Bloody Case* initiated public concern on copyright issues brought about by the spread of technology-based remix works. Commentators in China have not come to a unanimous conclusion yet. The adoption of the four-factor balancing test with focus on the first and fourth factors and the transformativeness analysis may help to examine whether fan fictions and remix works such as *The Steamed Bun Bloody Case* are considered to be fair use.

Undoubtedly, Hu Ge altered the contents of *The Promise* since he rearranged the film, added screenshots from TV programs, and dubbed voice-over narrations and background music that did not originally belong to the film. In order to win the case if he was sued, Hu Ge must prove that he had transformative intentions in the creation of the video. In other words, *The Steamed Bun Bloody Case* should convince the judges that it is a critique and satire on the film rather than entertainment for viewers which is the purpose of the original film. In watching the video, there are certain parts that actually ridiculed and commented on *The Promise*. For example, the video uncovered loopholes in the film plots by showing the heroine as a child eating the steamed bun at the beginning of the film, and the exact same steamed bun which appeared 20 years later in the hand of an evil man who attempts to seek revenge from the adult heroine, as well as dubbing a humorous voice-over which said, "how this steamed bun appear again as it was already eaten.... I am not clear about the steamed bun problem; it is design of the director."[32] In addition, the video criticized the outrageous characterization of the film by inserting commentaries such as "parents should educate their children to form a correct outlook on life; don't let their children follow an evil man who has harbored bitter resentment for 20 years." These adaptations made the video a parody and were likely to cater to a fair use defense. However, the criticism to the film itself does not make up a large proportion of the overall video which also contains satires of various social problems. Satire cannot be judged as fair use, as it derives the original work with the purpose to comment on other issues rather than the original work itself. Therefore, in litigation, the judges should determine whether the rearranged screenshots from *The Promise* play an appropriate role in commenting and criticizing the film which is the

[32]The video of *The Steamed Bun Bloody Case* is available on the Chinese broadcasting website www.tudou.com

main purpose of the video creation based on the evidence provided by the litigant so as to determine the transformative nature of the video.

Apart from remix works and fan fictions, the four-factor balancing test that analyzes transformativeness could also shed light on other kinds of cases, such as the Google Book Search litigation. Google made agreements with some major research libraries to digitize the books in their collections for the purpose of facilitating individuals to carry out searches on the indexed book results via the Google database.[33] For books in the public domain, the entire contexts are available for searchers; for books under copyright protection, only small parts of the entire text are made available. Google was sued for its book digitization by the relevant authors and publishers. The case was ultimately resolved by a settlement agreement reached by Google and the publishers. In taking the four-factor balancing and transformative purpose test into consideration, Google's condensation of the copyright books could be regarded as content alteration, but the courts can analyze Google's purpose for reproduction of the books in different ways by relying on the evidence provided. The courts may reach the conclusion that Google's use is transformative, as Google contributes to making book information individually searchable and accessible; or the use is not transformative, as Google's provision of partial contents of the books at the expense of the interest of the copyright holders is not different from the purpose of the authors to share their thoughts. The courts may then balance the purpose of the use against the other three factors. The four-factor balancing test alone cannot indicate the outcome. It facilitates the courts to concentrate on the determining factors and directly balance the first factor against the fourth while considering the second and third factors based on case facts and evidence.

Similar book search cases can also be found in China. In 2004, Zheng Chengsi and six other professors and scholars sued the Beijing Shusheng Digital Technology Company (thereafter Shusheng Company) for digitalizing and disseminating the copyright works of Zheng and his colleagues on its website (www.21media.com) [15]. The Shusheng Company argued that its business mode assimilated the reading mode found in libraries, under which readers could not download or distribute works except through a rather complex means of screenshots, and at maximum, only three people could simultaneously read the same book. Thus, according to the defense by the Shusheng Company, the business mode is similar to traditional libraries which complied with copyright limitations and should not be regarded as copyright infringement. However, Zheng claimed that the company's technology only restricted the number of people who could read the same book simultaneously, but did not prevent the reading of the same book simultaneously at different occasions. In addition, the Shusheng Company did not seek authorization from Zheng and his colleagues to use their works. Based on the evidence, the district court ruled against the Shusheng Company, holding that unlike traditional libraries which restrict the use of their collections due to material conditions, the business mode of the Shusheng Company did not reduce the risk of exploitation of copyright works.

[33] "Google Books Litigation and Settlements," available at http://copyright.columbia.edu/copyright/special-topics/google-settlement/ (visited May 17, 2014).

Therefore, digitalization and online distribution of academic works by the Shusheng Company did not comply with copyright limitations and their use of the works without authorization from the copyright holders committed copyright infringement. The appellate court later confirmed the lower court's opinion.[34] In this case, the court focused on the adverse impact that Shusheng Company's business mode would have on the potential market of the concerned books. In addition, the court can support its conclusion if it took the purpose and nature of the use into consideration. In contrast to the Google book search case in which Google made excerptions of the books, the Shusheng Company reproduced the whole work without any alterations and the purpose of their reproduction and distribution was not different from the original aims of the authors, namely, to educate readers and facilitate academic research.

5.3.3 *Importing Nonexclusive List of Exceptions as Minute Prescriptions*

In order to guarantee the flexibility and predictability of copyright limitations and applicability to the national conditions of developing countries such as China, legislations should also import a list of nonexclusive exceptions in addition to the general guidance provided by the four-factor balancing test. Uses that are considered to be under nonexclusive exceptions and comply with the four-factor balancing test can be recognized as fair and are thus free from copyright infringement. Since the list of exceptions is nonexclusive, uses that obviously do not fall within the scope shall be analyzed under the four-factor general test. The application of the general guidance and list of minute copyright limitations could provide more certainty to potential users and borrower-as-creators, as the list of exceptions reduces transaction costs that a user needs to clear multiple copyrights before publication of his/her new work and protects the user from litigations and uncertain case-by-case decisions.

There are two parts to minute prescriptions. The first is a list of nonexclusive exceptions for research, private study, comments, news reporting, fulfillment of governmental obligations, and reservation of collections in library, archives, museums, and galleries as regulated by fair dealing in some Commonwealth and continental European countries. The second part is permitted use under technological measures. The anti-circumvention rules of TPMs adopted by China and many other countries made non-infringing use unavailable to the large amount of copyright works stored in the digital form. In order to enjoy copyright limitations, the user or the borrower-as-creator must first obtain access to the protected works by circumventing the technological measures, which is deemed illegal under the current anti-circumvention rules. Those who support technological measures decline to import

[34] *Zheng Chengsi v. Beijing Shusheng Digital Technology Company* (in Chinese), Beijing First Intermediate People's Court (2005) Yi Zhong Min Zhong Zi No. 3643.

general exceptions for traditional copyright limitations under the digital network environment in fear that they cannot differentiate circumvention of technological measures for non-infringing use from circumvention for infringement. A proposal to revise the anti-circumvention rule by including a technological design to guarantee minimum use, legislative design to incorporate general copyright limitations and exceptions, judicial design to provide guideline for court decisions, and a scheme that takes into consideration issues beyond intellectual property, such as competition law, may help to address the problem.

5.3.3.1 List of Nonexclusive Exceptions

A legislative model that provides all possible copyright exceptions has been adopted by common law jurisdictions, such as the United Kingdom and Canada, and civil law jurisdictions, such as Germany and Taiwan. Only uses that are within the scope of the list can be regarded as fair dealing or exceptions. Copyright exceptions cannot apply to other circumstances outside the statutory scope. Hence, there have been criticisms that fair dealing in these countries are too restrictive and lack flexibility, since a static list cannot possibly contain all potential uses due to advancement in technology. However, the categories listed under fair dealing can illustrate the types of uses that are considered as fair so as to achieve the purpose of promoting the advancement of knowledge and learning in copyright.

The Copyright, Designs and Patents Act (CDPA) of the United Kingdom lists all permissible uses under Chapter III "Acts Permitted in Relation to Copyright Works." Sections 29 and 30 outline the fair dealing that are applicable for the purposes of research and private study, criticism or review, and reporting of current events. In order to weigh the fair dealing defense in litigations, judges will successively consider three issues: (1) whether the dealing in question falls within the scope of research and private study, criticism, review, and reporting of current events; (2) if the use falls within the scope, whether the dealing is fair based on various criteria developed from common law cases; (3) and whether the dealing meets additional statutory requirements, such as sufficient acknowledgment of the original works in the cases of research and private study, criticism, review, and reporting of current events and whether the original work has been made available to the public in the case of criticism or review.[35] Unlike the fair use model in the United States under which every case can be weighed according to the four-factor balancing test, weighing the factors in the United Kingdom only applies to a situation which already falls under the mandatory list of specified items. The determining factors which have been developed from various cases that are used to determine fairness include

[35] Copyright, Designs and Patents Act 1988, ss 29 and 30. No acknowledge is required in connection with fair dealing for the purpose of research and private study where this could be impossible for reasons of practicality or otherwise. No acknowledgment is required in connection with the reporting of current events by means of a sound recording, film, or broadcast where this would be impossible for reasons of practicality or otherwise.

whether the work was made available to the public, method through which the work was obtained, quantity and quality of the parts used, type and purpose of the use, consequence of the dealing, and whether the same objective can be achieved by using other means.[36] These factors have been adopted and used by the courts as a whole to make decisions. As Lord Denning opined in *Hubbard v. Vosper*, "it is impossible to define what is 'fair dealing'. It must be a question of degree. ... But after all is said and done, it must be a matter of impression."[37]

Fair dealing in Canada assimilates that of the CDPA in the United Kingdom. Section 29 of the Canadian Copyright Act provides that fair dealing for the purposes of "research or private study, criticism or review, and news reporting" does not infringe copyright. Similar to the approaches of the United Kingdom, courts in fair dealing cases must consider three elements: (1) whether the dealing falls into the list of a number of exceptions; (2) if the dealing is related to one of the purposes that are listed and fair based on criteria similar to the weighed factors in the US fair use model and the UK fair dealing model; and (3) whether acknowledgment such as the source and name of the creator is mentioned in criticism, review, and news reporting. Besides fair dealing, the Canadian Copyright Act also contains some exceptions for educational institutions, libraries, archives and museums, incidental inclusion, ephemeral recording, and reproduction of works for persons with perceptual disabilities.[38]

As a typical civil law jurisdiction from which China has mainly assimilated its copyright legislations, Germany precisely lists all exceptions in Chapter VI titled "Limitations on Copyright" in the Law on Copyright and Neighboring Rights (Copyright Law).[39] These exceptions are not restricted to fair dealing which is similar to the law of the United Kingdom, but include circumstances where equitable remunerations are required to be paid to the author or right owner. Exceptions in the German Copyright Law are permissible free use for administration of justice and public safety, public speeches, newspaper articles and broadcast commentaries, visual and sound reporting on events of the day, quotations, reproduction for private

---

[36] Song [16].

For the factor "whether the work was made available to the public," the unpublished nature of the work will be weighed against a finding of fair dealing. For the factor "by which method the work was obtained," obtaining the work by theft or breach of confidence will be weighed against a finding of fair dealing. In terms of "the quantity and quality of the parts taken," generally speaking, the less that has been taken means a more fair dealing. However, the courts may find that copying of the entire work to be fair as well. For the factor "the type and purpose of the use," the courts will consider whether the use is commercial or transformative. For "consequence of the dealing," the courts will consider the influence of the use on the market of the original work. If the dealing substitutes the original work, the courts will be less likely to rule in favor of fair dealing. For "whether the same objective can be achieved by using other means," alternatives available to the dealing will be weighed against a finding of fair dealing.

[37] *Hubbard v. Vosper* [1972] 1 All E.R. 1023 (CA).

[38] Canadian Copyright Act, ss 29–32.2.

[39] The German Copyright Law was enacted in 1965 and later revised many times. The latest version was issued in 2008 which is only available in German. The introduction and analysis of copyright limitations in Germany are based on the English version released in 1998.

and other personal uses, incidental works, catalog illustrations, works in public places, and portraits.[40] In the Google litigation case on the thumbnail images, the German Federal Supreme Court rejected Google's fair use argument with regard to unauthorized reproduction and scaling down of the images of two artists as thumbnails for search engines.[41] The court was reluctant to expand the existing list of exceptions under the Copyright Law: "The limitation and exception regulations of Arts 45 et seq. Copyright Act based on the social tie of intellectual property generally are to be interpreted in a narrow way so as to give the author a reasonable share in economic utilization of his works, and therefore, not to excessively restrict the exclusive rights due to him with regard to the exploitation of the work."[42]

Slightly different from the fair dealing model in common law jurisdictions and the exceptions adopted by Germany, copyright limitations in Taiwan not only enumerate specific situations in Articles 44–63 of the Taiwanese Copyright Act but also contain a general guiding provision, Article 65(2), which is applicable to circumstances listed in Articles 44–63 and other potential fair uses. The same four factors in the US fair use doctrine are included in Article 65(2) to determine fairness from the listed situations and other possible circumstances. The four factors are as follows: (1) the purpose and nature of the use, including whether the use is for commercial purposes or nonprofit education; (2) the nature of the work; (3) the amount and substantiality of the portion of the work used in relation to the entire work: and (4) the influence of the use on the potential market and the current value of the work.[43]

The comparative research on fair dealing or list of exceptions among typical common law and civil law jurisdictions illustrates that certain kinds of reproduction and communication to the public of the work are included in either way of legislative models. Common specific situations are research and private study, criticism or review, quotations, and reporting of current events, including public speeches and visual and sound reporting on events of the day as well as newspaper articles and broadcast commentaries on events that have a political, economic, or religious nature. Therefore, the inclusion of these situations into a list of nonexclusive exceptions complies with the actual needs and establishes clear instructions for relevant users to directly apply the statutory clauses. Exceptions allowed for research, criticism, and news reporting also help to achieve the purpose of the copyright system in promoting the advancement of knowledge and learning. In addition, the legislative approach of Taiwan which embodies both detailed descriptions and factors for general guidance may provide more certainty and flexibility in comparison with other models. The Taiwanese legislative model may enlighten other jurisdictions especially Mainland China in reforming her laws on copyright limitations and exceptions by importing means that are both rigid and elastic.

---

[40] German Copyright Law, ss 45–63.

[41] Google thumbnail case, the German Federal Supreme Court case no. IZR 69/08, judgment made of Apr.29, 2010.

[42] Ibid., p. 27.

[43] Taiwanese Copyright Act, Art 65(2).

5.3.3.2 Exceptions Under Technological Protection Measures

The widespread adoption of TPMs by copyright owners and the legitimization of anti-circumvention rules worldwide have disrupted the balance of interest in traditional copyright laws by impeding access of public users and fair use of protected works. For example, the DMCA of the United States and the 2006 Regulation of China both prohibit users from circumventing technological measures that copyright owners use to control access and copying of their works. Traditional copyright laws grant the copyright owner a series of exclusive rights based on use of the work such as the right to reproduce or distribute, or to perform and display the work in public, and limit these exclusive rights by allowing the public to engage in certain fair or other non-infringing uses of the work given access, but traditional copyright laws do not provide right of access to the work in the first place [2, p. 605]. With technological measures, one cannot engage in fair or other non-infringing uses of the work if there is no access. Although the 2006 Regulation of China contains a list of exemptions that allow certain institutions to circumvent technological measures for certain purposes, the legislation lacks a general provision of exceptions in the protected works. Without a fair use/ fair dealing safe harbor, exemptions for circumvention of technological measures are quite restricted and exclude numerous possible fair uses in the age of a creative remix culture.

On the contrary, if the legislation incorporates overly general exceptions which permit circumvention of any technological measure that protects copyright works, this provision will create the means for rampant copyright infringement, because it is difficult for a copyright holder or law executor to distinguish between actual fair use and infringing use prior to a circumvention act.

The proposal to revise the anti-circumvention rule by incorporating a technological component that guarantees minimum use, a legislative component to incorporate general exceptions for fair or other non-infringing uses, a judicial component to provide guidelines for court decisions, and a scheme that goes beyond intellectual property, such as competition law, may help to address the problem. With a technological component, users will be allowed to circumvent the technological measures for minimum uses such as browsing or reproducing 5–15 % of the protected works. After the initial duplication or use of the work, a technological measure will be put into place that prevents him/her from any further exploitation. With a legislative component, a general exception for fair or other non-infringing uses should be incorporated into copyright laws, by explicitly articulating that the anti-circumvention rule shall not constrain or impede the copyright limitations and exceptions. With a judicial component, the courts should follow the general exceptions in the legislation to decide on each case based on the purpose and characteristics of the final use. Finally, policymakers could consider other schemes rather than those of intellectual property to grant protection to technological measures, such as competition law.

5.4 Supplementary Schemes

The remix culture in the digital Internet era requires substantial tolerance of unauthorized uses [11, p. 497]. Apart from reconstructing fair use/fair dealing legislations, supplementary schemes should also be imported so as to expand the public's access and use of copyright works as well as avoid substantive damage to the interests of copyright owners.

There are three schemes that resemble fair use/fair dealing, which encourage reproduction and adaptation of copyright works without authorization from copyright holders. The first scheme is compulsory licensing, which statutorily confines the scope of the use and requires monetary remunerations to the copyright owners. The second scheme is copyright no action policy, a concept that borrows from property law and is recommended by some copyright scholars. It advocates tolerance of copyright owners on certain infringements by issuing a no action notice in the first place and enforces their rights against infringements later if necessary. The third scheme is community-based guidelines which encourage practices by the creative communities in defining and defending fair use/fair dealing.

5.4.1 Compulsory Licensing Scheme

The compulsory licensing regime allows a content user to use ex ante the protected work without authorization from the copyright owner, but should later pay certain remunerations and respect the moral rights of the author by quoting the source and author name. The compulsory licensing scheme can act as a supplement to fair use/ fair dealing to broaden access and exploitation of copyright work by users on the one hand and satisfy the desire of copyright owners to economically benefit on the other hand. It can resolve the difficulties brought on by mass individual-by-individual private licensing especially under the digital network environment and save on copyright transactions that rely on administration by copyright collecting societies. Several issues should be noted and well arranged in order to implement a compulsory licensing scheme.

5.4.1.1 Clarifying Scope of Compulsory Licensing Under Digital Network Environment

The Copyright Law of China already incorporates a compulsory licensing scheme for five situations, including (1) compilation of parts of published works, short written works, music works, or single copies of works of painting or photographic works into textbooks for implementation of the 9-year compulsory education system and national educational planning,[44] (2) reprinting the work already published in a

[44] Copyright Law of People's Republic of China (2010 Amendment), Art 23.

newspaper or periodical or printing its abstract or printing as reference material by other newspapers or periodical publishers,[45] (3) exploiting a musical work which has been lawfully recorded as a sound recording by a producer of another sound recording,[46] (4) broadcasting by a radio station or television station of a published work created by another,[47] and (5) broadcasting by a radio station or television station of a published recording.[48] The compulsory licensing scheme in China also applies to the digital network environment, under which distance education institutions can provide courseware that contains excerpts of a work, a short written work or music work, or a single work of fine arts or photographic work, if published, through the information network to registered students enrolled in national compulsory education or the plans of national education[49]; and network service providers can make available to the public in rural areas through the information network published works of Chinese citizens or entities that deal with topics which aid poverty-stricken areas such as cultivation and breeding, prevention and treatment of diseases, or prevention and reduction of disasters, or which satisfy the basic needs for culture.[50]

In the first Modified Draft of Copyright Law in China, Articles 45–47 list three kinds of compulsory licensing schemes for the reproduction and redistribution of published literary works by newspaper and periodicals, reproduction of video recordings by phonogram producers, and broadcasting published works by radio stations and television stations. Article 48 establishes several conditions for the compulsory licensing mentioned in Articles 45–47 under which users do not need permission from copyright owners, but are required to (1) apply for a record from the copyright administrative authorities of the State Council before use, (2) indicate the name of the author and the title and source of the work in the use, and (3) pay remuneration to copyright collecting societies according to the standards provided by the copyright administrative authorities of the State Council 1 month after the use and, at the same time, submit the name of the author and the title and source of the work.

The most heated discussion in the first Modified Draft is aroused by the provisions of compulsory licensing. Many famous Chinese songwriters have voiced that Articles 46 and 48 are detrimental to the interests of producers and songwriters of original music, because under Article 46, "any sound recording, after being published for 3 months, may be used by other recording producers, according to the process provided in Article 48, to produce their own sound recording, without the permission of its copyright owner."[51] The recording producers need to contact

[45] Copyright Law of People's Republic of China (2010 Amendment), Art 33 paragraph 2.

[46] Copyright Law of People's Republic of China (2010 Amendment), Art 40 paragraph 3.

[47] Copyright Law of People's Republic of China (2010 Amendment), Art 43 paragraph 2.

[48] Copyright Law of People's Republic of China (2010 Amendment), Art 44.

[49] Regulation on the Protection of the Right to Network Dissemination of Information, Art 8.

[50] Regulation on the Protection of the Right to Network Dissemination of Information, Art 9.

[51] "China's Proposed Copyright Reforms Prompt Widespread Comment," available at http://the-1709blog.blogspot.com/2012/04/chinas-proposed-copyright-reforms.html (visited May 12, 2012).

the copyright administration authority, specify the original author and source of recording, and submit remuneration to the copyright collecting society. According to Gao Xiaosong, a well-known songwriter, "the new amendment will encourage internet copyright infringement," and according to Zhou Yaping, CEO of a Beijing-based record company, "there will be a weakened purchasing position for record companies when bidding to assume a control of a copyright as the window is so short."[52] On the contrary, advocates of the provisions argued that "the current law has no time limit at all. Those who want to re-record the songs can do so on the day following its release."[53] Professor Feng Xiaoqing also supported the amendment, opining that "previously, it was hard for the users of sound recordings to find the copyright owners and pay them. The draft makes it much clearer and easier."[54]

To my understanding, it is preferable to not adopt and pass the controversial provisions which may intensify conflicts among different shareholders. However, a compulsory licensing scheme should still be maintained in copyright law. A compromise that is one sided which only benefits copyright owners will result in legal retrogression, thus neglecting the dual purpose of the copyright system. To amend the compulsory licensing scheme, additional situations could be taken into consideration to expand the scope of compulsory licensing. First, certain types of works could be listed under the compulsory licensing scheme for specific groups of individuals. For example, to benefit the minorities, compulsory licensing could include translation of a published work of a Chinese citizen or organization from Mandarin into any language of the minority ethnic groups for publication and distribution within China, as well as publication and distribution of translated works in the minority language via the information network within China. For perceptible disabilities, compulsory licensing could include transliteration of a published work into Braille, publication of the work so transliterated, and supply of the work to the blind through the information network in a way as particularly perceptible to the blind. For people who are incapable of reading foreign languages, compulsory licensing could include translation of works in foreign languages and published within the domestic market from foreign languages to the national language.

Secondly, a compulsory licensing scheme could be used to help construct digital libraries. Some scholars advocate for the adopting of private licensing or fair use/fair dealing to resolve the problem of obtaining authorization from copyright owners for accumulating collection of digital works. However, compared with compulsory licensing, private licensing and fair use/fair dealing are not the most appropriate way to settle the issue, because it is difficult and infeasible to implement individual-by-individual type of licensing among large volumes of digital works, while the applicable fair use/fair dealing with regard to libraries is restricted to digitalization

[52] Ibid.

[53] "Songwriters Say Copyright Draft Doesn't Protect," available at http://www.chinadaily.com.cn/china/2012-04/06/content_14986887.htm (visited May 12, 2012).

[54] Ibid.

of works already collected by a library for the purposes of preservation or display. The adopting of a compulsory licensing scheme for the construction of digital libraries can save costs in copyright transactions, increase the efficiency of obtaining authorization, and economically reward authors and copyright owners. If the authors or right owners do not agree to place their works under a compulsory licensing scheme for the construction of digital libraries, they can provide a declaration that prohibits the unauthorized exploitation of their works.

Thirdly, in light of the substantial amount of reproduction and distribution of articles from newspapers, periodicals, and websites through the information network, compulsory licensing should apply to the reproduction of online articles on the premises that the scope of works which are allowed to be reproduced is restricted, the works are published works, and the source and author names are mentioned. The scope of reproduced works shall be limited to literary works without extension to audiovisual works, because production of the latter works requires a large investment. Unauthorized reproduction and distribution of such works through the Internet may seriously affect their market. Typical situations in the case of reproduction of literary works include the following three types: reproduction of articles from affiliated newspapers and periodicals by a website, reproduction by a website of articles from other websites, and reproduction of articles from affiliated websites by newspapers and periodicals.

5.4.1.2 Establishing Declaration System for Copyright Owners

In light of the influence that a compulsory licensing scheme may bring to quite a number of works in libraries, newspapers or periodicals, and websites, establishment of a declaration system can better address the concerns of authors and right owners on potential copyright infringement caused by implementation of compulsory licenses. If an author does not wish to have his/her work used under a compulsory licensing scheme for the construction of digital libraries or reproduced in newspapers, periodicals, or websites, he/she can publish a declaration that prohibits the exploitation of the work. Establishment of a declaration system could better protect authors and balance the interests between creators and users. Generally, a compulsory licensing scheme will help authors to distribute their works and establish their reputation. However, under certain circumstances, authors may only want a particular newspaper or periodical to reproduce their works. A declaration system will satisfy this need.

Two items should be noted in the process of establishing a declaration system. First, only authors and right owners have the right to make the declaration. Declarations provided by publishers that do not own copyrights such as the press office cannot prohibit the reproduction of their work by other newspapers or periodicals. Secondly, the time to make the declaration can be flexible. Authors can make the declaration either before the publication of the work, at the same time during the publication, or after the publication.

5.4.1.3 Perfecting Compensation System

A dual-track compensation system could be implemented to perfect a compulsory licensing scheme. On the one hand, administrative authorities, such as the National Copyright Administration of China, should create a reasonable standard of remuneration and amend the standard from time to time to comply with the development of the economy and market rate. On the other hand, a remuneration negotiation mechanism should be incorporated to deal with exceptional circumstances under which payment of remuneration according to a statutory standard will lead to unfairness. In the negotiation mechanism, when the uniform compensation is considered too low for copyright owners or too high for users, the two parties can launch a negotiation to reach an agreement on compensation based on the actual situation. If consensus on the amount of compensation cannot be reached, the two parties can apply for an adjudication made by the copyright administrative authorities. If the two parties disagree with the adjudication, they can further file a civil litigation in the courts. In the process of judging the amount of compensation, efforts made by the user to exploit the work should be adequately taken into consideration.

5.4.1.4 Perfecting Mechanism of Copyright Collective Management

Copyright collecting societies have played an important role in collecting remuneration for copyright owners from the enforcement of compulsory licensing. To clarify the rights and responsibilities of copyright collecting societies in the process of implementing compulsory licensing is essential to guarantee the economic interests of copyright owners and an efficient procedure for authorization.

First, the laws and regulations should outline detailed operation procedures for receiving remunerations by the copyright collecting societies. For example, detailed provisions should be made in dealing with issues such as the charges, safekeeping, and assignment of royalties, as well as the allocation of rights, obligations, and liabilities between copyright collecting society and users. More detailed provisions mean that the compulsory license scheme is more manageable and feasible.

Secondly, a professional committee could be imported to help resolve the disputes in the process of charging remunerations, and the right to file litigation by the copyright collecting societies should be clearly regulated. A professional committee could be established to conclusively decide on disputes in the collection of royalties, whose members may include judges, officers in administrative organs, and lawyers. Parties that disagree with the standard remunerations can appeal to the professional committee. The standing as litigant by the copyright collecting societies shall be well regulated by law so as to ensure that the societies can initiate judicial proceedings in their own name.

Thirdly, supervision on copyright collecting societies should be well imposed in case there is an abuse of power by the societies, which would negatively impact the interests of the copyright owners and public users. The system of supervision can be in many forms, including those that pertain to pre- and post-supervision. In terms of situations that fall under pre-supervision, the establishment of copyright collecting societies should comply with certain conditions and procedures and be finally approved by administrative authorities. In terms of situations that take place post-supervision, punishment should be imposed on any illegal activities by copyright collecting societies and remedies should be provided for copyright owners and public users. Supervision from governments, right holders, and society is necessary to implement a justified, fair, and effective scheme for collection and allocation of remuneration.

5.4.2 Copyright No Action Policy

With regard to infringing uses that do not clearly fall within the category of either fair use/fair dealing or compulsory licensing, but copyright owners nonetheless tolerate the uses, the government may import a copyright no action policy for copyright holders. This policy requires the issuance of a no action notice by the copyright owner to hold the user non-liable for the infringement at issue. If the copyright owner does not submit a complaint, the user can safely exploit the copyright work.

The creation of a no action notice policy originates from the latent reason of tolerated use. Not all unauthorized uses will cause substantial economic loss to copyright holders. On the contrary, there are situations in which the infringement will economically complement the copyright work or enforcement will cost much more than the potential damage. Many of the tolerated uses may fall within the category of statutorily permitted use which even benefits the copyright owner. The problem and the slight differences between tolerated and fair use lie in the difficulty that people can hardly expect "how many of the mass infringement a court would find to be fair use" [17, p. 620]. There are numerous unauthorized uses of copyright works that clearly falls neither into the threshold of fair use/fair dealing nor into the realms of compulsory licensing. Taking fan fictions as an example again, many audiovisual online fan creations obviously infringe the original copyright works by simply compiling screenshots from films or TV series and dubbing them with voice-overs or sound and music. Nevertheless, many of the film or TV program producers do not take action to eliminate these infringing uses or sue the infringers for compensation. This lack of enforcement against fan fictions may illustrate that the copyright holders consider that the infringing uses will not cause substantive damage to their potential market and instead could further help propagate the copyright works. The no action policy could comprise notices posted on websites or elsewhere that detail the tolerated uses granted by copyright owners. As Professor Tim Wu interpreted, "in legal terms, the copyright no action policy is a unilateral, non-exclusive, potentially revocable license from the media owner to all members of the general public who meet its terms" [17, p. 628]. Wu thus indicated that the following contents could be written in a no action notice by copyright owners: "[the media owner] will not take any action against, and encouraged the creation of works based on its copyrighted works that fall into the following categories: non-commercial fan fiction…" [17, p. 628].

5.4.3 *Community Guidelines*

In addition to enforced laws that are positive, the creative communities have attempted to issue their own guidelines on fair use/fair dealing. Members of five filmmaker organizations of the United States in November 2005 released the Documentary Filmmakers' Statement of Best Practices in Fair Use which asserted four common situations for filmmakers that constitute fair use based on the judicial concept of transformativeness: "quoting media in order to critique or analyze it; quoting media to make a point about the culture; incorporation of copyrighted works in the process of filming something else; and quoting to make a historical point" [18]. The statement was successful in that "all major insurers of documentary film now routinely accept fair use claims" [18] as provided by the statement. In terms of filmmakers, similar attempts to issue creative community guidelines or statements of best practices in fair use are issued among film scholars, art teachers, and dance professionals [18]. For example, the Electronic Frontier Foundation released the "Fair Use Principles for User-Generated Video Content"[55] with the main proposition that "automated filters should not be used to block content unless both audio and video are matched as coming overwhelmingly from the same source, thus requiring human review for typical mashups and other remixes."[56] Meanwhile, the MacArthur Foundation launched an educational initiative for new digital forms, including guidance for teachers whose students would like to engage in the remix culture [11, p. 499]. Similar practices also work for amateur creators who do not have as adequate representation as the art professionals in the United States. The Organization for Transformative Works, a nonprofit tax-exempt organization, attempts to define and defend fair use for individual creators by "protecting and preserving noncommercial fan-created works such as fan fiction and fan art based on existing copyrighted materials" [11, p. 501]. These community-based practices prove that organized and self-reflective actions by borrower-as-creators help to promote the development of recreation works and recognize their social value.

5.5 Conclusion

The concerned limitations and exceptions are important in copyright systems to support the exploitation of preexisting works for future creation, achieve social functions, and promote social progress. The continuous expansion of copyright laws to extend the terms of protection and widen the scope of subject matters and exclusive rights seriously restricts the realm of limitations and exceptions. In addition, the three-step test imposed by international intellectual property conventions

[55] "Fair User Principles for User-Generated Video Content," available at https://www.eff.org/pages/fair-use-principles-user-generated-video-content (visited Dec 13, 2010).

[56] Ibid.

limits copyright exemptions to "special cases which do not conflict with a normal exploitation of the work and do not unreasonably prejudice the legitimate interests of the right holder."[57] The access and use of copyright works are more constrained in the digital network age, because of the widespread adoption of technological measures by copyright owners and the enactment of anti-circumvention rules against the unauthorized circumvention of access-control measures and trafficking of devices that facilitate circumvention of both access- and copy-control measures.

In terms of the copyright limitations and exceptions embodied in the Chinese Copyright Law, the exclusive list of specific exemptions no longer parallels the continuously emerging changes brought on by digital network technologies. Current Chinese laws and judicial decisions have not well addressed the issues aroused by the remix culture. Amateur works such as fan fictions and user-generated contents fall into a gray zone under which the legal status of these works is vague and it is unclear whether they constitute copyright infringement. Therefore, copyright limitations and exceptions can be revised by importing both legal flexibility and certainty which would help to widen the scope of non-infringing uses and resolve many new issues under the digital network environment and remix culture.

It is advisable for copyright systems to obtain legal flexibility and certainty by introducing the four-factor balancing test as an abstract guidance and a list of non-exclusive exceptions as the minute prescriptions. The proper adoption and administration of a fair use provision outside the United States or other English-speaking countries would "enable courts to deal with fact-specific situations falling outside the codified exceptions to copyright law's exclusive rights, which invariably occur in practice" [19, p. 1156]. The introduction of the four-factor balancing test neither entirely eliminates the possibility of making fair use adaptive to new situations nor totally excludes other potential circumstances. The importation of a list of detailed exceptions which meet national conditions will add more certainty to copyright limitations by providing statutory requirements that users can directly apply.

The revision of copyright limitations and exceptions supplemented by alternative schemes in support of non-infringing uses would turn many potential infringers into legitimate re-creators, thus promoting the accomplishments of amateur creations outside copyright industries, encouraging non-infringing uses in the digital network age, and restoring a balance of interest between proprietary holders and public users in copyright systems.

References

1. Goldstein, P. (2007–2008). Fair use in context. *Columbia Journal of Law and the Arts, 31*, 433–443.
2. Picker, R. (2007–2008). Fair use v. Fair access. *Columbia Journal of Law and the Arts, 31*, 603–616.

[57] TRIPS Agreement, Art 13.

3. Gordon, W. (1982). Fair use as market failure: A structural and economic analysis of the Betamax case and its predecessors. *Columbia Law Review, 82*, 1600–1657.
4. Gordon, W. (2002). Excuse and justification in the law of fair use: Commodification and market perspective. In N. Elkin-Koren & N. W. Netanel (Eds.), *The commodification of information* (pp. 149–192). The Hague: Kluwer Law International.
5. Ku, R. S. R. (2003). Consumers and creative destruction: Fair use beyond market failure. *Berkeley Technology Law Journal, 18*, 539–574.
6. Fisher, W. (1988). Reconstructing the fair use doctrine. *Harvard Law Review, 101*, 1659–1795.
7. Liu, J. P. (2007–2008). Two-factor fair use? *Columbia Journal of Law and the Arts, 31*, 571–585.
8. Parchomovsky, G., & Goldman, K. A. (2007). Fair use harbors. *Virginia Law Review, 93*, 1483–1532.
9. Lunney, G. (2002). Fair use and market failure: Sony revisited. *Boston University Law Review, 82*, 975–1030.
10. Beebe, B. (2008). An empirical study of U.S. Copyright fair use opinions, 1978–2005. *University of Pennsylvania Law Review, 156*, 549–624.
11. Tushnet, R. (2007–2008). User-generated discontent: Transformation in practice. *Columbia Journal of Law and the Arts, 31*, 497–576.
12. Heymann, L. A. (2007–2008). Everything is transformative: Fair use and reader response. *Columbia Journal of Law and the Arts, 31*, 445–466.
13. Leval, P. N. (1990). Toward a fair use standard. *Harvard Law Review, 103*, 1105–1136.
14. Reese, R. A. (2007–2008). Transformativeness and the derivative work right. *Columbia Journal of Law and the Arts, 31*, 467–495.
15. Wang, Q. (2008). *Internet copyright law*. Beijing: China Renmin University Press (in Chinese).
16. Song, S. H. (2011). *New challenges of Chinese copyright law under the digital age*. Alphen aan den Rijn: Wolters Kluwer.
17. Wu, T. (2007–2008). Tolerated use. *Columbia Journal of Law and the Arts, 31*, 617–635.
18. Aufderheide, P., & Jaszi, P. (2010). Fair use and best practices: Surprising success. Available at http://www.centerforsocialmedia.org/fair-use/best-practices/documentary/fair-use-and-best-practices-surprising-success. Visited 13 Dec 2010.
19. Reichman, J. H. (2009). Intellectual property in the twenty-first century: Will the developing countries lead or follow? *Houston Law Review, 46*, 1115–1185.

Chapter 6
Construction of Digital Commons and Exploration of Public Domain

6.1 Introduction

Traditional copyright laws have been developed with a one-size-fits-all approach to achieve their goal of promoting the progress of culture and useful arts. On the one hand, they grant an author with a series of exclusive rights to publicly reproduce, distribute, perform and display their works, make adaptations, and attribute the work to the creator him/herself. Copyright systems also endow authors with the right to assign or license copyright works. On the other hand, the systems incorporate fair use/fair dealing doctrines and compulsory licensing schemes to guarantee access and exploitation of copyright works by public users and encourage recreation. Copyright laws have established a limited term of protection upon expiration of which the copyright works will enter the public domain and will be free for all to use. The copyright systems have been established with the purpose to well maintain a balance between copyright owners and users, thus motivating creative activities by copyright owners and in the meantime promoting free dissemination of works and information.

The development of technology greatly enlarges the capability to access and the range of expressive means by ordinary users [1, pp. 445–461] and yet ironically expands the scope and duration of copyright protection. Subject matters under protection have expanded from traditionally paper-based works to many new types of media, such as digital music and motion pictures as well as software. The duration of protection has been extended from the original 14 years from publication of the work plus another 14 years if the author is alive to the creator's life plus 70 years. The emergence of digital technology and the Internet has exacerbated the tension between benefits reaped by copyright owners and the interests of public users. The DMCA of the United States imposes liability onto ISPs and punishes the circumvention of TPMs that control access and copying of copyright works as well as production and dissemination of technology or devices that facilitate the circumvention of technological measures. The European Union Information Society Directive, which was passed in 2001, addresses almost the same issues as

J.J. Hua, *Toward A More Balanced Approach: Rethinking and Readjusting Copyright Systems in the Digital Network Era*, DOI 10.1007/978-3-662-43517-5_6,

the DMCA, including the provision of very limited exceptions to exclusive rights held by copyright holders and protection of technological measures. China follows the copyright reforms in developed societies to deal with copyright problems in the digital network era by promulgating the 2006 Regulation.

The increase in the rights of copyright owners facilitated by digital network technology greatly reduces the means of users to obtain access and exploitation of the copyright information and work. Some commentators have explicitly questioned and criticized the traditional system by asserting that copyright laws have never provided benefits to society but rather serve to reward a few at the expense of creativity.[1] Copyright opponents further promote anti-copyright debates and draw public attention to the issue of copyright reforms. One famous instance of an anti-copyright movement was Grey Tuesday which occurred on February 24, 2004. The activists intentionally violated a copyright of EMI through *The White Album* by distributing MP3 files of a mashup album called *The Grey Album*.[2] Over 400 sites participated in the Grey Tuesday movement, with protesters stating that "The Grey Album illustrates a need in revision in copyright law to allow sampling under fair use of copyrighted material or proposing a system of fair compensation to allow for sampling."[3] Similar to *The Grey Album* activists, social and political groups also suggested proposals to their governments to reform the system of copyright enforcement and compensation. The French group, Association des Audionautes, proposed that France should legalize peer-to-peer file sharing and compensate artists with a surcharge on ISP fees.[4] In addition, seven Swedish Parliament members from the Moderate Party proposed the complete decriminalization of online file sharing in a Swedish tabloid.[5] Internet corporate entities, such as YouTube, Viacom, and Google, obviously would not oppose copyright and may cooperate to remove online copyright works upon request, but could decline to actively enforce copyright by asserting that they did not have the power to prevent uploading and downloading of copyright material.[6]

Commentators who do not support severe copyright protection and enforcement argue that authors create not only because of economic incentives and monetary compensation but also because of their desire to share thoughts and earn recognition from peers. Many authors have continued to write even if they do not think there is a market for publication. Current copyright laws discourage the wide dissemination of the works of authors. Other arguments perceive freedom of knowledge as a fundamental human right and advocate for the release of copyright for free culture and communication. In face of the widespread anti-copyright arguments and tendencies, scholars and critics therefore endeavor to search for solutions that could restore a balance of interest between copyright owners and public users both within and outside

[1] "Anti-copyright," available at http://en.wikipedia.org/wiki/Anti-copyright (visited Apr 15, 2010).

[2] Ibid.

[3] *See* n 1 above.

[4] *See* n 1 above.

[5] *See* n 1 above.

[6] *See* n 1 above.

traditional copyright regimes. Within the system, suggestions focus on allowing appropriate exceptions for circumvention of technological measures, establishing reasonable safe harbors for ISPs, and redefining copyright limitations and exceptions. Based on copyright doctrines and legal concepts outside the intellectual property regime, scholars have begun to import alternative schemes under which authors reserve only part of their exclusive rights and license public users who could then exploit their copyright works upon satisfying the conditions of the license.

This chapter will first introduce the alternative schemes that are established based on copyright norms, but outside traditional copyright frameworks. Well-known examples include open source software and the Creative Commons. Then, this chapter will take the Creative Commons as an example to further examine how this alternative scheme works, the benefits that it will bring to the dissemination of works and free communication, and whether it has latent disadvantages that should be of concern. Finally, this chapter will discuss the influence of alternative schemes on the public domain, in an attempt to point out the positive role that these digital commons play in enriching the public domain and the effect of the expansion of the public domain in turn to boost the use, remix, and recreation of copyright material.

6.2 Alternative Schemes: Digital Commons

In the late 1980s, Professor Richard Matthew Stallman from the Massachusetts Institute of Technology (MIT) proposed the term "free software" by launching the GNU's Not Unix! (GNU) project, in an attempt to create a free use for computer operation system. Later, in 1989, Stallman drafted the GNU General Public License (GNU GPL) under which software developers may publish their software with the license which allows anyone to freely use the software, make new revisions, run on new operating systems, share with others, or market the software. Relevant provisions in the GNU GPL also apply to the derivative software designed based on the original free software. A nonprofit organization, the Free Software Foundation, was established to support the operation of free software and dedicated to popularizing the concept of freeing and opening software. Stallman insisted on the ideal that all software should be freely available, analogous with "free" as in "free speech," not as in no cost, such as "free beer" [2, pp. 303–324]. In 1998, a group of individuals advocated that the term "free software" be replaced by "open source software" (OSS) as an expression which is less ambiguous and more in line with the corporate and business world.

Under the GNU licenses of free software and OSS, certain criteria must be fulfilled to distribute the license-governed software. First, the software under the license can be freely redistributed, either by means of making physical copies or disseminating via the Internet.[7] The software program must contain a source code which must

[7] Open Source Definition, Art 1 "Free Distribution," available at http://www.opensource.org/docs/osd (visited Mar 12, 2011).

be in a form that can be redistributed or modified by a subsequent programmer.[8] Computer language can be simply divided as source code and object code. The former is a higher programming language and the latter is the resulting machine language [2, pp. 303–324]. One only needs the latter to run a computer program, but in order to modify a program, one needs to change the former. The source codes of privately owned software are not freely available. In order to modify the original software or write new software based on the preexisting material, one must resort to the holder of the original source code for authorization. The availability of source codes reduces the cost and time that are required to create a new program. Secondly, licensees are allowed to modify the software and redistribute their derivative software in the modified form.[9] If redistributed, the modified program must be governed by the same license. Redistribution under different licenses is deemed as copyright infringement which will result in banning of further dissemination. This is the viral effect of the GPL [2, pp. 303–324]. Under the viral effect, software programmers are forbidden to exclusively control the GPL-governed software. The viral effect reflects Stallman's ideal of making all software freely available. Thirdly, additional conditions are not allowed to be added onto the license either by inserting additional words or through additional licenses.[10] Moreover, software can be distributed via any technology, either through physical copies or the Internet.[11] The terms of the open source license cannot state preference or decline certain technologies. Fourthly, commercial use will not be excluded by open source licensing.[12] Nor will certain persons or groups be excluded from access and use of OSS.[13]

There are several views that explain why digital commons such as OSS have become reality and are endorsed by many people. The mainstream view is that OSS will help to provide monetary or nonmonetary rewards in combination with business entrepreneurship and social functions. Although the writing of OSS may not directly reward the programmer, related activities are based on their access and use. For example, a dedication to the OSS community could help a programmer establish his/her reputation. The reputation will in turn benefit the professional development of the programmer. Corporations or companies could exploit OSS for their hardware production and earn profits. Hardware production could in turn promote the advancement of the industry. The OSS could also be used by governments or nonprofit organizations for certain needs and their own purposes, so that they will no longer need to spend their limited funds on purchasing expensive commercial software. Regardless of the specific reason that supports OSS, the open source model provides an alternative way that falls within legal frameworks but bypasses the series of exclusive rights under traditional intellectual property systems. This alternative way ameliorates the confrontation of interests between copyright holders and public users.

---

[8] Ibid., Art 2 "Source Code".

[9] *See* n 7 above, Art 3 "Derived Works."

[10] *See* n 7 above, Art 7 "Distribution of License."

[11] *See* n 7 above, Art 10 "License Must Be Technology-Neutral."

[12] *See* n 7 above, Art 6 "No Discrimination Against Fields of Endeavor."

[13] *See* n 7 above, Art 5 "No Discrimination Against Persons or Groups."

In following the free software and OSS movement, a series of projects or events have emerged that promote the anti-copyright tendencies of the public. Some typical projects include the Creative Archive License of the British Broadcasting Corporation which allows public users to download certain archived content for noncommercial use, Open Audio License created by the Electronic Frontier Foundation (EFF) and Etymotics Free Music License which make music works freely available to public users, and the Open Publication License of the Open Content Project which mainly provides free documents but offers licensors the option to restrict the distribution of derivative works. Influenced by the numerous digital commons projects that advocate for open access to copyright works and inspired in part by the GNU GPL, the Creative Commons was born and later became a world renowned licensing scheme that is widely used by creators, corporations, public users, as well as the aforementioned free access projects.

6.3 Construction and Promotion of Creative Commons

The Creative Commons, a nonprofit organization, was founded in 2001 by Professor Lawrence Lessig and a board of cyber law and intellectual property experts with financial support from the Center for the Public Domain. In 2002, the Creative Commons released a set of licenses and encouraged creators to adopt these licenses that authorize the public to freely exploit and revise their works upon complying with the licensing conditions. Based on the philosophy that "private rights (are used) to create public source," the Creative Commons aims to attain an appropriate balance between the copyright field where all rights are reserved and the public domain where no rights are reserved, that is, some rights reserved.

As the Creative Commons licensing was designed based on American copyright and the use of the licenses had spread internationally, the organization launched the Creative Commons International in 2003 with the purpose to facilitate the linguistic and legal localization of the original license provisions in jurisdictions other than the United States. The Creative Commons International allows slight revisions to the license provisions by importing countries according to their domestic copyright laws as long as the revisions are consistent with the philosophy of the standard licenses. The localized licenses are supposed to be publicly discussed in the domestic community and approved by the Creative Commons.

6.3.1 Creative Commons Licenses

The basic licenses of the Creative Commons (CC) contain four different elements: (1) Attribution, which means that users must give attribution as required to the creator of the work being used. Users are permitted to copy, distribute, display, and perform the copyrighted works as well as make derivative works. (2) NonCommercial, which means that users can only use the work for noncommercial purposes. Users must first obtain the creator's permission if their use is expected to be commercial. For example, "Gus published his photograph with a noncommercial license. Camille incorporates a piece of Gus's image into a collage poster. Camille is not allowed to sell her collage poster without Gus's permission."[14] (3) NoDerivatives, which means that users are allowed to fully use the work except to make derivative works. In the previous example, Camille must first obtain permission from Gus to incorporate his image into her own poster, if there is a NoDerivatives clause attached. (4) ShareAlike, which means that users who make derivative works based on the copyrighted work must distribute their derivations under the same terms that govern the original work. By using the previous example again, if the copyrighted photograph of Gus was licensed under a CC Attribution-NonCommercial-ShareAlike license, Camille, who incorporated the image of Gus as part of her collage poster, must also distribute her work under a CC Attribution-NonCommercial-ShareAlike license.

The Creative Commons licenses are a combination of these four fundamental elements. Twelve different combinations are possible. However, the elements NoDerivatives and ShareAlike cannot simultaneously appear in one license, since ShareAlike only applies to derivative works. If derivation is prohibited, there will not be any derivative work that can be licensed under the same terms that govern the original work. Therefore, there are in total 11 kinds of licenses in the 1.0 Version. They are Attribution, Attribution-NonCommercial, Attribution-NoDerivatives-NonCommercial, Attribution-NonCommercial-ShareAlike, Attribution-NoDerivatives, Attribution-ShareAlike, NonCommercial, NoDerivatives-NonCommercial, NonCommercial-ShareAlike, NoDerivatives, and ShareAlike. Since the data show that 98 % of licensors chose licenses that contained the element Attribution in the practical use, the updated 2.0 and 3.0 Versions all included Attribution as a required element, in combination with the remaining three elements to form six different licenses. The six licenses are Attribution, Attribution-NonCommercial, Attribution-NoDerivatives-NonCommercial, Attribution-NonCommercial-ShareAlike, Attribution-NoDerivatives, and Attribution-ShareAlike. The reduction of the type of licenses will make selection by copyright owners more focused and easier.

The Creative Commons licenses are available in three different ways: (1) Commons Deed, a plain-language summary of the license, complete with the relevant icons; (2) Legal Code, the fine print that the licensor needs to comply, so that the license will stand up in court; and (3) Digital Code, a machine-readable translation of the license that helps search engines and other applications to identify the licensor's work by its terms of use.[15]

Beyond the six fundamental licenses, the Creative Commons provides other types of licenses, including the Founder's Copyright, CC-GNU GPL, and CC-GNU LGPL. Some additional licenses such as Sampling License, Public Domain Dedication, and Developing Nations license once existed in the Creative Commons licensing scheme but were gradually withdrawn because they did not have

---

[14] Available at www.creativecommons.org (visited Dec 21, 2010).

[15] Ibid.

enough demand or conflicted with values that the organization deemed important.[16] The terms of the deprecated licenses still govern the existing works that were attached to these licenses before their termination, but the Creative Commons no longer provides these licenses for any future work.[17] As to the remaining alternative licenses, the Founder's Copyright allows copyright owners to transfer their copyrighted works to the Creative Commons for the one-dollar royalty. The duration of protection for these transferred works is 14 years or 28 years if the copyright owner chooses to extend the protection for another 14 years. Upon termination of the protection duration, works will enter the public domain. The CC-GNU GPL and CC-GNU LGPL developed from the GNU General Public License and the Lesser General Public License of the Free Software Foundation for computer programs.

Up to the present, over 70 countries or regions have established collaborative relationships with the Creative Commons. As more and more individuals and institutions adopt the Creative Commons licenses, the licensing scheme has spread widely over various cultural fields, which range from education to entertainment. The MIT launched the OpenCourseWare to freely provide educational contents for students and researchers all over the world. The MIT adopted Creative Common licenses for almost all its all coursewares and allowed MIT education resources to be widely available to those with access to the Internet. Inspired by MIT, ten other universities in the United States, Japan, and Vietnam also started to offer open courseware programs. Similarly, the Rice University launched the Connexions project, in an attempt to "create a commons of high-quality diverse content through grassroots collaboration facilitated by use of a Creative Commons Attribution license" [1, p. 453]. Connexions uses "modules" as the basic unit for network distribution and these modules can be organized and linked into courses. The Connexions design not only promotes material dissemination but also enhances "collaboration and community building in the educational context" [1, p. 453]. In addition to educational institutions, some entertainment intermediaries and websites also favor the Creative Commons licenses and the philosophy of the remix culture. The ccMixter, a music intermediary, encourages creators to distribute their sample work or musical tracks under the Creative Commons licenses to benefit the recreation of users-as-creators. Individual web users, such as bloggers, video producers, and photographers, also prefer to use works licensed under Creative Commons licenses or distribute their creations by Creative Commons licenses.

[16] Available at http://creativecommons.org/retiredlicenses (visited Dec 21, 2010). The Sampling License permitted the making of derivative works based on the original copyrighted work for commercial purposes. Under the Sampling License, the user could take a sample of a song to create new music or incorporate a sample of a photograph into a new collage. The Sampling License was withdrawn on June 4, 2007. Public Domain Dedication meant that the copyright owner relinquishes all exclusive rights under the copyright law by allowing users to freely exploit his/her work for noncommercial or commercial purposes. The Public Domain Dedication was withdrawn on October 11, 2010. The Developing Nations license allowed free use of copyrighted works in developing countries while reserving full copyright in developed countries. The Developing Nations license was withdrawn on June 4, 2007.

[17] Ibid.

The well-known website Flickr hosts a large number of digital photographs which are attached to Creative Commons licenses. The photographs distributed on Flickr not only invite exploitation by and recreation of amateurs but also attract collaboration from media conglomerates. One famous example is the National Broadcasting Company (NBC) television network of the United States, which used photos of ice crystals by Harvard scholar Doc Searls that was shared under the Creative Commons licenses on Flickr for the Vancouver Olympic Games [3]. The ice crystal pictures were shown in event information graphics, scoreboards, and many other graphic elements of the NBC's Olympic broadcasts that were viewed by audiences of millions. Searls indicated that this was a victory for the Creative Commons.

6.3.2 Creative Commons in Greater China

China is among the many countries that actively participate in the Creative Commons project. Each jurisdiction in the Greater China areas proposes its own schedule to incorporate the Creative Commons and localize the set of licenses.

Mainland China formally launched the Creative Commons program on March 26, 2006 in Beijing which was led and prepared by the Renmin University of China Law School.[18] After its launch, the Creative Commons China Mainland hosted many events to popularize the usage and strengthen public awareness on the local version of the licenses. It has organized Creative Commons salons, birthday parties, seminars, and annual photography contests to help more people become familiar with the Creative Commons.[19] It has also collaborated with various renowned media or institutions such as Sohu.com, Mozilla Online, CORE, Nphoto.net, and the Migrant Youth Performing Art and Performance Troup (MYPAPT).[20] Nphoto.net, a Chinese Flickr-like website for online picture storage and sharing, formally integrated the licenses of the Creative Commons China Mainland into its services. MYPAPT, a nonprofit folk art troupe established by several rural migrant workers, recorded their original works under the licensing of the Creative Commons China Mainland.

Taiwan began to adopt and localize Creative Commons licensing shortly after the launch of the Creative Commons International in 2003.[21] The Institute of Information Science, Academia Sinica, played the principal role in importing licenses and translating the English version into Chinese along with support from other partners.

---

[18] Available at http://cn.creativecommons.org/en/abouten/development-of-ccchina/ (visited Dec 23, 2010). Creative Commons China Mainland was officially translated in Chinese as "知識共享," meaning "Knowledge Sharing."

[19] Ibid.

[20] *See* n 18 above.

[21] Available at http://creativecommons.tw/ (visited May 14, 2014). Creative Commons Taiwan was officially translated in Chinese as "創用CC." The Chinese "創用" means "Creation and Public Use" and it maintains the abbreviation of Creative Commons "CC."

Similar to Mainland China, the Creative Commons Taiwan also held a series of events to promote the licensing by the Creative Commons. They organized "Free Culture Showcases," to invite submission of music works or video clips under "Attribution-ShareAlike." The One Laptop per Child (OLPC) program was established in Taipei to provide course materials for children under the Creative Commons licenses. Creative Commons Hong Kong was formally launched on October 25, 2008, hosted by the Journalism and Media Studies Center at the University of Hong Kong.[22] After its launch, Creative Commons Hong Kong carried out close collaborations with certain web media conglomerates, such as Wikipedia and Flickr, to promote the philosophy of the Creative Commons and the usage of its licenses.[23] Macau has not yet officially launched localized Creative Commons licensing, but its local project team hosted by the Macau University of Science and Technology Faculty of Law is undertaking the importing of research work by consultation with the Macao Intellectual Property Department and the Creative Commons teams in other jurisdictions within Greater China.[24]

Since Greater China has diversified jurisdictions of Creative Commons, my research chooses the Creative Commons China Mainland as an example for further discussion on its localized licenses, as well as the impact on local society and copyright reform in the digital network age.

6.3.3 Creative Commons China Mainland Licensing

Since current licenses in use within Mainland China have adopted Creative Commons Version 3.0,[25] the research will focus on the Creative Commons China Mainland Version 3.0 for further discussion.

The licenses of Creative Commons China Mainland contain six categories: (1) Attribution 3.0 China Mainland, under which the licensor allows users to reproduce, distribute, exhibit, perform, show, and broadcast his/her copyright work and derivative work based on the copyright work, as well as disseminate the copyright work and derivative work through the information network.[26] Users must maintain the attribution of the licensor to the original copyright work. For example, Hong licenses her photograph under Attribution 3.0 China Mainland. When Ming finds Hong's photograph and displays the picture on his website, Ming must keep Hong's name on the website along with the photograph[27]; (2) Attribution-NonCommercial

[22] Creative Commons Hong Kong was officially translated into Chinese as "共享創意," meaning "Sharing Creations."

[23] Available at http://hk.creativecommons.org/ (visited Dec 23, 2010).

[24] Available at http://mo.creativecommons.org/ (visited Dec 27, 2010). Creative Commons Macau was officially translated into Chinese as "創意共用澳門," meaning "Creation Sharing Macau."

[25] Available at http://creativecommons.net.cn/licenses/meet-the-licenses/ (visited Nov 13, 2013).

[26] Available at http://cn.creativecommons.org/licenses/licenses_exp/ (visited Dec 28, 2010).

[27] Ibid.

3.0 China Mainland, under which the licensor allows users to reproduce, distribute, exhibit, perform, show, and broadcast his/her copyright work and derivative work based on the copyright work, as well as disseminate the copyright work and derivative work through the information network, but users must attribute the licensor to the original copyright work and the use must not be for any commercial purposes. In the previous example, if Hong licenses her photograph under Attribution-NonCommercial 3.0 China Mainland, Ming must not display the photograph on his website for any commercial purposes in addition to keeping Hong's attribution; (3) Attribution-NoDerivatives 3.0 China Mainland, under which the licensor allows users to reproduce, distribute, exhibit, perform, show, and broadcast his/her copyright work, as well as disseminate the copyright work through the information network, but users must maintain the licensor's authorship and cannot alter the copyright work or make any derivative work based on the original copyright work. For example, if Hong chooses to license her photograph under Attribution-NoDerivatives 3.0 China Mainland, Ming cannot incorporate Hong's photograph as part of his collage. Ming can only display the exact original photograph on his website with Hong's name mentioned in connection with the photograph; (4) Attribution-ShareAlike 3.0 China Mainland, under which the licensor allows users to reproduce, distribute, exhibit, perform, show, and broadcast the copyright work and derivative work based on the copyright work, as well as disseminate the copyright work and derivative work through the information network, but users must maintain the licensor's attribution and distribute the derivative works under the same terms as the license that governs the original copyright work. For example, if Hong publishes her photograph under the Attribution-ShareAlike 3.0 China Mainland license and Ming uses Hong's photograph to create his own collage, Ming must license his collage under the Attribution-ShareAlike 3.0 China Mainland license and indicate Hong's authorship of the original photograph; (5) Attribution-NoDerivative-NonCommercial 3.0 China Mainland, under which the licensor allows users to reproduce, distribute, exhibit, perform, show, and broadcast the copyright work as well as disseminate the copyright work through the information network, but users must respect the authorship and cannot alter the copyright work or make any derivative work based on the copyright work. Furthermore, users cannot exploit the original copyright work for any commercial purposes; and (6) Attribution-NonCommercial-ShareAlike 3.0 China Mainland, under which the licensor allows users to reproduce, distribute, exhibit, perform, show, and broadcast the copyright work and derivative work based on the copyright work, as well as disseminate the copyright work and derivative work through the information network, but users should maintain the licensor's attribution and license the derivative works under the Attribution-NonCommercial-ShareAlike 3.0 China Mainland license. In addition, the use cannot be for any commercial purposes.

The six categories of licensing vary according to the licensor's authorization, but they share several common areas that merit clarification. First of all, Creative Commons licenses work within the frameworks of copyright and contract laws. Copyright laws grant authors with a series of exclusive rights to reproduce, distribute, exhibit, perform, show, and broadcast their works as well as disseminate the works through the information network and make derivative works based on the originals. Contract law permits the right holders to assign the entire or a part of their exclusive rights through contracting or licensing. Upon the breach of the contract or license, contract law provides remedies for the injured party. By licensing the copyright works under Creative Commons licenses, the authors assign the main part of their exclusive rights to public users. As long as users comply with the conditions of the licenses, they can freely reproduce, distribute, exhibit, perform, show, and broadcast the copyright works as well as disseminate the works through the information network. Upon breaching the conditions of the licenses, the licenses and the rights granted hereunder will automatically terminate.[28] However, the Creative Commons has not established any enforcement system which could help licensors prohibit the breach of licenses and search for compensation. Secondly, Creative Commons licenses do not intend to affect "limitations on the exclusive rights of the copyright owner under copyright law" such as fair use/fair dealing. Thirdly, Creative Commons licenses give users certain obligations under which users must include a copy or the uniform resource identifier (URI) of the license with every copy of the original copyright work and must keep all notices that refer to the license intact and to the disclaimer of warranties with every copy of the original copyright work.[29] In addition, users cannot set up any technological measures that control access or use of the copyright work in a manner inconsistent with the terms of the licenses,[30] because the Creative Commons was established with the purpose of promoting wide distribution of copyright works while technological measures impede the exploitation of copyright works by users. Fourthly, if users wish to engage in activities that are prohibited by the licenses such as making derivative works under Attribution-NoDerivatives and Attribution-NoDerivatives-NonCommercial or exploiting the copyright work for commercial purposes under Attribution-NonCommercial and Attribution-NonCommercial-ShareAlike, they must acquire additional authorization from the author or the licensor. Finally, the legal effect of Creative Commons licenses will automatically expire at the end of the work's copyright term of protection.[31] Upon becoming effective, Creative Commons licenses cannot be revoked by any person, even the licensor.

Creators in Mainland China can license their works under the Creative Commons scheme by selecting a license from their official website and China Mainland as the jurisdiction. Once the license terms are selected, there will be several lines of HTML codes that creators need to copy and paste onto their websites. Thereafter, the Creative Commons license logo will be found on the works of the creators on their website along with a clause that contains a hyperlink to the license's brief and complete related text. Users can search for works distributed under Creative Commons licenses by entering a search query into the Creative Commons search engine on their official website and choosing the appropriate work formats. The Creative

[28] Creative Commons license, Art 7(a).

[29] Creative Commons license, Art 4(a).

[30] Ibid.

[31] Creative Commons license, Art 7(b).

Commons search engine works in connection with several popular websites, including Google for web texts and images, Flickr for images, blip.tv for videos, Jamendo for music, and SpinXpress for all kinds of media.[32]

6.3.4 Positive and Negative Impacts of Promoting Creative Commons in Mainland China

In addition to increased sanctions and self-help measures against copyright infringement, public respect for copyright protection may be increased in circumstances where control and exploitation of a copyright work is deemed fair. Creative Commons licensing provides an alternative way to control and use licensed works that can be perceived as fair by the public. Public compliance with the terms of Creative Commons licensing and public use of the licensed works may better help achieve the goal of copyright as promoting cultural progress and learning. However the Creative Commons licensing scheme has advantages and disadvantages. Thus, the promotion and implementation of Creative Commons licensing in different jurisdictions will have both positive and negative impacts on local societies.

6.3.4.1 Positive Impacts

First, the simple and feasible licensing pattern of the Creative Commons could facilitate information flow and alleviate the conflict of interest between copyright owners and public users. By offering license templates for copyright holders and the public, Creative Commons makes the authorization process transparent and clear. Both sides who have an interest will understand the kinds of rights that are reserved by the copyright owner and the categories of rights that have been authorized to the user through licensing. Due to the standard contract format of Creative Commons licensing and publishing on the Creative Commons official website, anyone in the public can become a licensee, obtaining access to and making exploitation of the copyright works released under Creative Commons licensing. Anyone can find works authorized under Creative Commons licensing through search engines, which promote wide dissemination of copyright works and free flow of information.

Creative Commons licenses are applicable to copyright works distributed in the traditional media, but more importantly, they serve digital works disseminated on the Internet and other new types of media, such as websites, online music, online literature, movies, and digital photographs. The creative licensing scheme resolves certain technical difficulties that networks bring to traditional copyright systems, such as feasibility of authorization of copyright works distributed online, compensation of royalty for copyright works provided by nonprofit websites, and verification of

[32] Available at http://search.creativecommons.org/# (visited Dec 30, 2010).

copyright for works disseminated through the information network. The authorization logos attached to the works released under Creative Commons licenses well inform the public the appropriate scope and methods of the permitted use. The Creative Commons licensing scheme greatly decreases the cost that users need to pay for authorization and ameliorate copyright protection under the digital network environment, hence, alleviate the conflict of interest between copyright holders and public users.

Currently, more than ten million digital network works have adopted Creative Commons licenses, from movies, popular music, and digital books to news archives of broadcasting companies and open coursewares of universities. After being imported and localized in Mainland China, Creative Commons can provide a significant amount of sources for creations for youths and creative groups in China, spurring the production of more excellent works and enriching cultural life. Furthermore, educational institutions in China could learn from the experience of open courseware programs offered by MIT and the Rice University and release their own courseware or self-compiled teaching material under Creative Commons licenses so as to offer educational sources to the public who can benefit from open education.

Secondly, the Creative Commons can promote the development of creative industries in China. Creative industries refer to "those industries which have their origin in individual creativity, skill and talent and which have a potential for wealth and job creation through the generation and exploitation of intellectual property" [4, p. 4]. The Chinese government often pays attention to cultural and creative industries and supports them. With the continual growth and development of economic and national power, "China has ambition to shift its image from one of low-cost production for others to that of a world leader with its own global brands; a move from Made in China to Created in China."[33] Chinese creative industries, including clusters in films, TV, animation, performing arts, design, publishing, music, and digital media, are growing rapidly, which makes China the third largest exporter of creative industries after the United States and the United Kingdom.[34] Governments and companies continuously invest and explore the potential for creative industries, especially the sectors that have extensive connections with high technology such as digital and mobile music, Internet games, and animation. Creative industry parks are established in many metropolitans, such as Beijing, Shanghai, Chengdu, and Shenzhen, to attract capital and talent. Many young people are also involved in the creative industries, establishing small enterprises, propagandizing their own creations, and participating in competitions and activities sponsored by the governments. The importation of Creative Commons licensing into China could provide more opportunities for creative young people and industries to absorb new ideas and free their creative potential and capabilities. In additional to

[33] "The Creative Industries in China: IVCA Report- March 2010," available at http://www.ivca.org/ivca/live/news/2010/develop-your-business-in-china-join-the-ivca-trade-mission-to-shanghai/IVCA_Report_-_The_Creative_Industries_in_China.pdf (visited Jan 19, 2011).

[34] Ibid.

the creative industries, the Creative Commons could also implant creative elements into other businesses and economic activities, thus strengthening the value-added potentials of various industries.

6.3.4.2 Negative Impacts

The foremost disadvantages of the Creative Commons are the terms of non-revocability and non-enforceability, due to which the copyright holder who anticipates to acquire commercial benefits will not prematurely adopt Creative Commons licensing to distribute his/her work. Once a copyright holder chooses to disseminate his/her work under a particular Creative Commons license, s/he cannot change or revoke the license applicable to his/her work. The effect of the license will not expire until the end of the copyright term of protection. The copyright holder cannot stop the continuous use and exploitation of his/her work, as long as the use and exploitation does not violate the terms of the license. The copyright holder also cannot remove the licensed work from circulation, regardless of the type, which can be either a copy of the individual work or in a collection or a copy of the derivative work created based on the original work. The choice of the copyright holder to place the same work under other nonconflicting Creative Commons licenses will not influence the effect of the current license in use.

In addition, the terms of the Creative Commons licenses are voluntarily executed by the copyright holder and the licensee who makes use of the work. The Creative Commons does not establish a dispute resolution or enforcement scheme to bind the two parties under its licenses. If users infringe certain exclusive rights reserved by the copyright holder, such as the rights of attribution and making commercial use, the copyright holder cannot safeguard his/her rights through the Creative Commons and obtain compensation. In order to look into the liability of infringement, the copyright holder must file litigation in court.

Due to the features of non-revocability and non-enforceability in Creative Commons licensing, the copyright holder who wishes to commercially benefit from his/her creation cannot simply adopt a Creative Commons license to disseminate the copyright work. Even though the copyright holder does not anticipate acquiring commercial benefits but rather promote his/her work and gain a reputation through Creative Commons licensing, conditions in the licenses will impede the future use of the work by the copyright holder for any commercial purposes. Furthermore, the licensing scheme will not be accepted and approved by publishers who earn benefits for selling copyright works, major record labels, and well-known performers and artists in a short period of time.

Secondly, the Creative Commons has conflict of benefit with copyright collecting societies. Creative Commons licenses are nonexclusive, thus permitting public users to freely exploit copyright work upon compliance with the licensing terms. If the author assigns his/her work through exclusive licenses to a third party, such as a publisher or copyright collecting society, s/he can no longer place the same work under Creative Commons licenses, and vice versa. Particularly, in some jurisdictions, the author must authorize copyright collecting societies to manage all of his/her works. Under such circumstances, the author cannot assign parts of his/her works to collecting societies and release the remainder for Creative Commons licensing to be freely exploited by the public. S/he must choose one or the other, that is, assign all the work to collecting societies, or choose to distribute the works under Creative Commons licensing.

Currently, there are several copyright collecting societies in Mainland China, including the Music Copyright Society of China, China Audio-Video Copyright Association, China Written Works Copyright Society, Images Copyright Society of China, and Chinese Film Copyright Association (Collective). Many writers, musicians, photographers, as well as phonogram and audiovisual program producers are members of these copyright collecting societies which assist to manage most of their copyright works. Hence, if these authors intend to license their works under proxy management through the Creative Commons, this will conflict with the interests of the collecting societies. Although the Creative Commons has earned recognition and support by certain copyright collecting societies, such as the Recording Industry Association of America and Motion Picture Association of America, it takes time for copyright collecting societies in China to approbate and promote the Creative Commons licensing scheme.

Finally, the governing of the works by the authors themselves under Creative Commons licensing may not fully promote public access to the works and their exploitation. Statistical data show that over 50 % of the licensors chose Attribution-ShareAlike for their works, among which around 60 % chose a noncommercial element [5]. Attribution-NonCommercial-ShareAlike is thus the most popular license. By adopting this license, the authors are able to disallow all subsequent users to commercially exploit their own derivative works created based on the original licensed work. Around 30 % of the licensors prefer to license their works under Attribution-NoDerivative, which prohibits the making of derivative works by subsequent users based on their works, among which a majority chose Attribution-NonCommercial-NoDerivative [5].

6.3.4.3 Conclusion: Proposed Improvement for Creative Commons in Mainland China

Despite its negative impacts, non-revocability guarantees exploitation of the licensed works by subsequent users. If licenses are revocable by authors at any time, subsequent users may not be able to exploit the works in accordance with the terms of the license in the event that they will be held liable for copyright infringement because of the expired licenses. The potential detriment to subsequent users justifies the non-revocability feature which in turn increases public reliance on the Creative Commons.

Enforceability is more important when third parties are involved especially under the ShareAlike feature. It is not enough to merely guarantee enforceability against the direct licensees, since works under Creative Commons licensing are likely to be reused over and over again. Leaving subsequent indirect users out of the contract restrictions will cause the Creative Commons licenses to lose effectiveness. Authors will not be likely to license their works under the Creative Commons if third parties can use their works against their will. For example, if a licensor who adopts the NonCommercial clause cannot enforce the license against a third party who makes commercial use of the work, s/he can neither prohibit the third party's commercial use nor be compensated from the subsequent commercial use of his/her work. Consequently, the licensor will no longer be willing to place his/her works under a Creative Commons license. Moreover, without enforceability against third parties, authors have to establish licenses with every subsequent user of their works, which decreases efficiency and fails to meet the goal of the Creative Commons in promoting sharing and exploitation.

In order to resolve the problems of non-enforceability and potential conflict with copyright collecting societies, the administrative organ of the Creative Commons can assist authors in enforcing their rights against direct or indirect licensees who breach the contract and commit copyright infringement and to negotiate with collecting societies. The administrative organ can establish monitoring and supervision mechanisms that monitor the compliance of licensees with the licensing terms. Upon finding that there is noncompliance or upon receiving complaints about breach of contract, the administrative organ can send cease-and-desist letters to the infringers or require them to compensate. If the infringers ignore the warnings and requests for compensation, the administrative organ can represent the authors in filing litigation against the infringers in court. In addition, the administrative organ can help the authors to negotiate with copyright collecting societies and withdraw certain works from collective management if the authors wish to place those works under Creative Commons licensing. Although the proposed administration may increase the expenses of the Creative Commons, it is likely to reduce the cost by authors that is spent on enforcing their rights under the licensing, thus, attracting more authors to submit their creations to the Creative Commons.

6.4 Impact of Digital Commons on Public Domain

The digital commons developed under copyright regimes can positively influence the public domain which is extensively correlated with intellectual property. The term "public domain" refers to "a true commons comprising elements of intellectual property that are ineligible for private ownership" [6, p. 975] in the context of intellectual property. Under copyright regimes, the public domain contains works that are not protectable by copyright, including those finished prior to the release of copyright laws and regulations, such as the Chinese literature masterpiece, *Dream of the Red Chamber*; works that were once copyrightable but their copyright terms of protection have expired; and works that are ineligible for copyright protection, such as works which do not meet the minimum requirement of originality or infringe upon the copyrights of other authors.

There are also some "murky terrain near the boundaries of the public domain," which contain intellectual creations that are protectable by intellectual property but are treated as in the public domain for various purposes [7, p. 149]. These intellectual creations include copyrightable works voluntarily distributed by the right holder publicly through the Internet or other channels without charging fees or establishing restrictions on the use, portions of the creations that are exploited under copyright limitations, works that are licensed without remuneration of royalties, and creations available via digital commons such as the OSS and the Creative Commons.

Due to borrowing in the process of creation, a prolific public domain plays a significant role in supporting copyright regimes and helping to achieve the goal of promoting the progress of culture and useful arts. Digital commons such as the Creative Commons to some degree contribute to the public domain, especially in the digital Internet era when copyright protection has been significantly increased.

6.4.1 Necessity of Public Domain

A work is eligible for copyright protection once it is created. In order to ensure the newly created work is exempt from litigation, the author must own the original authorship of the work. Originality is the fundamental requirement of copyright protection. To be original, the substantial expression of the work must own its origin to the author and must not be copied from other sources. The dichotomy of idea and expression ensures that copyright law only forbids the creator from copying expressions of other authors, not prohibit independent creation based on similar ideas. Therefore, examination of copying determines whether the work owns its originality and whether the author commits infringement of the copyright of former authors. Nonetheless, to determine what constitutes copying and use of prior sources may appear theoretically simple, but in practice, it is difficult to execute, because authors often borrow ideas, facts, or plots from preexisting material rather than fully independently create works out of thin air. New cultural texts are often built upon existing cultural texts. Composers create music by borrowing existing tunes and sounds; writers create literature by borrowing existing cultural and social texts as well as combining their own experiences; audiovisual program producers create films, TV series, or animations by borrowing existing plots, stories, and scenes; software programmers create new programs based on the source code used in other software; and photographers, sculptors, and architects are all involved in the process of borrowing, transformative imitating, and remixing already existing material and sources in various forms. This is the main feature of authorship and original creation.

Problems will emerge when part of the work at issue is generated from the creator's subconsciousness based on preexisting works that s/he had previously encountered. Consider the example that may often happen in the process of creation: two musicians heard a song when they attended a concert during their youth. Neither of them deliberately memorized the song. As time passed by, the first musician has entirely forgotten the tune, but the second musician had subconsciously absorbed the music into his mind. Both musicians compose works which embody a piece of the music that is similar to the tune in question. The similarity of the first musician's work is merely a coincidence so that the first musician owns a copyright of his creation. In contrast, the second musician is inspired by his subconsciousness to create his work and thus cannot be entitled to copyright, because he has copied from this preexisting tune and is liable for infringement. Similar situations may also take place in the process of writing a book, painting a picture, producing a film, designing a software program, etc. The paradox of such a situation lies in the difficulty of distinguishing the state of mind of different creators in reality. Furthermore, the state of mind does not influence the determination of originality or copyright infringement. Therefore, courts follow procedural rules and allocation of burden of proof to determine originality of a work in the face of such paradoxes.

In litigations, the plaintiff must collect evidence to demonstrate that the defendant once obtained access to preexisting work and substantially assimilated the exact work in order to prove copyright infringement. The defendant could refute the plaintiff's argument by introducing evidence that s/he independently created the work in question neither deliberately nor subconsciously copied from the plaintiff's work. It is possible for the defendant to disprove access to the plaintiff's work, but it is paradoxical to disprove his/her subconscious copying or assimilation. In light of such a dilemma, the defendant could bypass the problem about subconscious copying and instead, address the originality of the plaintiff's work, and prove that the plaintiff had exposure to other sources and substantially copied from them. If the plaintiff does not own the origin of his/her work and is not entitled to copyright protection, s/he cannot pursue legal action against the defendant for copyright infringing liability. However, the borrowing of authorship and process of creation will complicate the verification of originality, hence making the concept of originality unascertainable.

Professor Jessica Litman named the borrowing of creation as a "romantic model of authorship" [6, p. 1008]. This romantic model makes creative processes magical and likely to produce unique expression [6, p. 1008], since authors will use "words, musical notes, shapes or colors to clothe impulse that come from within her singular inner being" [6, p. 1008]. The magical inner being may store impressions, experiences, and works of other authors and the author transforms all of the raw material into something distinct and unrecognizable [6, p. 1008]. An author's impression and expression are subconsciously affected by what s/he had experienced, by other works and information that s/he read, and by the interaction of these two factors. The interaction combines all pieces of an author's experiences and knowledge as an entirety, even though the author him/herself cannot separate one memory from another. When an author engages in creation, his/her complicated memories will be transformed into his/her expressions. Therefore, it is not difficult to understand that parts of the author's work will mirror the works of others. If each author intends to enforce copyright protection on everything in his/her work, everyone could be accused as committing infringement.

Mapping an appropriate public domain could help to resolve this problem. The situating of ideas, theories, concepts, processes, plots, and some of the once copyrightable works into the public domain removes the apprehension of authors in borrowing from their peers and be inspired by them and provides access for the public to retrieve and exploit preexisting resources. Due to the public domain, it is assumed that each author acquired his/her concepts and raw material from the public domain rather than subconsciously copied from the prior works of others. The public domain relieves the burden of authors in searching for origins and independently verifying creations.

In litigations, the overprotection of plaintiff copyright restricts defendants in efficiently uncovering information and facts from the public domain. It is unfair to penalize the defendants who inadvertently exploit raw material found in the commons. The public domain benefits potential defendants who in good faith absorb parts of the authorship of others in the production of their own expressions. The public domain will also benefit potential plaintiffs, in cases that s/he is required by defendants to prove the originality of his/her work, because the material absorbed by the defendant may have also previously existed in other works of authorship. If it is assumed that all of the plaintiffs need to prove the originality of their works in order to win copyright infringement suits, they will not be likely to enforce their rights through judicial procedures. Due to the difficulties and challenges in proving originality, the lack of a public domain will impede copyright holders to pursue protection. As a neutral party, the court will also rely on the public domain to make a decision that places raw material, idea, and plots into the commons. If the court grants that all prior authors own raw material, this will block the creations of future authors.

In other words, the public domain is associated with copyright protection, which helps the individuals involved in the creation to resolve dilemmas. The public domain reserves enough literature in the commons, thus guaranteeing access and exploitation of prior material to establish original authorship.

6.4.2 Shrinking Public Domain in Digital Age: Threats from Second Enclosure

The public domain is not an unchanging terrain because it varies according to time and jurisdictions. The public domain expands when copyrights expire or some of the literature is excluded from copyright protection by legislation or judicial decisions, such as theories, processes, or simple compilation of facts. The public domain shrinks when the US government enacts bills to extend the copyright term of protection and excessively extends protection to technological measures or when the European Union issues a directive to grant *sui generis* protection to databases. In some sense, the relationship between copyright and the public domain is that when one goes down, the other goes up.

The emergence of intellectual property systems which incorporate intangible intellectual commons with property rights is regarded by Professor James Boyle as "the second enclosure movement," compared with the first enclosure movement that privatized common lands as individual property in England [8]. In the second enclosure movement, intellectual property continues to expand: subject matters of copyright and patents were increased; copyright terms of protection were lengthened; and technological measures against circumvention of access and use of copyright works were protected and widely adopted by copyright owners. The expansion of intellectual property especially in the area of copyright is a response to the advancement of technology. The strength of intellectual property rights must inversely vary with the cost of copying [8, p. 42]. In the age without copying machines, there were no copyrights, since producing manuscripts used almost the same amount of labor as writing a book. The invention of copying machines spurred the enactment of the first copyright act, the Statute of Anne. Digital technology and the Internet impelled the promulgation of the DMCA, CTEA, European Union Information Society Directive, and European Database Directive. Extending copyright to everything seriously reduces resources in the commons, thus shrinking the public domain.

The CTEA was issued by the US Congress in 1998 to extend 20 years to the duration of the original copyright protection, changing the term of protection to creator's life plus 70 years. The CTEA thus blocks works which are near expiration from entering the public domain. The CTEA influences the copyright status of a pyramid of works. It also impedes a large number of parodies and recreation based on works of which the terms of copyright protection have been lengthened. In the famous case *Suntrust v. Houghton Mifflin*,[35] the plaintiff as the trustee of the Mitchell Trust sued the defendant for copyright infringement because of its publication of *The Wind Done Gone*, a novel created based on *Gone with the Wind* by Margaret Mitchell. According to the laws prior to the CTEA, the literature masterpiece *Gone with the Wind* shall belong to the public domain after 1999 and be free for all to use. The CTEA maintained copyright protection of *Gone with the Wind* for decades and indirectly affected the determination of copyright infringement. Although the influence of the CTEA is primarily on works in traditional formats and non-digital aspects of the public domain, the influence on the digital terrain of copyright and the public domain will be reflected by librarians in establishing digital libraries that collect books and articles which have expired from copyright protection.

The DMCA encourages copyright owners to adopt technological measures that provide an extra layer of protection to their digital works and information. The DMCA prohibits circumvention of technological measures and distribution of devices that can circumvent technological measures. Technological measures not only control copying of the protected work but also control access to the work. Although the DMCA aims to protect technological measures that control access and use of copyright works only, it also impedes consumer access and exploitation of material in the public domain, because on the one hand, technological measures will

[35] *Suntrust v Houghton Mifflin Co.* 252 F.3d 1165 (11th Cir. 2001).

continue to play a role after the expiration of the copyright of protected works; on the other hand, distribution of circumvention-facilitated devices is completely banned under the DMCA, regardless whether the device is used to circumvent technological measures of copyright works or bypass control of information in the public domain. More seriously, the DMCA does not enforce technological measures to enable fair use or other privileged uses that exist in the traditional copyright regime. Many American scholars agree that the DMCA would be unconstitutional without allowance of circumventing technological control for fair use purposes [8].

The anti-circumvention rule of the DMCA has been imported and localized by many overseas jurisdictions through bilateral free trade agreements or domestic legal transplant. The US Free Trade Agreements reached after the DMCA compelled many of the developed and developing countries to enact anti-circumvention laws, including Jordan, Chile, Singapore, Australia, Morocco, Bahrain, Central America (CAFTA),[36] and the Free Trade Area of the Americas (FTAA) [9]. In areas where no such free trade agreement is signed, legislatures or governments were active in borrowing the legal model of anti-circumvention rules from the United States. China implemented an anti-circumvention law in its 2006 Regulation with provisions similar to those in the DMCA. The widespread adoption of technological measures and importation of the anti-circumvention legislative model of the DMCA exacerbate problems which negatively influence public domains worldwide.

In addition to the CTEA and the DMCA, the European Union Database Directive represents another challenge to the digital public domain. The Database Directive grants those who make qualitatively and quantitatively substantial investment in compiling a database a *sui generis* right, under which a database compiler enjoys 15 years of protection that prohibits the extraction and reutilization of the entire or substantial parts of the database contents.[37] Any substantial change which can be considered as a substantial new investment will result in renewing the term of database protection, which could in principle make the term of protection perpetual.[38]

The United States later introduced the database protection law, the Collections of Information Anti-Piracy Act (CIAA), which was similar to the European Union Database Directive. Although the CIAA broadened the exceptions for extraction and utilization of data from the protected database for the purposes of scientific research, education, news reporting, and verification, it largely expanded database protection to public domain works as long as they fall within the legislative definition of "data."[39] As they realized the threats that the CIAA would bring to the public domain, scientists and Internet industries lobbied against the release of such a law. Thus, the CIAA was not promulgated. The US Congress later replaced the CIAA

[36] Central America Free Trade Agreements with agreement countries including Costa Rica, the Dominican Republic, El Salvador, Guatemala, Honduras, and Nicaragua.

[37] European Union Database Directive, Arts 7 and 10.

[38] Ibid, Art 10.

[39] H.R. 354, ss 1401, 1402, 1403.

with bill H.R. 1858 which prohibits copying a corporation's database and participating in direct competition against that corporation.[40] The bill would still influence the public domain. However, by narrowing the criterion down to corporation databases, it alleviated the serious tension between the protection of databases and the preservation of the public domain brought on by the CIAA.

Each of these legislations challenges the digital public domain, but it is difficult to tell which legislation provides the most serious challenge. The CTEA extended the term of copyright protection and hinders information from entering the public domain. The DMCA protects technological measures and bans trafficking of devices that control access to both copyright works and information in the public domain. The European Union Database Directive and the CIAA/H.R. 1858 grant the database compiler with exclusive rights to prohibit others to use his/her data as long as s/he has substantially invested in obtaining the contents regardless whether the contents are original or mere facts extracted from the public domain. Synergies and interaction among these legislations will more seriously diminish the public domain. Any invested compilation of digital information under the protection of the European Union Database Directive or the CIAA could be covered by an additional layer of protection of technological measures in the DMCA. Even though the database compiler has authorized the public to extract and utilize his/her digital compilation, users must have hacking skills to circumvent the technological measures. Otherwise, in reality, the users will barely be able to use the database without hacking devices, as distribution of circumvention-facilitated devices is illegal under the DMCA.

6.4.3 Constructing Public Domain in Digital Age: Influence of Digital Commons

In light of the threats posed by the expansion of copyright, many initiatives outside the legislative spectrum have been spontaneously launched by institutes or groups of scholars to mitigate the serious shrinking of the public domain in the digital environment. Academic and educational institutions have established legal information institute (LII) projects, making ordinances, regulations, court opinions, arbitration decisions, and law reform material freely available on the open website.[41] The LII projects have spread among numerous jurisdictions and regions, including Hong Kong (HKLII), Australia and Asia (AustLII and AsianLII), the United Kingdom and Ireland (BAILII and IRLII), Canada (CanLII), New Zealand (NZLII), the Pacific Islands (PacLII), South Africa (SAFLII), the Commonwealth (CommonLII), and the world (WorldLII).[42] Scientists have created databases that keep scientific data free of private control and help cultivate a research common [10].

[40] H.R. 1858.

[41] Available at http://www.hklii.org/ (visited Feb 24, 2011).

[42] Ibid.

Libraries and cultural preservation organizations were prone to digitalize their collections and opened access to the public. These initiatives will help nurture and preserve the public domain under the digital network environment.

In addition to governmental or nonprofit institutions, individuals are actively engaging in making material and information available through the Internet, including material that is protectable by copyright and that originally in the public domain. Scholars attach the hyperlinks of their academic articles in their biography webpages or write academic works on their online blogs; writers and reporters provide commentaries or news reporting for Internet journals; professionals submit their discussions on professional bulletin board systems; and artists distribute their self-created music, videos, and short films through online broadcasting. Individuals who are willing to share thoughts and creations without asking for monetary compensation add great value to the public domain as well as help preserve the public domain under the digital network environment through the aid of technology.

Among the knowledge sharing programs or individual behaviors, the initiatives of the OSS and the Creative Commons represent the most popular and interesting contributions to the digital public domain. Although software or works distributed under the OSS and the Creative Commons still deserve copyright protection subject to terms of the licenses, assigning part of the important rights by copyright owners to the public provides more fundamentals for the creations of future authors, thus increasing resources in the public domain. The OSS helps future innovation by opening up the source code instructions of each software licensed under the program. By complying with the GPL, subsequent software programmers who develop new software based on the preexisting OSS must also open up the source code of the new software subject to the terms of licensing. Those who exclusively control the new software are considered to breach the terms of the GPL and infringe intellectual property rights of the original program. The GPL clearly states: "Here is this copyrighted body of work; you may use it, add to it, modify it, or copy it- all of these uses are legal, but only if you comply with the terms of the GPL."[43] In the licensing model of the OSS, one preexisting open source program could be followed by many derivative open source programs, and then each derivative attracts more follow-up software. Hence, the OSS takes advantage of the intellectual property system to preserve a commons that allows some of digital resources to fall within the public domain.

The Creative Commons is a project similar to the OSS but adapts its licensing to other kinds of works, such as literature, music, photography, and video. Authors choose Creative Commons licenses to disseminate their works by giving up some of the most important exclusive rights, including right of reproduction, distribution, and making derivative works based on the original work. In contrast to the OSS, the Creative Commons provide six different categories of licenses with terms that range from flexible to strict. Thus, any author can select the most appropriate license without worrying that users will exploit the licensed works in a way that does not benefit

[43] GNU Library General Public License, available at http://www.gnu.org/copyleft/library.html (visited Nov 17, 2011).

him/her. Under the license with the most flexible terms, the authors permit the public to fully exploit their works even for commercial purposes, as long as the public respect the authorship and attribution. Although the copyright of these works does not end, the authors dedicate them to the commons and offer remix and recreation resources for future authors. Under the licenses that have the "ShareAlike" clause, potential licensees are required to distribute their derivative works based on the original work subject to the same terms of the original license. Derivatives of the licensees are expected to be exploited and adapted by future users. Similar to the chain effect of the OSS, the Creative Commons continues to keep follow-up works open and helps to extend the digital public domain.

Digital commons such as the OSS and the Creative Commons establish a model that avoids the potential damages of abolishing intellectual property systems with everything unprotected by copyright. Under the model, the price for admission to the copyright works is the commitment by authors to make their innovation part of the ecology of open sources [8, p. 65]. This model is successful because it does not simply provide everything free which will harm creation and innovation incentive but runs its norms based on the legal system. Authorized access to copyrightable works at a low price or even without payment could respect original authorship on the one hand and allow for subsequent borrowing and recreation on the other hand. As Professor James Boyle indicated, the old dividing line between intellectual property and the public domain had been between the realm of property and the free, but the new dividing line is between the realm of individual control and distributed creation, management, and enterprise [8]. The new model is "constructed around the twin notions of preventing monopoly control over network protocols in order to preserve innovation, while still allowing for the type of collective management" [8] which avoids the tragedy of weakening creative passion and underinvestment. It is protected by a liability rule in which a user will be accused of infringement only after his/her use does not comply with the licensing terms, rather than the property rule in which a user's conduct will be deemed infringement as long as his/her use of a work has not been authorized by the author.

Digital commons are by no means perfect. They have shortcomings of non-revocability and non-enforceability as discussed above. The emergence of such a model to form an e-commons is spurred by the serious concern about the continuing worldwide expansion of intellectual property. Digital commons are mostly supported by individual creators or small enterprises that need resources for their innovation. Conglomerates in creative industries are still reluctant to entirely accept the operation mode of the OSS and the Creative Commons. In addition, one small problem of the digital commons that is a concern to scholars is that it is not very clear how they fit into "the binary opposition between intellectual property on the one hand and the public domain on the other" [8]. Despite the potential defects, the contribution to the public domain under the digital network environment made by the digital commons is confirmed. They open a window for the public to consider possible means which alleviate strict intellectual property protection outside the legislative regime and judicial procedures.

6.5 Conclusion

Apart from the amendment and reconstruction of copyright systems with regard to exceptions under anti-circumvention rules, safe harbors for technological intermediaries and copyright limitations, creation of digital commons based on copyright and contract laws, but outside the traditional intellectual property realm would also help to counter the continuous expansion of copyright protection and recover the public domain which contains existing information and data in support of knowledge storage and future creation. Although digital commons such as the Creative Commons still have drawbacks due to the lack of revocability and enforceability, they can expand user access and right to appreciate, disseminate and exploit copyright works. The borrowing by users and their recreation based on the preexisting material would in turn add to enriching cultural goods and promoting cultural progress. By properly administrating and utilizing digital commons, developing countries such as China would well cultivate and stimulate their creative and innovative sectors that are beneficial to social and cultural progress.

References

1. Carroll, M. W. (2007). Creative commons as conversational copyright. In K. Y. Peter (Ed.), *Intellectual property and information wealth: Issue and practices in the digital age* (Copyright and related rights, Vol. I). Westport: Praeger Publisher.
2. Schellekens, M. (2006). Free and open source software: An answer to commodification? In G. Lucie & P. B. Hugenholtz (Eds.), *The future of the public domain: Identifying the commons in information law*. The Hague: Kluwer Law International.
3. Hietanen, H. (2010, August 12–13). Creative commons Olympics. In: *Presentation at the 10th annual intellectual property scholars conference* organized by Berkeley Center for Law and Technology, Berkeley, CA, USA.
4. Department of Culture, Media and Sport of the United Kingdom. (2001). *Creative industries mapping document 2001* (p. 4). Available at http://webarchive.nationalarchives.gov.uk/+/http://www.culture.gov.uk/global/publications/archive_2001/ci_mapping_doc_2001.htm. Visited 17 Nov 2011.
5. Elkin-Koren, N. (2005). What contracts can't do: The limits of private ordering in facilitating a creative commons. Available at http://papers.ssrn.com/sol3/papers.cfm?abstract_id=760906. Visited 25 Mar 2013.
6. Litman, J. (1990). The public domain. *Emory Law Journal, 39*, 965–1023.
7. Samuelson, P. (2003). Mapping the digital public domain: Threats and opportunities. *Law and Contemporary Problems, 66*, 147–171.
8. Boyle, J. (2003). The second enclosure movement and the construction of the public domain. *Law and Contemporary Problems, 66*, 33–74.
9. Chander, A. (2006). Symposium: Cyberpersons, propertization, and contract in the information culture- exporting DMCA lockouts. *Cleveland State Law Review, 54*, 205–217.
10. Reichman, J., & Uhlir, P. (2003). A contractually reconstructed research commons for scientific data in a highly protectionist intellectual property environment. *Law and Contemporary Problems, 66*, 315–462.

Conclusion

Main Findings

The expansion of copyright systems is influenced by the development of technology. New technology induces new kinds of works based on new types of media and significantly decreases the cost of reproducing and disseminating works. Such technological advancements change the interests between copyright owners and public users. Users are exposed to more opportunities brought on by digital network technology to obtain access to copyrightable works and exploit them. If copyright laws do not expand the protected subject matters and categories of exclusive rights, the authors cannot be adequately compensated under a digital network environment. Copyright laws can no longer function as incentive for creation, if there is a lack of revision and appropriate expansion. Hence, copyright laws have extended protection to new subject matters such as computer programs and databases, granted right holders new kinds of rights such as right of rental and right to network dissemination of information, established indirect infringing liability for ISPs, and expanded protection to technological measures. These measures were adopted to mitigate the threat posed by increasing opportunities to access and exploit various works.

However, copyright expansion should not be unlimited and should cease when appropriate access to work is at risk and future creation is jeopardized. Expansion of copyright protection is only justified when the access and use of works from the public threatens incentive for creation and recovery of economic rewards. Overexpansion of copyright protection would again disrupt the balance if access to works is narrowly restricted. Accessibility plays a central role in copyright systems to fulfill the dual purposes of encouraging creation on the one hand and advancing knowledge and learning on the other hand. Without appropriate accessibility, copyright works cannot be reproduced and disseminated. Thus, the goal of promoting knowledge and learning cannot be well achieved.

Accessibility to copyright works and information is stifled due to the continuous expansion of copyright protection by enacting laws against circumvention of

J.J. Hua, *Toward A More Balanced Approach: Rethinking and Readjusting Copyright Systems in the Digital Network Era*, DOI 10.1007/978-3-662-43517-5,

technological measures, increasing conditions for the safe harbors of ISP liability, and narrowing copyright limitations and exceptions.

Anti-circumvention rules have been adopted by international copyright conventions and various jurisdictions to protect effective technological measures, such as encryption or other similar devices that are employed by copyright holders to control unauthorized access and reproduction of copyright works. The WIPO Internet Treaties for the first time granted protection to technological measures at a multinational level, obligating member countries to provide adequate legal protection and effective legal remedies against the circumvention of effective technological measures that are used by authors in connection with the exercise of their copyright while leaving room for member countries to make detailed regulations. The legislative model that involves the anti-circumvention rule in the DMCA of the United States represents the most typical and popular legal approach which has been widely imported by many jurisdictions through multilateral or bilateral agreements and legal transplant.

The anti-circumvention rule in the DMCA prohibits unauthorized circumvention of access-control technological measures and production and distribution of any technology, service, or device that is primarily used to circumvent the technological measures that control access and copying of copyright work. The DMCA includes some exceptions to balance the increased control of copyright works, such as preventing circumvention of access controls, incorporating a general provision of copyright limitations, providing a list of specific exceptions for prohibition on circumvention and trafficking of circumvention devices, and establishing an ongoing administrative rulemaking proceeding to evaluate the impact of the prohibition against the circumvention of access controls. However, these measures cannot well balance the interests of public users against those of copyright holders. Non-infringing uses that originally existed in traditional copyright systems are largely restricted due to the anti-circumvention access controls and anti-trafficking of circumvention devices, since public users cannot enjoy fair use/fair dealing privileges without first obtaining access to the protected works or without any device to aid them in conducting the circumvention. Furthermore, the anti-circumvention rule also imposes restrictions on right of notice and privacy as well as fair competition in the secondary market for interoperable devices by technically controlling access to computer programs in the products for their normal operation. These disadvantages outweigh the balanced scheme established in the anti-circumvention rule and adversely affect appropriate access to copyright works.

In response to the conventional requirement of protecting the right of communication to the public and widespread online copyright piracy, copyright laws and policies among different jurisdictions have extended infringing liability to technological intermediaries which induce the infringing activities of their subscribers. Technological intermediaries such as ISPs will be held liable for direct copyright infringement by their subscribers if the ISPs have knowledge of the infringement, obtain direct financial benefit from the activities, and have the ability to supervise the direct infringement, or the ISPs have authorized the infringement or have a common design with the direct infringers. Judicial decisions in landmark cases such as

Napster, *Aimster*, and *Grokster* have witnessed this trend of stifling technology and given copyright industries the support to address any new media that facilitate Internet users to reproduce and disseminate copyright works. Although safe harbors have been developed from judicial practices and incorporated into legislations, proceedings such as the notice and takedown approach, and subpoena procedures, would still affect information dissemination and infringe individual privacy because of the risk of erroneous takedown and abuse of power by the right holders.

In addition, the graduated response policy initiated by the French government and ISP injunctions granted by a couple of European courts exacerbate the weak position of new media forms. Under the graduated response policy, the administrative authority will warn the ISPs to cease the infringing activity of their subscribers in question after receiving complaints from copyright owners. Otherwise, the ISPs will be held indirectly liable. Such a policy not only increases conditions for ISP safe harbors but also negatively affects due process, freedom of expression, individual privacy, and balance of interest in the copyright system. In addition to France, the graduated response policy has already been adopted by a range of jurisdictions including the United Kingdom, South Korea, and Ireland. This also additionally establishes restrictions on the dissemination of copyright information and development of new communication technologies.

With the purpose to advance knowledge and promote future creations, copyrights contain limitations and exceptions for the exclusive rights of copyright owners, mostly allowing social functions such as personal study, scientific research, classroom teaching, news reporting, and preservation of collections by nonprofit organizations. Although different jurisdictions adopt different legislative models with regard to limitations and exceptions, they shall comply with the international conventional obligations to confine copyright limitations and exceptions to certain special cases which do not conflict with normal exploitation of the work and do not unreasonably prejudice the legitimate interests of the right holder. The United States has adopted the fair use doctrine which includes four items as guiding factors for courts to make decisions case by case. Other common law jurisdictions such as the United Kingdom and Canada and several civil law jurisdictions such as Germany and China have adopted the list of exceptions which describe in detail the situations that are particularly suitable for fair dealing. The United States model contains more flexibility as judges can use the guiding factors to decide each case subject to specified conditions, but lacks certainty because there is no specified guidance as to how these factors in the multifactor test can be weighed and balanced. The list of detailed exceptions provides more certainty as uses that can be deemed fair are clearly stipulated, but lacks flexibility since a static list cannot embody all possible non-infringing uses especially in the remix culture. Without adequate flexibility and certainty, copyright limitations and exceptions cannot well guarantee the social function of copyright systems and future creations.

More seriously, nowadays, copyright is controlled by a few entertainment conglomerates due to media concentration. Media concentration has constrained the creative freedom that people are used to enjoy. Before copyright industries monopolized the market and endeavored to strike infringement, the public was free to view existing information, borrow from previous material, create, and comment on works of others as they felt appropriate. The emergence of the Internet increased such personal freedom. Millions of individual Internet surfers embraced the new way of expression and communication by writing novels, blogging ideas and daily experiences, composing songs, clipping and editing videos, or producing short movies. People usually engage in such creative activities by working on their personal computers or accessing the Internet at home or in private places. As long as people do not use their creations based on copyright works for commercial purposes, their activities are like private or face-to-face communications in ordinary life, which impose no harm to the interests of copyright owners. Furthermore, such individual creativity forms part of the nonmainstream and mass culture. To overly impose liability and restrictions on personal uses negatively affects privacy, personal freedom, and free expression.

This is the time when the networked world transfers from being digital to being human. According to Xiaoxiang Shi, being human means that "networked individuals are becoming more involved in cultural creativity, innovation and communication through the use of information technology and the Internet. This tendency has increased as a result of the growing public digital literacy, and the rise of a 'participative web'. The production of arts and literature works is no longer considered a 'privilege' of social and cultural elite, but a daily engagement for mass individuals, which is enjoyable and provides for instance, communication, entertainment, creative play and self-development" [1]. Therefore, laws and policies should be reconsidered and amended to balance copyright systems.

Contributions of the Study

In order to recover a balance of interest among right holders, technological intermediaries, and public users under the digital network environment, it is time for policymakers to rethink the current copyright system and summon the courage to carry out a new round of legal reforms. Policymakers should be concerned in the process of reforms about the form of the digital future and how the future will be shaped. Policymakers should take into consideration appropriate accessibility, dissemination, and permission of recreation of copyright works. The concerns and considerations are not only relevant for China, one of the developing countries which is heavily discussed in this book, but also benefit other jurisdictions which aim to change their existing copyright systems toward a more balanced form, thus satisfying their domestic social demands. Specific proposals addressed by this book include revision of the anti-circumvention rule, amendment of ISP liability, importing both legal flexibility and certainty into copyright limitations and exceptions, and promoting the digital commons based on voluntary licensing schemes, such as the Creative Commons.

Revision of Anti-circumvention Rule

My input for the revision of anti-circumvention rules is to basically amend current copyright laws by including a general exception provision that can guide the decision-making of judges with regard to the circumvention of TPMs for non-infringing uses based on generalized exceptions and conditions on protection of TPMs and include certain requirements under anti-circumvention laws that will fall into more general areas of laws, such as the competition law. The amendment of legal mechanisms could be assisted by improvements in technology which would install automatic decoding equipment thus allowing minimum fair use and transferring technology so that circumvention devices are available for fair users to circumvent TPMs for non-infringing uses.

First, the definition of TPMs should be simplified and clarified, avoiding ambiguity and lengthiness. TPMs should simply refer to effective technologies, devices, or components used by the right owners to prevent access and reproduction of copyright works without prior authorization, because a series of acts such as browsing, approaching, running, or making available of works through the information network regulated in the relevant laws of China can be embodied into a general classification of two types of activities, namely, access and reproduction. In addition, simplified language complies with the terms that define the TPMs in international conventions and will make the terminology easier to understand.

Secondly, a technological mechanism can be installed into TPMs to allow users' circumvention of access controls and copy controls for minimum use such as browsing or reproducing 5–15 % of the protected works. Under such a mechanism, users only need ordinary knowledge and skills to partially circumvent the TPMs and use the authorized minimum amounts of protected works. Then, the partially circumvented TPMs will go back to function as protection against access or copying of the remaining parts of the works. To design such a technological arrangement, the issue on the creation and invention of appropriate software is left to technology developers and experts. Other issues with regard to the definition and scope of minimum use for different kinds of copyright works could be resolved through negotiations among various stakeholders including legislatures, copyright owners, technology developers, nonprofit organizations, and consumers.

Thirdly, copyright laws should establish a general condition on the protection of TPMs, stipulating that only TPMs that guarantee the legitimate interests of copyright owners in copyright laws are under statutory protection. In addition, a general exception should also be incorporated into copyright laws, explicitly articulating that anti-circumvention laws will not constrain and impede limitations and exceptions to the exclusive rights of copyright owners, including fair use or fair dealing. Prohibition on trafficking of circumvention devices should only apply to devices which are primarily designed or produced for the purpose of circumventing a TPM, have only limited commercially significant purpose or use other than to circumvent, and are marketed to be used to circumvent. Provision of devices which are not primarily designed for circumvention and have commercially significant purposes other than mere circumvention should not be banned, even though the devices may be occasionally used to circumvent TPMs. The general exception should be able to embody all potential situations that may be deemed fair or non-infringing under the digital network environment and guide judicial decisions on whether the questionable acts of circumvention or trafficking of circumvention devices violate copyright laws.

Fourthly, when litigations on circumvention issues are filed to the courts, judges should decide whether the use of TPMs satisfies the prerequisite on TPM protection and whether the acts of circumvention or trafficking of circumvention devices are for uses that fall within the scope of limitations and exceptions in the exclusive rights of copyright owners. In countries where precedent is the legal tradition, courts can refer to previous landmark cases to examine whether the decision should be for or against circumvention acts. In countries where precedent is not the decisive factor for judicial determinations, such as China, the Supreme Court can release judicial interpretations to specify the norms for courts to comply when making decisions.

Finally, policymakers should consider alleviating the negative effect of the TPMs on use of copyright material by importing anti-circumvention rules into more general laws such as the competition law other than copyright laws as carried out in Japan where the copyright law only prohibits circumvention of copy-control technological measures while anti-circumvention of access controls and anti-trafficking of circumvention devices are regulated under the competition law.

Amending Internet Service Provider Liability and Safe Harbors

Several suggestions are made to modify ISP liability and safe harbors, including settling the determinative factors in indirect liability principles, revising and clarifying the procedure of notice and takedown, adopting the Norwich Pharmacal procedure as carried out by Hong Kong, postponing the importing of a graduated response policy, granting injunctions against ISPs cautiously, and absorbing heterogeneous approaches combined with legislative measures to better achieve certainty of ISP liability.

First, certain standards on the following factors should be settled in either common law indirect liability principles or statutory liability regulations of ISPs: the knowledge of ISPs on the primary infringement, obtaining of direct financial benefits from the primary infringement, and the ability of the ISPs to control or supervise infringing activity. Therefore, ISP knowledge shall include both actual knowledge and awareness of apparent infringing activity for the first item. The emergence of certain situations should be deemed as apparent infringing activity, including abnormally high traffic on the network, appearance of terms like "pirated" or "bootleg" in the file title, inclusion of names of copyright works in the file title of which the uploader is obviously not the copyright owner, and the repeated appearance of material that has been targeted by statutory takedown notices. However, mere knowledge of the prevalence of infringing activity in general should not be deemed as awareness of apparent infringement. As for the second factor, direct financial benefits should be shown by a very close relationship between the ISPs and the alleged infringing activity. Situations such as the attraction of advertising probably due to the popularity of the infringing material shall not be deemed adequate to prove a close relationship with an alleged infringer. As for the third factor, the ability to control or supervise subscriber activity could mean that the ISPs have the prerequisite ability to block access to the infringing material.

Secondly, the notice and takedown regime can be reformed in a stepwise manner by incorporating a reasonable grace period for suspected subscribers to defend themselves and establish certain exemptions for ISPs if they fail to take down the suspected infringing material. In the first step, a reasonable grace period can be incorporated for suspected subscribers to defend themselves prior to the removal of their material by the ISPs. A reasonable grace period could be around 4 or 5 days, which are neither too short for the subscribers to prove their innocence nor too long for copyright holders and ISPs to monitor suspected subscribers and address the infringement. Under circumstances in which the suspected subscriber does not respond during the grace period after receiving the notice from the ISP, the ISP should expeditiously take down the material in the event that it will be liable for the infringement. The period of time within the expeditious takedown would be better if defined as 24 h. In the second step, some exceptions can be established in the grace period, including special circumstances under which ISPs can immediately take down the suspected material without waiting for the end of the grace period. Examples include circumstances where copyright owners have already suffered great losses due to the unauthorized online transmission of their works. In the third step, special exemptions can be established, which allows ISPs to be still protected by safe harbors even if they fail to take down suspected material after the notice and the grace period. Such exemptions include circumstances where enforcement of the takedown will cause great economic loss or impose undue burden to the ISPs.

Thirdly, a comparative discussion between the "subpoena procedure" and "Norwich Pharmacal" discovery procedure shows that the latter has more relevance for the protection of privacy due to the prerequisite in which a person who is seeking for a court order should have the genuine intent to commence a proceeding. Therefore, the "Norwich Pharmacal" procedure should be imported to balance the interests of different parties. On the one hand, district or intermediate courts could be appointed as authoritative organs to decide whether the information of alleged infringers shall be disclosed upon the request of copyright holders. On the other hand, ISPs should be required by law to record the information of suspected infringers when a judicial procedure is triggered.

Fourthly, countries which have not yet imported the graduated response policy should think twice and well examine and balance the positive and negative factors that will affect copyright owners, ISPs, and Internet users. Even if governments intend to adopt the graduated response system, several key factors should be taken into consideration as mentioned in the previous chapter: an "independent review" mechanism, "educative and rehabilitative" purposes, and maintaining of "reasonable alternative access" to the Internet; minimization of "collateral damages"; safeguarding of "proportionality" and "flexibility"; and the use of "internet disconnection as a last resort."

Fifthly, judicial decisions involving granting ISP injunctions should well consider the proportionality of the order and balance the protection of interests of copyright owners against other fundamental rights held by users and ISPs, such as freedom of expression, right to privacy, right to receive and impart information, and technology intermediaries' freedom of conducting business. Several important factors should be taken into consideration to determine the proportionality of the injunction, including the cost and time to implement the blocking and filtering technology, the targeted websites of the injunction, the impact of the injunction to the ISPs' transmission service, the scale of the infringement, and ISPs' knowledge about the infringement.

Finally, heterogeneous approaches combined with legislative measures can better achieve the certainty of ISP liability and the free flow of information. In addition to revision of copyright laws and regulations, various feasible methods should be adopted, including revision of other relevant laws such as the competition law and privacy law, government policy, and industry guidelines, as well as introduction of public consultation and multiparty forums so as to make these mechanisms collaboratively work on the issues of ISP liability, free dissemination of information, and protection of privacy in the digital network environment. When applying heterogeneous approaches into digital legal reforms, it is important for policymakers to avoid potential overlapping and conflicts between the different methods and try to merge the various approaches so that they can systematically and consistently resolve legal issues under the digital network environment.

Importing Legal Flexibility and Certainty into Copyright Limitations and Exceptions

As for statutory limitations and exceptions for exclusive rights under which copyright works are allowed to be exploited without authorization and without payment of remuneration to the right holders, legal flexibility and certainty should be imported by incorporating the four-factor balancing test with focus on the first and fourth factors as abstract guidance and a list of nonexclusive detailed exceptions as minute prescriptions.

The four factors in the balancing test are the purpose and character of the use, nature of the copyright work, amount and substantiality of the use, and effect of use on the market of the original copyright work. In comparing the association of the four factors to fair use cases, the first and fourth factors have more direct and determinative influence on decisions as opposed to the other two factors. A large number of cases show that the works in question are creative, as copyright is primarily concerned with originality and creativity, and courts are not likely to favor a fair use defense if a large volume of the copyright work is used. Adoption of the four-factor test with focus on the purpose and character of the use as well as the effect of the use on the market will bring more certain and clearer guidance to judges and public users. Due to the emerging remix culture and mass participation in recreation, determining the transformativeness in the purpose and character of use becomes more and more important. Analyses on different cases illustrate that transformation of purpose is far more important than transformation of the contents of the original works.

In order to guarantee predictability and offset the different abilities of judges, a list of nonexclusive exceptions should also be added to supplement the four-factor balancing test. Uses that fall within the scope of the list of exceptions shall be regarded as fair or non-infringing. Uses that fall outside the scope shall be examined under the four-factor balancing test. A comparative study on fair dealing or exceptions among common law jurisdictions such as the United Kingdom and Canada and civil law jurisdictions such as Germany, Taiwan, and Mainland China demonstrates that the typical specified situations of fair use or fair dealing include research and private study, criticism or review, quotations, and reporting of current events including public speeches and visual and sound reporting on events of the day as well as newspaper articles and broadcasted commentaries on events that have a political, economic, or religious nature.

Moreover, three schemes supplement fair use/fair dealing, which encourage reproduction and adaptation of copyright works without authorization from copyright holders should also be incorporated. The first one is compulsory licensing schemes that statutorily confine the scope of the use and require monetary remunerations for the copyright owners. The second one is no action notice in which the concept borrows from property law and is recommended by some copyright scholars. It advocates toleration by copyright owners on certain infringements by using no action notice in the first place and enforcement of their rights against these infringements later if necessary. The third is community-based guidelines which encourage the practices of creative communities in defining and defending fair use/fair dealing.

To better implement a compulsory licensing scheme, focus should be placed on literary works that may help to serve the interests of minorities or disabled people, constructing digital libraries and promoting distribution of articles in newspapers, periodicals, and websites. A series of schemes should also be established to perfect the statutory licensing. A declaration system can exclude works that are not allowed by copyright owners based on fair reasons from compulsory licensing schemes. A dual-track remuneration system which contains both a statutory remuneration standard and multilateral negotiations can ensure that copyright owners are fairly compensated and users are not unfairly prejudiced. An effective and robust administrative mechanism on copyright collecting societies can well protect the interests of copyright owners and public users as well as prevent the abuse of power of collecting societies.

Promoting Digital Commons Projects

Digital commons projects based on voluntary licensing schemes such as the Creative Commons can better promote the dissemination of copyright works and recreation which relies on preexisting material. Although digital commons projects embody non-revocability and nonenforceability and may have conflicts of benefit with copyright collecting societies, they work as a feasible mean to facilitate information flow, alleviate the conflict of interests between copyright holders and public users, and advance the development of creative industries which significantly rely on the encouraging and borrowing of new ideas and innovative expressions. Furthermore, digital commons projects can very much contribute to the public domain by placing copyright works under a series of voluntary and automatic licensing schemes under which exploitation of works can be carried out without further authorization or restriction from right holders. Future authors can freely use the existing material within digital commons projects and formulate their own creations as long as they comply with terms of the licenses. Therefore, encouraging the development of digital commons is a good way to encourage future creations outside the traditional means of revising and amending laws and legal practices. The problems of nonenforceability and potential conflicts with copyright collecting societies can be resolved by the assistance of the administrative organ in the Creative Commons in helping authors to enforce their rights and negotiate with collecting societies.

Concluding Remarks

It is time to rethink and amend copyright systems under the digital network environment. Based on comparative research on international and regional conventions as well as laws, regulations, policies, and cases among different jurisdictions, this book suggests proposals to attain a balance of interest among copyright holders, transmission intermediaries, and public users in accessing, distributing, and exploitation of copyright works. Four specific issues are discussed and reform proposals are suggested in the book: anti-circumvention rule for the protection of technological measures, indirect infringing liability for ISPs and safe harbor regulations, copyright limitations and exceptions, and digital commons projects which promote distribution and adaptation of copyright works placed under voluntary licensing schemes. The analysis of these issues and corresponding reform proposals are not only to reverse the trend of worldwide copyright expansion so as to make copyright law appropriately respond to digital network challenges and emerging remix culture in general but also to encourage developing countries such as China to rethink and amend their copyright system so as to restore a robust public domain where existing information and data can be used to produce future intellectual assets in particular.

Reference

1. Shi, S. X. Chinese copyright law, peer production and the participatory media age: An old regime in a new world. Available at http://ses.library.usyd.edu.au/bitstream/2123/2359/1/CopyrightAsiaPacific_Ch13.pdf. Visited 15 May 2012.

List of Legislations[1]

Administrative Measures for Software Products (P.R.C. 2009)
Agreed Statement Concerning the WIPO Copyright Treaty (1996)
Agreement of Trade-Related Aspects of Intellectual Property Rights (1994)
Amendment to the Copyright Act, 1957 (India 2010)
Anti-Counterfeiting Trade Agreement (2011)
Australian Copyright Amendment (Digital Agenda) Act 2000 (Australia 2000)
Berne Convention for the Protection of Literary and Artistic Works (1886)
Canadian Copyright Act (Canada 1921)
Copyright (Amendment) Bill (Hong Kong 2011)
Copyright (Amendment) Bill (Hong Kong 2014)
Copyright Amendment (Digital Agenda) Bill (Australia 1999)
Copyright, Designs and Patent Act 1988 (U.K. 1988)
Copyright Law of Japan (Japan 2010)
Copyright Law of the People's Republic of China (2010 Amendment) (P.R.C. 2010)
Copyright Law of the People's Republic of China (Modified Draft) (P.R.C. 2012)
Copyright Law of the People's Republic of China (2nd Modified Draft) (P.R.C. 2012)
Copyright Law of the People's Republic of China (Reviewing Modified Draft) (P.R.C. 2014)
Copyright Term Extension Act (U.S.A. 1998)
Decision of the Standing Committee of the National People's Congress on Amending the Copyright Law of the People's Republic of China (P.R.C. 2010)
Digital Economy Act 2010 (U.K. 2010)
Digital Millennium Copyright Act (U.S.A. 1998)
Directive 96/9/EC of the European Parliament and of the Council of March 11, 1996, on the Legal Protection of Databases (E.U. 1996)
Directive 2000/31/EC of the European Parliament and of the Council of June 8, 2000, on Certain Legal Aspects of Information Society Services, in Particular Electronic Commerce, in the Internal Market (E.U. 2000)

[1] The list of legislations includes international and regional conventions, national laws, regulations, judicial explanations, and revision draft of law amendments.

J.J. Hua, *Toward A More Balanced Approach: Rethinking and Readjusting Copyright Systems in the Digital Network Era*, DOI 10.1007/978-3-662-43517-5,

Directive 2001/29/EC of the European Parliament and of the Council of May 22, 2001, on the Harmonization of Certain Aspects of Copyright and Related Rights in the Information Society (E.U. 2001)
Directive 2004/48/EC of the European Parliament and of the Council of April 29, 2004, on the Enforcement of Intellectual Property Rights (E.U. 2004)
Explanatory Memorandum to the Digital Agenda Bill (Australia 1999)
General Principles of the Civil Law of the People's Republic of China (P.R.C. 1986)
German Copyright Law (Germany 1998)
H.R. 354—Collections of Information Antipiracy Act (U.S.A. 1999)
H.R. 1858—Consumer and Investor Access to Information Act (U.S.A. 1999)
Interpretations of the Supreme People's Court on Several Issues Concerning the Application of Law in the Trial of Cases Involving Copyright Disputes (P.R.C. 2006)
Marrakesh Treaty to Facilitate Access to Published Works for Persons Who Are Blind, Visually Impaired, Otherwise Print Disabled (2013)
Measures for the Administrative Protection of Internet Copyright (P.R.C. 2005)
Measures for the Implementation of Copyright Administrative Punishment (P.R.C. 2009)
Opinions of the European Data Protection Supervisor on the Current Negotiations by the European Union of an Anti-Counterfeiting Trade Agreement (ACTA) (2010)
Preliminary Proposals for Strengthening Copyright Protection in the Digital Environment (Hong Kong 2007)
Proposals for Strengthening Copyright Protection in the Digital Environment (Hong Kong 2009)
Protect IP Act (U.S.A. 2011)
Provisions of the Supreme People's Court on Certain Issues Related to the Application of Law in the Trial of Civil Cases Involving Disputes over Infringement of the Right to Network Dissemination of Information (P.R.C. 2012)
Rulemaking of DMCA Anti-Circumvention Law of 2000, 2003, 2006, 2009, 2012 (USA)[2]
Regulation on the Collective Management of Copyright (P.R.C. 2005)
Regulation on the Implementation of the Copyright Law of the People's Republic of China (P.R.C. 2002)
Regulation on the Protection of Computer Software (P.R.C. 2002)
Regulation on the Protection of the Right to Network Dissemination of Information (P.R.C. 2006)
Stop Online Piracy Act (U.S.A. 2011)
Taiwan Copyright Act (2003 Amendment) (Taiwan 2003)
The Copyright (Amendment) Bill, 2012 (India 2012)
The United States Constitution (U.S.A. 1787)
The United States Copyright Act (U.S.A. 1976)
The Universal Declaration of Human Rights (1948)
WIPO Copyright Treaty (1996)
WIPO Performances and Phonograms Treaty (1996)

---

[2] It is a triennial rulemaking proceeding to evaluate the impact of the prohibition against the act of circumventing access-control measures.

List of Cases

A&M Records Inc. v. Napster Inc. 239F.3d 1004 (9th Cir. 2001)

Australasian Performing Right Association Ltd. v. Jain (1990) 18 IPR 663

Beijing Jingdiao Company Ltd. v. Shanghai Naikai Electronic Technology Company Ltd. Shanghai First Intermediate People's Court (2006) Hu Yi Zhong Min Wu (Zhi) Chu No. 134

Beijing Jingdiao Company Ltd. v. Shanghai Naikai Electronic Technology Company Ltd. Shanghai High People's Court (2006) Hu Gao Min San (Zhi) Zhong Zi No. 110

Bill Graham Archives v. Dorling Kindersley 448F.3d 605 (2nd Cir. 2006)

Campbell v. Acuff-Rose Music 510 U.S. 569 (1994)

Capitol Records, Inc. v. Thomas-Rasset, Memorandum of Law & Order, Civil File No. 06-1497 (MJD/LIB), document 457 (D. Minn. 2011)

Cary v. Kearsley (1802) 170 Eng. Rep. 679

Castle Rock Entertainment v. Carol Publishing Group 150F.3d 132 (2nd Cir. 1998)

Chamberlain Group v. Skylink Technologies 292F. Supp. 2d 1023 (N.D. Ill. 2003)

Chamberlain Group v. Skylink Technologies 381F. 3d 1178 (Fed. Cir. 2004)

Chan Nai Ming v. HKSAR [2007] 10H.K.C.F.A.R. 273 (C.F.A.)

Columbia Pictures Industries Inc. v. Miramax Films Corp. 11F. Supp. 2d 1179 (1998)

Dish Network LLC & Others v. Zentek International Co. Ltd. & Another [2009] HKEC 220

Donaldson v. Beckett (1774) 1 Eng. Rep. 837

Donaldson v. Beckett (1813) 17 Cobbett's Parl. Hist. 953

Dr. Seuss Enterprises, L.P. v. Penguin Books 109F.3d 1394 (9th Cir. 1997)

Falcon v. Famous Players Film Co. Ltd. [1926] 2KB 474 (CA)

Folsom v Marsh 9F. Cas. 342 (C.C.D. Mass. 1841)

Google thumbnail case, the German Federal Supreme Court case no. IZR 69/08

Harper & Row Publishers Inc. v. National Enterprises (1985) 471 U.S. 539

Hubbard v. Vosper [1972] 1 All E.R. 1023 C.A.

In re Aimster Copyright Litigation 334F.3d 643 (7th Cir. 2003)

J.J. Hua, *Toward A More Balanced Approach: Rethinking and Readjusting Copyright Systems in the Digital Network Era*, DOI 10.1007/978-3-662-43517-5,

Kelly v. Arriba Soft Corp. 336F.3d 811 (9th Cir. 2003)
Lexmark International v. Static Control Components 253F. Supp. 2d 943 (E.D. Ky. 2003)
Lexmark International v. Static Control Components 387F. 3d 522 (6th Cir. 2004)
Mazer v. Stein 347 U.S. 201 (1954)
MDY Industry LLC v. Blizzard Entertainment Inc. 629F.3d 928 (9th Cir. 2010)
Metro-Goldwyn-Mayer Studios Inc. v. Grokster Ltd. 380F.3d 1154 (9th Cir. 2004)
Metro-Goldwyn-Mayer Studios Inc. v. Grokster Ltd. 545 U.S. 913 (2005)
Millar v. Taylor (1976) 98 Eng. Rep. 201
Music Copyright Society of China (MCSC) v. Guangzhou NetEase Inc. and China Mobile Beijing Ltd. Beijing Second Intermediate People's Court (2002) Er Zhong Min Chu Zi No. 03119
Nunez v. Caribbean International News Corp. 235F.3d 18 (1st Cir. 2000)
Perfect 10 Inc. v. Amazon.com, Inc. 508F.3d 1146 (9th Cir. 2007)
Scarlet Extended SA v. SABAM (European Court of Justice c-70/10, 2011)
Sega Enterprises Ltd. v. Accolade, Inc. 997F.2d 1510 (9th Cir. 1992)
Sony Corp. v. University City Studios Inc. 464 U.S. 417 (1984)
Stevens v. Kabushiki Kaisha Sony Computer Entertainment and Others [2005] HCA 58
Stowe v. Thomas 23F. Cas. 201 (C.C.E.D. Pa. 1853)
Suntrust v. Houghton Mifflin Co. 252F.3d 1165 (11th Cir. 2001)
Twentieth Century Fox Film Corp. v. British Telecommunications plc [2011] EWHC 1981 (Ch)
Twentieth Century Music Corp. v. Aiken 422 U.S. 151 (1975)
UMG Recording Inc. v. MP3.com Inc. 92F. Supp. 2nd 349 (S.D.N.Y. 2000)
United States v. Dove 585F. Supp. 2d 865, (W.D. Va. 2008)
Universal City Studios v. Reimerdes 111F. Supp. 2nd 294 (S.D.N.Y. 2000)
Universal City Studios Inc. v. Sony Corporation of America 659F. 2d 963 (9th Cir. 1981)
University of New South Wales v. Moorhouse (1975) 133 CLR 1
Viacom International Inc. v YouTube, Inc. 718F.Supp.2d 514 (2010)
Wheaton v. Peters 33 U.S. 591 (1834)
Zheng Chengsi and Others v. Beijing Shusheng Digital Technology Company Beijing First Intermediate People's Court (2005) Yi Zhong Min Zhong Zi No. 3643

Bibliography

Books

1. Aplin, T. (2005). *Copyright law in the digital society: The challenges of multimedia*. Oxford/Portland: Hart Publishing.
2. Barbosa, R. G. (2006). *International copyright law and litigation: A mechanism for improvement*. Ann Arbor: ProQuest Information and Learning Company.
3. Bettig, R. V. (1996). *Copyrighting culture: The political economy of intellectual property*. Boulder: Westview Press.
4. Betts, C. (1994). *Jean-Jacques Rousseau discourse on political economy and the social contract*. Oxford: Oxford University Press.
5. Boyle, J. (2008). *The public domain: Enclosing the commons of the mind*. New Haven: Yale University Press.
6. Brown, R. S., & Denicola, R. C. (2009). *Copyright: Unfair competition, and related topic bearing on the protection of works of authorship (Tenth Edition Statutory Supplement)*. New York: Foundation Press.
7. Bugbee, B. W. (1967). *The genesis of American patent and copyright law*. Washington, DC: Public Affairs Press.
8. Cohen, J. E., Loren, L. P., Okediji, R. L., & O'Rourke, M. A. (2010). *Copyright in a global information economy* (3rd ed.). New York: Wolters Kluwer.
9. Cooter, R., & Ulen, T. (1997). *Law and economics* (2nd ed.). Reading: Addison-Wesley Educational Publishers Inc.
10. Cooter, R., & Ulen, T. (1991). *Law and economics* (Zhang Jun, etc., Trans.). Shanghai: Joint Publishing (in Chinese).
11. Drahos, P. (1996). *A philosophy of intellectual property*. Aldershot: Dartmouth Publishing Company.
12. Elkin-Koren, N., & Netanel, N. W. (Eds.). (2002). *The commodification of information*. The Hague: Kluwer Law International.
13. Feng, P. (1997). *Intellectual property in China*. Hong Kong: Sweet & Maxwell Asia.
14. Feng, X. (2006). *Balance of interest theory of intellectual property law*. Beijing: China University of Political Science and Law Press (in Chinese).
15. Ganea, P., & Pattlock, T. (2005). *Intellectual property law in China* (C. Heath, Ed.). The Hague: Kluwer Law International.
16. Gantz, J., & Rochester, J. B. (2008). *Pirates of the digital millennium* (Zhou Xiaoqi, Trans.). Beijing: Law Press (in Chinese).
17. Gervais, D. (Ed.). (2006). *Collective management of copyright and related rights*. The Hague: Kluwer Law International.

J.J. Hua, *Toward A More Balanced Approach: Rethinking and Readjusting Copyright Systems in the Digital Network Era*, DOI 10.1007/978-3-662-43517-5,

18. Goldstein, P. (1996). *Copyright's highway: From Gutenberg to the celestial jukebox*. New York: Hill and Wang.
19. Goldstein, P. (2006). *International legal material on intellectual property* (2006 ed.). New York: Foundation Press.
20. Guibault, L., & Hugenholtz, P. B. (Eds.). (2006). *The future of the public domain: Identifying the commons in information law*. The Hague: Kluwer Law International.
21. Hauser, A. (1952). *The social history of art*. New York: Knopf.
22. Hegel, G. W. F. (1991). *Elements of the philosophy of right* (A. W. Wood, Ed.). Cambridge: Cambridge University Press.
23. Jiang, K. (2008). *Music copyright administration and litigation of China*. Beijing: Intellectual Property Publishing House (in Chinese).
24. Kim, M. (2005). *An analysis of the creative commons as a solution for copyright protection in the digital era*. Ann Arbor: ProQuest Information and Learning Company.
25. Kong, Q. (2005). *WTO, internalization and the intellectual property rights regime in China*. Singapore: Marshall Cavendish Academic.
26. LaFrance, M. (2009). *Global issues in copyright law*. St. Paul: Thomson Reuters.
27. Lessig, L. (2008). *Remix: Making art and commerce thrive in the hybrid economy*. London: Bloomsbury Academic.
28. Li, D., Yang A. et al. (2008). *Copyright strategy, administration and litigation*. Beijing: Law Press (in Chinese).
29. Li, Y. (2005). *International and comparative intellectual property: Law, policy and practice*. Hong Kong: LexisNexis.
30. Liu, C. (Ed.). (2003). *Intellectual property law* (2nd ed.). Beijing: Higher Education Press and Peking University Press (in Chinese).
31. Locke, J. (1974). *Two treaties of civil government*. New York: Hafner.
32. McJohn, S. M. (2006). *Intellectual property: Examples and explanations* (2nd ed.). New York: Aspen Publishers.
33. Melendez-Ortiz, R., & Roffe, P. (Eds.). (2009). *Intellectual property and sustainable development: Development agendas in a changing world*. Cheltenham/Northampton: Edward Elgar Publishing Inc.
34. Merges, R. P., Menell, P. S., & Lemley, M. A. (2010). *Intellectual property in the new technology age* (5th ed.). New York: Wolters Kluwer.
35. Nan, Z., & Liu Chunlin. (2003). *Research on intellectual property academic frontier issues*. Beijing: China Books Press (in Chinese).
36. Netanel, N. W. (2008). *Copyright's paradox*. New York: Oxford University Press.
37. Patry, W. (2009). *Moral panics and the copyright wars*. Oxford: Oxford University Press.
38. Pendleton, M. D., & Lee, A. (2001). *Intellectual property: A guide to the law in Hong Kong*. Hong Kong: Butterworths Asia.
39. Posner, R. A. (1998). *Economic analysis of law* (5th ed.). New York: Aspen Law & Business.
40. Posner, R. A. (1997). *Economic analysis of law*. Beijing: Encyclopedia China Publishing House (Chinese version).
41. Rajan, M. T. S. (2006). *Copyright and creative freedom: A study of post-socialist law reform*. London/New York: Routledge.
42. Reyman, J. (2010). *The rhetoric of intellectual property: Copyright law and the regulation of digital culture*. New York: Routledge.
43. Ricketson, S., & Ginsberg, J. C. (2006). *International copyright and neighbouring rights: The Berne Convention and beyond* (2nd ed.). Oxford: Oxford University Press.
44. Ricketson, S. (1999). *The law of intellectual property: Copyright, designs and confidential information*. Sydney: LBC Information Services.
45. Rousseau, J. J. (1762). Social contract. Available at http://www.constitution.org/jjr/socon.htm
46. Schollin, K. (2008). *Digital rights management: The new copyright*. Stockholm: Jure Forlag AB.
47. Shan, H. (2008). *The protection of trade secrets in China*. Alphen ann den Rijn: Wotlers Kluwer.
48. Song, S. H. (2011). *New challenges of Chinese copyright law in the digital age*. Alphen ann den Rijn: Wotlers Kluwer.

49. Stamatoudi, I. A. (Ed.). (2010). *Copyright enforcement and the Internet*. Alphen aan den Rijn: Kluwer Law International.
50. Stokes, S. (2009). *Digital copyright law and practice* (3rd ed.). Oxford/Portland: Hart Publishing.
51. Strowel, A. (Ed.). (2009). *Peer-to-peer file sharing and secondary liability in copyright law*. Cheltenham/Northampton: Edward Elgar Publishing Inc.
52. Tang, G. H. (2011). *Copyright and the public interest in China*. Cheltenham: Edward Elgar Publishing Inc.
53. The Editorial Committee. (2008). *Counseling edition of "National Intellectual Property Strategy Outline"*. Beijing: Intellectual Property Publishing House (in Chinese).
54. The Editorial Committee of China IP Protection Handbook. (2008). *China IP protection handbook*. Beijing: Intellectual Property Publishing House.
55. Tian, Y. (2009). *Rethinking intellectual property: The political economy of copyright protection in the digital era*. London/New York: Routledge-Cavendish.
56. Von Lewinski, S. (2008). *International copyright law and policy*. Oxford/New York: Oxford University Press.
57. Wang, Q. (2008). *Internet copyright law*. Beijing: Remin University of China Press (in Chinese).
58. Wang, Q. (2007). *Comparative research on copyright limitations system*. Beijing: People's Publishing House (in Chinese).
59. Wu, H. (2008). *Multidimensional interpretation of intellectual property*. Beijing: Peking University Press (in Chinese).
60. Wu, H. (Ed.). (2007). *Blue Book of intellectual property in China (2005–2006)*. Beijing: Peking University Press (in Chinese).
61. Wu, H. (Ed.). (2007). *Research on intellectual property international protection system*. Beijing: Intellectual Property Publishing House (in Chinese).
62. Xu, J. (2006). *Intellectual property protection in the Internet and E-commerce*. Beijing: People's Court Press (in Chinese).
63. Xue, H., & Zheng, C. (2002). *Chinese intellectual property law in the 21st century*. Hong Kong: Sweet & Maxwell Asia.
64. Yi, J. (2009). *Technology development and copyright expansion*. Beijing: Law Press (in Chinese).
65. Yu, P. K. (Ed.). (2007). *Intellectual property and information wealth: Issue and practices in the digital age* (Copyright and related rights, Vol. I). Westport: Praeger Publisher.
66. Yu, P. K. (Ed.). (2007). *Intellectual property and information wealth: Issue and practices in the digital age* (International intellectual property law and policy, Vol. IV). Westport: Praeger Publisher.
67. Zhang, J. (Ed.). (2008). *Report on the development of creative industry in China (2008)*. Beijing: China Economic Publishing House (in Chinese).
68. Zheng, C. (2007). *Intellectual property*. Beijing: Social Science Academic Press (in Chinese).
69. Zheng, C. (2003). *Intellectual property law* (2nd ed.). Beijing: Law Press (in Chinese).
70. Zhong, Y., & Ma, C. (2007). *Report on frontier issues of intellectual property laws: Research and enlightenment on frontier issues of intellectual property law under the globalization and informatization background*. Beijing: China Economic Publishing House (in Chinese).

Journal Articles, Book Chapters, Online Material and Conference Presentations

71. ACTA- Anti-counterfeiting Trade Agreement. Available at http://trade.ec.europa.eu/doclib/docs/2011/may/tradoc_147937.pdf
72. Agency of Cultural Affairs of Japan. Responding to copyright policies for a new era. Available at http://www.bunka.go.jp/english/pdf/h21_chapter_07.pdf

73. Analysis of WIPO Marrakesh Treaty to facilitate access to published works for persons who are blind, visually impaired, or otherwise print disabled. Available at http://www.ifrro.org/content/analysis-wipo-marrakesh-treaty-facilitate-access-published-works-persons-who-are-blind-visua
74. Angela Wang & Co. IP Law-Application for Norwich Pharmacal Relief in respect of Online Infringement of Copyright-China (3 December 2009). Available at http://www.hg.org/article.asp?id=7729
75. Annual Report of the Intellectual Property Cases in the Supreme People's Court (2011). Available at http://www.hljcourt.gov.cn/lawdb/show.php?fid=147063 (in Chinese).
76. Arewa, O. B. (2007). Copyright and borrowing. In P. K. Yu (Ed.), *Intellectual property and information wealth: Issue and practices in the digital age* (Copyright and related rights, Vol. I, pp. 33–52). Westport: Praeger Publisher.
77. Aufderheide, P., & Jaszi, P. Fair use and best practices: Surprising success. Available at http://www.centerforsocialmedia.org/fair-use/best-practices/documentary/fair-use-and-best-practices-surprising-success
78. Band, J. Cell phone unlocking: A legal primer. Available at http://www.districtdispatch.org/wp-content/uploads/2013/03/band-cell-phone-unlocking-08mar13.pdf
79. Bao, Y., Chen, D., & Liang, J. (2010). Balance of interest in copyright and development of copyright industry under the digital environment. *Journal of Beijing Institute of Graphic, 18*, 16–19 (in Chinese).
80. Beebe, B. (2008). An empirical study of U.S. Copyright fair use opinions, 1978–2005. *University of Pennsylvania Law Review, 156*, 549–624.
81. Beebe, B. (2007–2008). Does judicial ideology affect copyright fair use outcome?: Evidence from the fair use case law. *Columbia Journal of Law and the Arts, 31*, 535–590.
82. Besek, J. M. (2004). Anti-circumvention laws and copyright: A report from the Kernochan Center for Law, Media and Arts. *Columbia Journal of Law and the Arts, 27*, 385–519.
83. Bill Summary & Status, 112th Congress (2011–2012), H.R. 3261, CRS Summary. Available at http://www.webcitation.org/643NehNoc
84. Borland, J. Student faces suit over key to CD locks. *CNET News* (9 October 2003). Available at http://news.cnet.com/2100-1025_3-5089168.html
85. Boyle, J. (2003). Foreword: The opposite of property? *Law and Contemporary Problems, 66*, 1–32.
86. Boyle, J. (2003). The second enclosure movement and the construction of the public domain. *Law and Contemporary Problems, 66*, 33–74.
87. Brainard, T., Deng, S., & Miller, M. Abolishment of copyright law promotes social justice. Available at http://www.ethicapublishing.com/confronting/5CH16.pdf
88. Brief of Kenneth J. Arrow, Ian Ayres, Gary Becker, William M. Landes, Steven Levitt, Douglas Lichtman, Kevin Murphy, Randal Picker, Andrew Rosenfield, and Steven Shavell, as Amici Curiae in Support of Petitioners, MGM Studios, Inc. v. Grokster Ltd., No. 04-480 (U.S. Supreme Court, filed January 24, 2005). Available at http://www.copyright.gov/docs/mgm/kenneth-Arrow-et-al.pdf
89. Brief of Jessica Litman, Keith Aoki, Ann Bartow, Dan Burk, Julie Cohen, Christine Haight Farley, Laura N. Gasaway, Shubha Ghosh, Paul J. Heald, Peter Jaszi, Dennis Karjala, Lydia Pallas Loren, Michael Madison, Ruth Okedji, L. Ray Patterson, Pamela Samuelson, Alfred C. Yen and Dianne Zimmerman, as Amici Curiae in Support of Reversal of Napster Inc. v. A & M Records Inc., Nos. 00-16401 and 0016403 (U.S. Court of Appeals Ninth Circuit). Available at http://www-personal.umich.edu/~jdlitman/briefs/Amicus.pdf
90. Brief of Deirdre K. Mulligan, as Amici Curiae in Support of Reversal of Stephen J. Barrett M.D., ET. AL v. Ilena Rosenthal, No. S122953 (Supreme Court of California). Available at https://www.eff.org/sites/default/files/filenode/Barrett_v_Rosenthal/law_professors_amicus_brief.pdf
91. Brown, I. (2006). The evolution of anti-circumvention law. *International Review of Law, Computers and Technology, 20*, 239–260.
92. Burger, J. Filtering & graduated response against online infringers. Available at http://www.dvd-and-beyond.com/features/feature.php?feature=118

93. Burk, D. L. (2003). Anticircumvention misuse. *UCLA Law Review, 50*, 1095–1140.
94. Carroll, M. W. (2007). Creative commons as conversational copyright. In P. K. Yu (Ed.), *Intellectual property and information wealth: Issue and practices in the digital age* (Copyright and related rights, Vol. I, pp. 445–461). Westport: Praeger Publisher.
95. Chander, A. (2006). Symposium: Cyberpersons, propertization, and contract in the information culture- exporting DMCA lockouts. *Cleveland State Law Review, 54*, 205–217.
96. China Internet Network Information Center. Semiannual survey report on development of China's Internet (January 2001). Available at http://www.cnnic.cn/hlwfzyj/hlwxzbg/200906/P020120709345368965113.pdf (in Chinese).
97. China Internet Network Information Center. 17th statistical survey report on the Internet development in China (January 2006). Available at http://www.cnic.cas.cn/qkbg/cnnictjbg/cnnictjfz/200601/P020090819615860278077.pdf (in Chinese).
98. China Internet Network Information Center. 28th statistical survey report on the Internet development in China (July 2011). Available at http://www1.cnnic.cn/IDR/ReportDownloads/201209/P020120904421102801754.pdf (in Chinese).
99. China's proposed copyright reforms prompt widespread comment. Available at http://the-1709blog.blogspot.com/2012/04/chinas-proposed-copyright-reforms.html
100. Cloke, J. ISPs getting comfortable with blocking injunctions (6 March 2013). Available at http://blogs.dlapiper.com/mediaandsport/?p=490
101. Copyright Reform Bill Targets Anti-circumvention. Available at https://www.cdt.org/blogs/andrew-mcdiarmid/1005copyright-reform-bill-targets-anti-circumvention
102. Craig, C. J. (2002). Locke, labour and limiting the author's right: A warning against a Lockean approach to copyright law. *Queen's Law Journal, 28*, 1–60.
103. Delrahim, M. Forcing firms to share the sandbox: Compulsory licensing of intellectual property rights and antitrust (10 May 2004). Available at http://www.justice.gov/atr/public/speeches/203627.htm
104. Department of Culture, Media and Sport of the United Kingdom. Creative industries mapping document 2001. Available at http://webarchive.nationalarchives.gov.uk/+/http://www.culture.gov.uk/global/publications/archive_2001/ci_mapping_doc_2001.htm
105. Diplomatic conference to conclude a Treaty to facilitate Access to published works by visually impaired persons and persons with print disabilities. Available at http://www.wipo.int/dc2013/en/
106. Dopplick, R. Consumer advocates and industry endorse cellphone unlocking bill at House Judiciary Committee Hearing (7 June 2013). Available at http://techpolicy.acm.org/blog/?p=2838
107. DRM in the Draft Copyright Amendments. Available at http://spicyipindia.blogspot.com/2010/03/drms-in-draft-copyright-amendments.html
108. Efroni, Z. (2011). Anticircumvention laws. In Efroni, Z. (Ed.), *Access-right: The future of digital copyright law* (pp. 287–398). Oxford/New York: Oxford University Press.
109. Elkin-Koren, N. (2006). Exploring creative commons: A skeptic view of a worthy pursuit. In L. Guibault & P. B. Hugenholtz (Eds.), *The future of the public domain: Identifying the commons in information law* (pp. 325–377). The Hague: Kluwer Law International.
110. Elkin-Koren, N. What contract can't do: The limits of private ordering in facilitating a creative commons. Available at http://papers.ssrn.com/sol3/papers.cfm?abstract_id=760906
111. Fisher, W. Digital music: Problems and possibilities. Available at http://www.law.harvard.edu/faculty/tfisher/Music.html
112. Fisher, W. (1988). Reconstructing the fair use doctrine. *Harvard Law Review, 101*, 1659–1795.
113. Frieden, R. (2008). Internet packet sniffing and its impact on the network neutrality debate and the balance of power between intellectual property creators and consumers. *Fordham Intellectual Property Media & Entertainment Law Journal, 18*, 633–675.
114. Gao, L., & Huang, S. J. (2008). Navigating China's online world. *China IP Focus* 97–99.
115. Geist, M. Estimating the cost of a three-strikes and you're out system. Available at http://www.michaelgeist.ca/content/view/4731/135
116. Ginsburg, J. C. (2003). From having copies to experiencing works: The development of an access right in U.S. copyright law. *Journal of the Copyright Society of the USA, 50*, 113–131.

117. Ginsburg, J. C. (2005, August). *Legal protection of technological measures protecting works of authorship: International obligations and US experience* (Columbia Law School Public Law & Legal Theory Working Paper Group (Paper Number 05-93)). Available at http://ssrn.com/abstract=785945
118. Ginsburg, J. C. (2008). Separating the Sony sheep from the Grokster goats: Reckoning the future business plans of copyright-dependent technology entrepreneurs. *Arizona Law Review, 50*, 577–609.
119. Ginsburg, J. C. (2007, February). The pros and cons of strengthening intellectual property protection: Technological protection measures and Section 1201 of the US Copyright Act (Columbia Law School Public Law & Legal Theory Working Paper Group (Paper Number 07-137)). Available at http://ssrn.com/abstract=960724
120. Ginsburg, J. C. (2010). User-generated content sites and Section 512 of the US Copyright Act. In I. A. Stamatoudi (Ed.), *Copyright enforcement and the Internet* (pp. 183–198). Alphen aan den Rijn: Kluwer Law International.
121. Ginsburg, J. C., & Ricketson, S. (2006). Inducers and authorisers: A comparison of the US Supreme Court's Grokster decision and the Australian federal court's KaZaa ruling. *Media and Arts Law Journal, 11*, 1–25.
122. Goldstein, P. (2005–2006). Copyright's commons. *Columbia Journal of Law and the Arts, 29*, 1–10.
123. Goldstein, P. (2007–2008). Fair use in context. *Columbia Journal of Law and the Arts, 31*, 433–443.
124. Google Books Litigation and Settlements. Available at http://copyright.columbia.edu/copyright/special-topics/google-settlement/
125. Gordon, W. (2002). Excuse and justification in the law of fair use: Commodification and market perspective. In N. Elkin-Koren & N. W. Netanel (Eds.), *The commodification of information* (pp. 149–192). The Hague: Kluwer Law International.
126. Haber, E. (2010). The French revolution 2.0: Copyright and the three strikes policy. *Journal of Sports and Entertainment Law, 2*, 297–339.
127. Hardin, G. (1968). The tragedy of the commons. *Sciences, 162*, 1243–1248.
128. Hardy, T. (2001). Not so different: Tangible, intangible, digital, and analog works and their comparison for copyright purposes. *University of Dayton Law Review, 26*, 211–245.
129. Hardy, T. (1996). Property (and copyright) in cyberspace. *University of Chicago Legal Forum*, 217–260.
130. Hebei: The graduated response system may inhibit online infringement and piracy. Available at http://www.sipo.gov.cn/wqyz/dfxx/201104/t20110407_595456.html (in Chinese).
131. Hess, C., & Ostrom, E. (2003). Ideas, artifacts, and facilities: Information as a common-pool resources. *Law and Contemporary Problems, 66*, 111–145.
132. Hennessey, W. O. (2009–2010). Protection of intellectual property in China (30 years and more): A personal reflection. *Houston Law Review, 46*, 1257–1300.
133. Heymann, L. A. (2007–2008). Everything is transformative: Fair use and reader response. *Columbia Journal of Law and the Arts, 31*, 445–466.
134. Hietanen, H. *Creative commons Olympics*. Presentation at the 10th annual Intellectual Property Scholars conference organized by Berkeley Center for Law and Technology, Berkeley CA, USA, 12–13 August 2010.
135. Hoffer, A. (2011, Summer). A matter of access: How bypassing DRM does not always violate the DMCA. *Washington Journal of Law, Technology & Arts, 7*, 13–25.
136. Hua, J. (2009). The construction and promotion of creative commons mechanism: Creative commons in Hong Kong. *Journal of Chongqing University of Posts and Telecommunications (Social Sciences), 21*, 27–31 (in Chinese).
137. Huang, C, & Yang, M. (2009). Analysis on private reproduction in the copyright law: Balance of interest under the digital technology. *Rule of Law and Society,* No. 9, 131–132 (in Chinese).

138. House of Representatives Standing Committee on Legal and Constitutional Affairs. Advisory report on Copyright Amendment (Digital Agenda) Bill 1999. Available at http://www.aph.gov.au/Parliamentary_Business/Committees/House_of_Representatives_Committees?url=/laca/digitalagenda/contents.htm
139. India introduces Major Copyright Reform Bill. Available at http://www.michaelgeist.ca/content/view/4974/196/
140. India's digital copyright reform plan for digital locks. Available at http://www.michaelgeist.ca/content/view/4923/125/
141. Internet Law-Developments in ISP Liability in Europe. Available at http://www.ibls.com/internet_law_news_portal_view.aspx?id=2126&s=latestnews
142. Investigation of status quo of copyright protection in the network age: Severe burden of proof makes protection of rights difficult. Available at http://www.ce.cn/xwzx/gnsz/gdxw/201104/01/t20110401_22340359_1.shtml (in Chinese).
143. Jackson, M. (2007). Finding safe harbor for speech: Internet service providers and copyright law. In P. K. Yu (Ed.), *Intellectual property and information wealth: Issue and practices in the digital age* (Copyright and related rights, Vol. I, pp. 307–320). Westport: Praeger Publisher.
144. Jondet, N. *The French Copyright Authority (HADOPI), the graduated response and the disconnection of illegal file-sharers*. Presentation at the 10th annual Intellectual Property Scholars conference organized by Berkeley Center for Law and Technology, Berkeley CA, USA, 12–13 August 2010.
145. Kerr, I. (2007). To observe and protect? How digital rights management systems threaten privacy and what policy makers should do about it. In P. K. Yu (Ed.), *Intellectual property and information wealth: Issue and practices in the digital age* (Copyright and related rights, Vol. I, pp. 321–344). Westport: Praeger Publisher.
146. Khanna, D. S. Phone unlocking made legal. Available at http://www.nationalreview.com/article/349379/phone-unlocking-made-legal
147. Khanna, D. The law against unlocking cellphones is anti-consumer, anti-business, and anti- common sense (11 February 2013). Available at http://www.theatlantic.com/business/archive/2013/02/the-law-against-unlocking-cellphones-is-anti-consumer-anti-business-and-anti-common-sense/272894/
148. Kreiss, R. A. (1995). Accessibility and commercialization in copyright theory. *UCLA Law Review, 43*, 1–76.
149. Ku, R. S. R. (2003). Consumers and creative destruction: Fair use beyond market failure. *Berkeley Technology Law Journal, 18*, 539–574.
150. Lai, S. *Copyright and wrongs in the digital economy: Getting the balance right*. Presentation at the Global Forum on Intellectual Property organized by Singapore IP Academy, Singapore, 6–7 January 2011.
151. Lange, D. (1981). Recognizing the public domain. *Law and Contemporary Problems, 44*, 147–178.
152. Lessig, L. (2004). Commentary: The creative commons. *Montana Law Review, 65*, 1–13.
153. Leval, P. N. (1990). Toward a fair use standard. *Harvard Law Review, 103*, 1105–1136.
154. Lichtman, D. (2006, February). *Defusing DRM* (Chicago John M. Olin Law & Economics Working Paper Group No. 282 (2nd series)). Available at http://ssrn.com/abstract=883676
155. Lichtman, D. KaZaA and punishment. *Wall Street Journal* (10 September 2003). Available at http://papers.ssrn.com/sol3/papers.cfm?abstract_id=1472199
156. Lichtman, D. & Posner, E. (2004, July). *Holding Internet service providers accountable* (Chicago John M. Olin Law & Economics Working Paper Group No. 217 (2nd series)). Available at http://papers.ssrn.com/sol3/papers.cfm?abstract_id=573502
157. Lichtman, D. & Landes, W. (2003). Indirect liability for copyright infringement: An economic perspective. *Harvard Journal of Law and Technology, 16*, 395–410.
158. Liebowitz, S. J. Alternative copyright systems: The problems with a compulsory license. Available at http://www.serci.org/2003/liebowitz2.pdf

159. Litman, J. (2007). Lawful personal use. *Texas Law Review, 85*, 1871–1902.
160. Litman, J. (2011). Readers' copyright. *Journal of the Copyright Society of the USA, 58*, 325–353.
161. Litman, J. (2009). The copyright revision act of 2026. *Marquette Intellectual Property Law Review, 13*, 249–262.
162. Litman, J. (1990, Fall). The public domain. *Emory Law Journal, 39*, 965–1023.
163. Liu, G. The ins and outs of China's accession to international copyright conventions. Available at http://www.gapp.gov.cn/chinacopyright/contents/537/20672.html (in Chinese).
164. Liu, J. P. (2007–2008). Two-factor fair use. *Columbia Journal of Law and the Arts, 31*, 571–585.
165. Liu, Z. (2007). Thinking on reconstruction of copyright fair use system in the digital age. *Information Science, 25*, 1472–1477 (in Chinese).
166. Lunney, G. (2002). Fair use and market failure: Sony revisited. *Boston University Law Review, 82*, 975–1030.
167. Madison, M. J. (2007). Fair use and social practice. In P. K. Yu (Ed.), *Intellectual property and information wealth: Issue and practices in the digital age* (Copyright and related rights, Vol. I, pp. 177–200). Westport: Praeger Publisher.
168. Martin, T. S. (2009–2010). Vicarious and contributory liability for Internet host providers: Combating copyright infringement in the United States, Russia and China. *Wisconsin International Law Journal, 27*, 1–35.
169. McCullagh, D. Senate bill amounts to death penalty for websites. *CNET* (12 May 2011). Available at http://news.cnet.com/8301-31921_3-20062398-281.html
170. McDiarmid, A. Copyright reform bill targets anti-circumvention (10 May 2013). Available at https://www.cdt.org/blogs/andrew-mcdiarmid/1005copyright-reform-bill-targets-anti-circumvention
171. McDiarmid, A. The DMCA should not stand in the way of phone unlocking (14 March 2013). Available at https://www.cdt.org/blogs/andrew-mcdiarmid/1503dmca-should-not-stand-way-phone-unlocking
172. Meyer, D. Europe 'will not accept' three strikes in ACTA treaty. *ZDNet* (26 February 2010). Available at http://www.zdnet.co.uk/news/networking/2010/02/26/europe-will-not-accept-three-strikes-in-acta-treaty-40057434/
173. Menell, P. S. (2008–2009). Indirect copyright liability and technological innovation. *Columbia Journal of Law and the Arts, 32*, 375–399.
174. Mick, J. Wikileaks airs U.S. plans to kill pirate bay, monitor ISPs with multinational ACTA proposal. Available at http://www.dailytech.com/article.aspx?newsid=11870
175. Mtima, L., & Jamar, S. D. (2010–2011). Fulfilling the copyright social justice promise: Digitizing textual information. *New York Law School Review, 55*, 77–108.
176. Netanel, N. W. (1996). Copyright and a democratic civil society. *Yale Law Journal, 106*, 283–387.
177. Netanel, N. W. (2003). Imposing a noncommercial use levy to allow free peer-to-peer file sharing. *Harvard Journal of Law and Technology, 17*, 1–84.
178. Netanel, N. W. (2007). Temptations of the walled garden: Digital rights management and mobile phone carriers. *Journal on Telecommunications & High Technology Law, 6*, 75–99.
179. Noguchi, Y. Anti-circumvention regulation in Japan. Available at http://cyberlaw.stanford.edu/blogs/noguchi
180. Norwich Pharmacal orders: A quick guide. Available at http://ld.practicallaw.com/0-211-3137
181. Pandey, A. Development in India IP Law: The Copyright (Amendment) Act 2012 (22 January 2013). Available at http://www.ip-watch.org/2013/01/22/development-in-indian-ip-law-the-copyright-amendment-act-2012/
182. Papageorgiou, E., & Nandi, J. (2008). The complexities of online copyright. *China IP Focus*, 41–44.
183. Parchomovsky, G., & Goldman, K. A. (2007). Fair use harbors. *Virginia Law Review, 93*, 1483–1532.
184. Parodies of Harry Porter. Available at http://en.wikipedia.org/wiki/Parodies_of_Harry_Potter
185. Picker, R. C. (2007–2008). Fair use v. fair access. *Columbia Journal of Law and the Arts, 31*, 603–616.

186. Qiu, Q. (2010). Promoting benign development of video development: Youku formally released 2010 'Co-Plan 3.0' copyright strategy proposal. *China Advertising,* No. 5, 146 (in Chinese).
187. Radia, R. 3 Cell phone unlocking bills introduced- what would they accomplish? (16 March 2013). Available at http://techliberation.com/2013/03/16/3-cell-phone-unlocking-bills-introduced-what-would-they-accomplish/
188. Reese, R. A. (2007–2008). Transformativeness and the derivative work right. *Columbia Journal of Law and the Arts, 31*, 467–495.
189. Reichman, J. H. (2003). A contractually reconstructed research commons for scientific data in a highly protectionist intellectual property environment. *Law and Contemporary Problems, 66*, 315–462.
190. Reichman, J. H., Dinwoodie, G. B., & Samuelson, P. (2007). A reverse notice and takedown regime to enable public interest uses of technically protected copyrighted works. *Berkeley Technology Law Journal, 22*, 981–1060.
191. Reichman, J. H. (2009). Intellectual property in the twentieth-first century: Will the developing countries lead or follow? *Houston Law Review, 46*, 1115–1185.
192. Remarks of FCC Commissioner Ajit Pai at the cellphone unlocking forum hosted by TechFreedom and the Competitive Enterprise Institute (17 June 2013). Available at http://transition.fcc.gov/Daily_Releases/Daily_Business/2013/db0617/DOC-321641A1.pdf
193. Rogoyski, R. S. (2008). Learning the hard way: The anti-circumvention amendments to the Hong Kong copyright ordinance. *Tulane Journal of Technology and Intellectual Property, 11*, 35–57.
194. Rogoyski, R. S., & Basin, K. (2009). The bloody case that started from a parody: American intellectual property and the pursuit of democratic ideals in modern China. *UCLA Entertainment Law Review, 16*, 237–264.
195. Rose, C. M. (2003). Romans, roads, and romantic creators: Traditions of public property in the information age. *Law and Contemporary Problems, 66*, 89–110.
196. Samuelson, P. (2003, April). DRM (and, or, vs.) the law. *Communications of the ACM, 46*, 41–45.
197. Samuelson, P. (2003). Mapping the digital public domain: Threats and opportunities. *Law and Contemporary Problems, 66*, 147–171.
198. Samuelson, P. (2007). Preliminary thoughts on copyright reform. *Utah Law Review, 3*, 551–571.
199. Samuelson, P. Toward more sensible anti-circumvention regulations. Available at http://people.ischool.berkeley.edu/~pam/papers/fincrypt2.pdf
200. Samuelson, P., Reichman, J. H., & Dinwoodie, G. (2008, February). How to achieve (some) balance in anti-circumvention laws. *Communications of the ACM, 51*, 21–25.
201. Samuelson, P., & Schultz, J. Should copyright owners have to give notice of their use of technical protection measures? Available at http://people.ischool.berkeley.edu/~pam/papers/drmnotice.pdf
202. Schellekens, M. (2006). Free and open source software: An answer to commodification? In L. Guibault & P. B. Hugenholtz (Eds.), *The future of the public domain: Identifying the commons in information law* (pp. 303–324). The Hague: Kluwer Law International.
203. Shi, S. X. Chinese copyright law, peer production and the participatory media age: An old regime in a new world. Available at http://ses.library.usyd.edu.au/bitstream/2123/2359/1/CopyrightAsiaPacific_Ch13.pdf
204. Songwriters say copyright draft doesn't protect. Available at http://www.chinadaily.com.cn/china/2012-04/06/content_14986887.htm
205. Sookman, B., & Glover, D. Graduated response and copyright: An idea that is right for the times. Available at http://www.barrysookman.com/2010/01/20/graduated-response-and-copyright-an-idea-that-is-right-for-the-times/
206. State Council of People's Republic of China. Outline of the national intellectual property strategy. Available at http://english.gov.cn/2008-06/21/content_1023471.htm
207. Summary of the Berne Convention for the protection of literary and artistic works (1886). Available at http://www.wipo.int/treaties/en/ip/berne/summary_berne.html

208. Sun, X. (2010). Analysis on balance of interest of information sharing and copyright protection. *Hebei Law Science, 28*, 108–110 (in Chinese).
209. The creative industries in China: IVCA report- March 2010. Available at http://www.ivca.org/ivca/live/news/2010/develop-your-business-in-china-join-the-ivca-trade-mission-to-shanghai/IVCA_Report_-_The_Creative_Industries_in_China.pdf
210. The Digital Millennium Copyright Act of 1998: US Copyright Office Summary. Available at http://www.copyright.gov/legislation/dmca.pdf
211. The Twentieth Century Fox v BT Decision: A new development in the debate about ISP obligations to prevent copyright infringement (2011). *Communications Law Bulletin, 30*. Available at http://www.hdy.com.au/Media/docs/DOC121011-5a25b007-23a0-4ea6-a465-241cd4090c2d-0.pdf
212. Tushnet, R. (2007). Creating in the shadow of the law: Media fans and intellectual property. In P. K. Yu (Ed.), *Intellectual property and information wealth: Issue and practices in the digital age* (Copyright and related rights, Vol. I, pp. 251–268). Westport: Praeger Publisher.
213. Tushnet, R. (2007–2008). User-generated discontent: Transformation in practice. *Columbia Journal of Law and the Arts, 31*, 497–516.
214. United States-Section 110(5) of the US Copyright Act Report of the Panel (WT/DS160/R) (15 June 2000). Available at http://www.wto.org/english/tratop_e/dispu_e/1234da.pdf
215. VerSteeg, R. (2007). Originality and creativity in copyright law. In P. K. Yu (Ed.), *Intellectual property and information wealth: Issue and practices in the digital age* (Copyright and related rights, Vol. I, pp. 1–32). Westport: Praeger Publisher.
216. Wang, C. *Function of legal transplant in Chinese social transition and legal development*. Presentation at 2011 annual general conference of the European China Law Studies Association organized by Science Po, Paris France, 28–29 September 2011.
217. Wang, Q. (2011). The justification of copyright law protection on technological measures. *Chinese Journal of Law*, No. 4, 86–103 (in Chinese).
218. Weinberg, M. Three strikes, exile, and Judge Dredd. Available at http://www.publicknowledge.org/news-blog/blogs/three-strikes-exile-and-judge-dredd
219. Wienand, P. ISPs and injunctions- An update on the courts' control of online content (13 December 2012). Available at http://www.farrer.co.uk/News/Briefings/ISPs-and-injunction--n-update-on-the-Courts-control-of-online-content/
220. WIPO Director General addresses the future of copyright. Available at http://www.wipo.int/pressroom/en/articles/2011/article_0005.html
221. Wu, H. (2009). Copyright industry and copyright protection issues in the network age. *Intellectual Property*, No. 1, 54–57 (in Chinese).
222. Wu, H. (2008). Economic thinking on basic system of intellectual property. In Wu, H. (Ed.), *Multidimensional interpretation of intellectual property* (pp. 171–186). Beijing: Peking University Press (in Chinese).
223. Wu, H. (2008). Philosophical interpretation of intellectual property law by Jurists. In Wu, H. (Ed.), *Multidimensional interpretation of intellectual property* (pp. 157–170). Beijing: Peking University Press (in Chinese).
224. Wu, T. The copyright paradox. Available at http://papers.ssrn.com/sol3/papers.cfm?abstract_id=828784
225. Wu, T. (2007–2008). Tolerated use. *Columbia Journal of Law and the Arts, 31*, 617–635.
226. Xie, L. (2011). Analysis of online copyright infringement regulations in 'Digital Economy Act 2010' of the United Kingdom. *China Copyright*, No. 4, 47–49 (in Chinese).
227. Xu, S. (2010). Analysis of balance of interest in the copyright protection. *Economic and Social Development*, No. 8, 110–112, 124 (in Chinese).
228. Yu, P. K. (2006). Anticircumvention and anti-anticircumvention. *Denver University Law Review, 84*, 13–77.
229. Yu, P. K. (2010). Digital copyright reform and legal transplants in Hong Kong. *University of Louisville Law Review, 48*, 693–770.

230. Yu, P. K. (2007). Five disharmonizing trends in the international intellectual property regime. In P. K. Yu (Ed.), *Intellectual property and information wealth: Issue and practices in the digital age* (International intellectual property law and policy, Vol. IV, pp. 73–112). Westport: Praeger Publisher.
231. Yu, P. K. (2009). Intellectual property reforms in China. In R. Melendez-Ortiz & P. Roffe (Eds.), *Intellectual property and sustainable development: Development agendas in a changing world* (pp. 37–50). Cheltenham/Northampton: Edward Elgar Publishing Inc.
232. Yu, P. K. (2010). The graduated response. *Florida Law Review, 62*, 1373–1430.
233. Van Alstyne, W. W. (2003). Reconciling what the First Amendment forbids with what the Copyright Clause permits: A summary explanation and review. *Law and Contemporary Problems, 66*, 225–238.
234. Zavin, J. Twentieth Century Fox Film Corp. v. British Telecommunications plc. Available at http://www.lexology.com/library/detail.aspx?g=6cbbb90c-f32f-4dbe-a4ef-8ef993e1aea6
235. Zhang, G., & Zhang, G. (2008). Finding a balance in IP enforcement. *China IP Focus*, 69–72.

MIX
Papier aus verantwortungsvollen Quellen
Paper from responsible sources
FSC® C105338

If you have any concerns about our products,
you can contact us on
ProductSafety@springernature.com

In case Publisher is established outside the EU,
the EU authorized representative is:
Springer Nature Customer Service Center GmbH
Europaplatz 3, 69115 Heidelberg, Germany

Printed by Libri Plureos GmbH
in Hamburg, Germany